CHILE

and the

NAZIS

CHILE

and the

NAZIS

From Hitler to Pinochet

Graeme S. Mount

Montréal/New York/London

Black Rose Books No. EE301

Hardcover ISBN: 1-55164-193-3 (bound) Paperback ISBN: 1-55164-192-5 (pbk.)

Canadian Cataloguing in Publication Data

Mount, Graeme S. (Graeme Stewart), 1939-
Chile and the Nazis : from Hitler to Pinochet

Includes bibliographical references and index.
Hardcover ISBN: 1-55164-193-3 (bound) Paperback ISBN: 1-55164-192-5 (pbk.)

1. Fascism--Chile. 2. National socialism--Influence. 3. Chile--Foreign relations--1920-1970. 4. World War, 1939-1945--Chile. I. Title.
F3099.M68 2001   983.06'42   C2001-901164-4

Thanks to the Spanish Archives at the Alcalá de Henares for the use of photos pp.xiv,xv.

Cover design by Associés libres, Montréal

BLACK ROSE BOOKS

C.P. 1258	2250 Military Road	99 Wallis Road
Succ. Place du Parc	Tonawanda, NY	London, E9 5LN
Montréal, H2W 2R3	14150	England
Canada	USA	UK

To order books:

In Canada: (phone) 1-800-565-9523 (fax) 1-800-221-9985
email: utpbooks@utpress.utoronto.ca

In United States: (phone) 1-800-283-3572 (fax) 1-651-917-6406

In the UK & Europe: (phone) London 44 (0)20 8986-4854 (fax) 44 (0)20 8533-5821
email: order@centralbooks.comin

Our Web Site address: http://www.web.net/blackrosebooks

A publication of the Institute of Policy Alternatives of Montréal (IPAM)

Printed in Canada

The Canada Council | Le Conseil des Arts
for the Arts | du Canada

TABLE OF CONTENTS

To the people of Chile and to those who fought the Nazis.

ACKNOWLEDGMENTS

It is impossible to write a book without the help of many, many people. First and foremost must be my highly encouraging wife, Joan, who allows me to take the trips necessary for research and who gives quiet time at home. Rose May Démoré, Secretary of Laurentian University's History Department, and Ashley Thomson of the Library are always indispensable, as is Paulette Dozois of the National Archives of Canada. Special thanks for helpful suggestions go to colleagues Bill Glover, Edelgard Mahant, and Dieter Buse, and to graduate students Andrew Lefebvre and Jason Zorbas. As Andy and Jason did their work, they shared information, which I then could use. Andre Laferriere, who helped with the index, also introduced me to historian Christel Krause Converse, who had written her Ph.D. thesis on Nazis in Chile. Cyril Doherty checked for mistakes. Most helpful in understanding the thinking of German-Chileans were Ignacio Kuschel, a Deputy in the Chilean House of Representatives; and Totila Lintz, a hardware merchant in Puerto Montt. Reporter Quintin Oyarzo Leiva of *La Nación*, whom I first met in Puerto Montt and encountered again in Santiago, shared insights and information. Joan, Rupert and Elisabeth Cook, and Mike and Marjory Mulloy joined me at various stages during a stay in Chile and opened my eyes to points which I might have missed on my own. Chilean diplomat Luis Palma, as counselor at the Chilean embassy in Ottawa, arranged for me to use the documents at Chile's Ministerio de Relaciones Exteriores (Foreign Office). Professor Hank Nelson of the Australian National University opened doors in Canberra. John Armstrong of the National Archives of Canada alerted me to the existence of intercepted diplomatic messages between wartime Tokyo and Santiago.

The Laurentian University Research Fund provided money so that I could go to Chile, and Linda Barton and Dimitri Roussopoulos of Black Rose Books converted the manuscript into a book which could reach a wider audience. Clint MacNeil helped to prepare the index and the map. I am grateful to all.

Any mistakes, of course, are my responsibility.

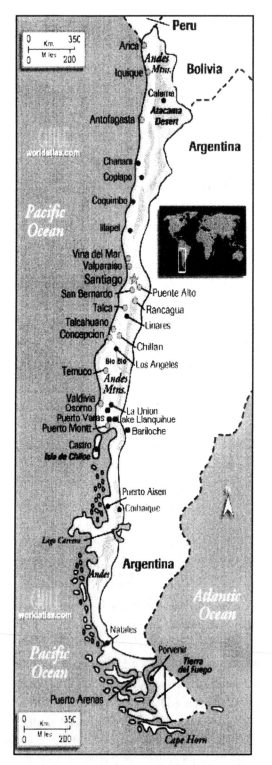

Photographs
by
Graeme Mount

German Schools have flourished throughout southern Chile since the arrival of the first German settlers in the mid-19th century. During the Nazi era they presented a threat to Chilean sovereignty and democratic values, but by the end of the 20th century, they offered the highest quality secondary-level education available in Chile. This picture shows the German School in Puerto Varas.

Valdivia, which in many respects resembles such German Rhineland communities as Bonn, was a centre of Nazi activity in Chile before and during World War II. Subsequently site of southern Chile's principal university, its insubordination antagonized the administration of General Augusto Pinochet (1973-1990), which preferred to invest public money in Puerto Montt.

In the second half of the 20th century, the Federal Republic of Germany sponsored a German Colonial Museum in Frutillar. The water wheel pictured here indicates the source of energy utilized by the earliest German pioneers.

The market of Valparaíso (March 1997). In less happy times, Valparaíso's *Baltimore* incident of 1891 had poisoned US-Chilean relations. During the Nazi era, Valparaíso was home to a number of Hitler's agents.

Bariloche, Argentina—across the Andes from Osorno—became home to many fugitives from the Third Reich. The leader of the German community for many years was former SS Captain Erich Priebke, listed in Bariloche's telephone directory as "Erico Priebke". Priebke and his wife established a maternity clinic on 24 of September Street (number 167) and lived upstairs until his arrest in 1994. In 1997, an Italian court convicted him of the murder of 335 Italians on the outskirts of Rome.

The Lutheran Church at Puerto Montt, rebuilt after the earthquake of 1960 when the pastor was the Nazi-friendly Karl Steybe. The caption, undoubtedly referring to the aftermath of the earthquake, says in German, "See! I make all things new." Steybe also served as pastor during World War II at the Lutheran Church at Osorno. The FBI was concerned about his behaviour and closely monitored Steybe's activities.

A plaque in honour of the 55 young Nazi "martyrs" who died during a failed *Putsch* 5 September 1938 is attached to the Ministry of Justice building opposite the presidential palace in Santiago. The caption above the names says in Spanish, "It does not matter, comrades. Our blood will save Chile!" After the list of names is the sentence, "They died for the people."

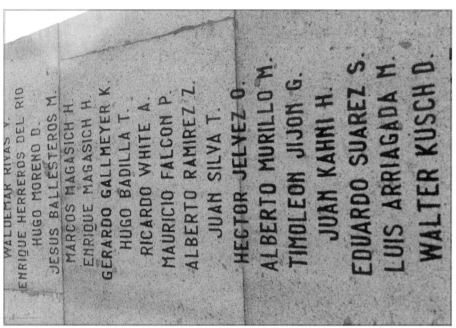

An examination of the names on the Nazi monument at the Santiago General Secretary demonstrates that comparatively few had German surnames.

Nazis also have a monument at the Santiago General Cemetery, where they hold a memorial service for the 55 "martyrs" every 5 September.

Note the Falange symbol on a Roman Catholic Church in Spain. During the short-lived Spanish Republic (1931-1939), many clergy had died violent deaths, when churches were torched. To Pope Pius XII and other Roman Catholic leaders, Franco's triumph over the Republicans was a welcome event.

Ramón Serrano, brother-in-law of Spanish leader Francisco Franco, was Foreign Minister of Spain from 1940 to 1942, when collaboration between Spain and Hitler's Germany was at its height. Note the Falange symbol (the collection of arrows) on his uniform. Until the Normandy landings of mid-1944, Franco did not anticipate a German defeat.

Spanish clergy outside the cathedral in Seville celebrate Franco's triumph in the Spanish Civil War, April 1939.

(Photographs on this page, and on the previous page, courtesy of the Spanish Archives at the Alcalá de Henares.)

This sign, erected in 1996 on the 140th anniversary of Frutillar's settlement by German pioneers, says in German, "All men become brothers." The bottom line, in Spanish, says, "And song unites us." Frutillar is a heavily German community on the shore of Lake Llanquihue. Until 1941, private Nazi armies had war games around Lake Llanquihue, attended on occasion by Ambassador Wilhelm von Schön.

The author stands outside the final home of Eric Honecker (8978 Carlos Silva Vildosola St. in the Santiago suburb of La Reina), leader of East Germany for almost thirty years. Honecker had granted political asylum to refugees from Pinochet's Chile, one of whom married his daughter. In 1990, Pinochet stepped down as Chile's president, and the German Federal Republic absorbed the German Democratic Republic. Honecker's daughter, then his wife Margot, moved to Santiago. German authorities launched criminal charges against Honecker in connection with deaths at the Berlin Wall but let him go into exile in Chile on compassionate grounds because of his health. Honecker died of cancer in May 1994. (Photo by Joan Mount.)

INTRODUCTION

There were nine principal neutrals of World War II: in alphabetical order Argentina and Chile, the Irish Free State (now the Irish Republic), Portugal and Spain, Sweden and Switzerland, the Vatican and Turkey. Belligerents could send diplomats and spies to those countries to observe what the other side was doing. This is the story of one of those neutrals, Chile, its efforts to maintain neutrality, its abandonment of neutrality, and the significance —long-term and short-term—of those actions.

German settlers, some of the earliest of whom were liberals, had migrated to Chile since 1846. A distinct society within Chile, these unassimilated people continued for decades to speak German and to retain fond memories of the Fatherland. Some had migrated to escape Germany's problems and sought to keep them at arm's length. Some saw more opportunity for themselves and their families in Chile than in Germany but retained positive thoughts of Germany. Whatever Germany's problems, Germany was more than its current government. As the United States was greater than the incumbent occupant of the White House, so too Germany was greater than the Weimar Republic or Hitler.

Nazi Germany maximized its opportunities in such an environment. It influenced Chilean politicians and military officers as well as the Chilean media. It influenced school teachers and won friends among the clergy, Roman Catholic and Protestant. Imperial Japan proved a beneficiary of German success for, despite the absence of an ethnic Japanese community in Chile, Japan could maintain its legation in Santiago a full year after the closure of its embassies and legations in all other Western Hemisphere capitals except Buenos Aires, Argentina.

Among those Chilean leaders of 1942 who exhibited strong tolerance of Nazi Germany were Carlos Ibáñez, Tobias Barros, and Conrado Ríos. In 1942, Ibáñez—a military officer and former president—was an unsuccessful presidential candidate. Tobias Barros, another military officer, was Chile's ambassador in Berlin. Conrado Ríos was Chile's ambassador in Argentina. Ambassador Ríos believed that Chile and Argentina should share a common foreign policy, notwithstanding tolerance of the Axis on the part of Argentina's current leaders.

THE PROBLEM

After the 7 December 1941 Japanese attack on Pearl Harbor and Hitler's subsequent declaration of war upon the United States, the administration of President Franklin Delano Roosevelt asked governments of the twenty Latin American republics to sever diplomatic ties with the Axis belligerents. Following an Inter-American conference of hemispheric foreign ministers at Río de Janeiro in January 1942, all except Argentina and Chile obliged. At Río the foreign ministers voted unanimously "to consider any act of aggression on the part of a non-American State against one of them as an act of aggression against all of them."[1] They also agreed unanimously to "recommend the breaking of their diplomatic relations with Japan, Germany and Italy, since the first-mentioned State attacked and the other two declared war on an American country."[2] Yet, Chile continued to maintain diplomatic relations with the Axis powers until January 1943, Argentina until January 1944.

Questions arise. What did the Axis belligerents learn in Chile? How useful was the information? Did the diplomatic rupture of January 1943 affect the flow of information from Chile to Germany and Japan? What was the relevance of the delay and of the reasons for the delay to the subsequent history of Chile? This book will endeavour to answer those questions.

One of the indications of Chilean tolerance of the Axis certainly was Chile's reluctance to sever diplomatic relations with the three principal Axis belligerents. Despite persuasive evidence that the Axis governments were using Chile as a base from which to spy on Allied shipping and the rest of the Western hemisphere, Chile maintained a "business as usual" approach toward Berlin, Tokyo, and Rome—one full year longer than any other Western Hemisphere country except Argentina. When it did make the break, it did so only under strong pressure from the Roosevelt administration in the United States. Earlier research has indicated that Chile was not as important for purposes of German intelligence as Spain, Sweden, Switzerland, Portugal, Turkey, or even Argentina.[3] However, Chile *was* a factor in a bitterly fought contest in which, to use understatement, much was at stake.

U.S. authorities saw the lack of co-operation from Chile as making a difference. At the insistence of its director, J. Edgar Hoover, the Federal Bureau of Investigation (FBI) was responsible for intelligence gathering within most of the Western Hemisphere. The Office of State Security (OSS) covered the rest of the world. A report written in March 1943 for the FBI included the following paragraph:

> Chile is important to the war effort. Her vast copper mines and other mineral resources furnish strategic materials for the United States' war production. With an increased productivity of her agricultural potentialities, Chile can help to feed the world. Chile has many problems, and particularly troublesome ones, in connection with her large German population. During the long months of Chilean neutrality this nation, with Argentina, was a haven for Axis representatives, a hotbed of Axis intrigue.[4]

"Neutrality," in terms of World War II jargon, referred to the period when Chile had diplomatic relations with both Allied *and* Axis belligerents [1939-1943]. With the closure of the Axis missions, Chile became a non-belligerent, and it maintained that status until it declared war on Germany and Japan in February 1945.

SOURCES

It is now possible to study the impact of Chile's ongoing relationship—why it continued and why it mattered that the Axis belligerents were not as isolated as Washington thought they should have been. U.S. documents have long been available to present the inside story as to why the Roosevelt administration sought the diplomatic rupture and what it did to promote that rupture. The U.S. army captured relevant German documents at the end of World War II. Americans, Britons, and Canadians intercepted Japanese diplomatic traffic, which is now available in Washington, London, and Ottawa. Because of Australia's geographic position, British authorities kept Australian officials well informed about developments in Chile, and the documentation is available in Canberra. Chilean and Spanish materials have become available in recent years. They add perspective to the events of 1942, when official Washington wanted the rupture, Chilean authorities resisted, and the British were relatively indifferent. The documents are highly compatible with one another, and each complements the others, thus contributing to the total story. They demonstrate that Nazi Germany saw Chile as a possible window on the Western Hemisphere and thought that, given Chile's geography and political culture, such a window might be fairly secure. Germany must invest heavily in Chile and persuade a substantial number of Chileans of Hitler's merits, but through bribes and infiltration the goal, thought officials from Nazi Germany, might be attainable. Imperial Japan benefitted from Germany's success and regarded Chile as a place from which it could maintain contact with expatriate Japanese in Peru—and spy. Eventually the German, Japanese, and Italian diplomats had to cease their efforts, and because of circumstances elsewhere, their friends were not of much assistance. Diplomatic isolation did make a difference.

This book evolved as sources became available. When I was writing *Canada's Enemies: Spies and Spying in the Peaceable Kingdom*,[5] John Armstrong of the National Archives of Canada suggested that I examine the records of Canada's Wartime Examination Unit.[6] I did, and found a marvellous collection of Japanese diplomatic correspondence for those years, conveniently translated into English. Some documents dealt with the Japanese consulate in Vancouver and the Japanese legation in Ottawa in the months leading to Pearl Harbor, and these proved useful for the seventh chapter of *Canada's Enemies*. Many more dealt with Japanese diplomatic traffic to occupied and neutral countries around the Pacific, particularly Chile. These documents traced the activities of Keyoshi Yamagata, Minister in charge of Japan's legation in Santiago de Chile, and his relations with other Axis diplomats stationed in Chile and certain Chilean politicians.

Armed with this information, I approached the Chilean embassy in Ottawa for permission to examine the 1942 files of Chile's Foreign Office. Patricio Aylwin had won Chile's presidential election of 1989, and with his inauguration in 1990, military rule came to an end and democracy returned. Counselor Luis Palma at the Ottawa Embassy arranged that I should see the appropriate information, and he kindly provided names and addresses of people who would be waiting for me. By the time I arrived in Chile it was 1994. Aylwin's term had expired, and his duly elected successor, Eduardo Frei Ruiz-Tagle, occupied the Moneda—Chile's equivalent of the White House. The Foreign Office documents certainly complemented the Canadian intercepts and provided fascinating insights into German activities, diplomatic and otherwise, throughout Chile in 1942.

Additional information was available. With Nazi Germany's unconditional surrender in 1945, the United States Army had captured a substantial portion of Germany's Foreign Office documents from unification in 1871 to the collapse at the end of World War II. In Washington scholars organized and microfilmed them. Once relations between West Germany and the United States became friendly, the originals returned to the custody of the Foreign Office (Auswärtiges Amt) in Bonn, but the National Archives and Records Administration of the United States maintained the microfilms. Correspondence to and from Baron Wilhelm von Schön, Nazi Germany's Ambassador to Chile in 1942, confirmed much of what the Canadian and Chilean documents had said and provided additional details.

Other documents were available or quickly became so: correspondence between U.S. Ambassador Claude Bowers in Santiago and his superiors in

Washington, much of it housed at the Franklin D. Roosevelt presidential archives in Hyde Park, New York; FBI files on Chile, 1942-1943, also stored at Hyde Park; British intercepts of Chilean diplomatic traffic, located at the Public Record Office in the London suburb of Kew Gardens, and British diplomatic correspondence house at the Australian Archives in Canberra. The MAGIC collection at the National Archives and Records Administration in College Park, Maryland, gives some insight into Japanese links with Chile after the rupture, and Spanish Foreign Office records in Madrid are open to indicate what services Franco's diplomats may have rendered to Hitler, Mussolini, or Tojo. The aforementioned British intercepts were particularly useful. In 1993-1994, the Public Record Office released the daily collections of intercepted diplomatic correspondence handed to Winston Churchill on a daily basis.[7]

Newspapers provided insights into what was visible to the interested public. Interviews with residents of Chile's Tenth Region—the most German part of Chile—during a sabbatical from Laurentian University in 1997 proved most useful. Particularly helpful have been Paulette Dozois and John Armstrong at the National Archives of Canada in Ottawa and Linda Macfarlane at the Australian Archives in Canberra. Thanks are in order to Professor Hank Nelson of Australian National University, who suggested that a trip to Canberra might be worthwhile and then pointed me in the right direction. At last it has become possible to have some reasonable insight into what had been a highly contentious issue in 1942. To what extent did Chile harm the Allied cause by maintaining diplomatic relations with the Axis? President Roosevelt, Under-Secretary of State Sumner Welles, and Ambassador Bowers repeatedly charged, publicly and privately, that Chile and Argentina—the only Latin American republics to host Axis diplomats after January 1942—were providing Hitler and the Japanese militarists with a window on the Western Hemisphere from which they could endanger Allied shipping. Chilean authorities disputed this, and British officials seemed indifferent. At last it became possible to see who knew what and when, and why (or whether) such information could affect the outcome of the war.

A word about Chilean surnames is in order. Chilean males, like other people in the Western world, have multiple given names. Like other Hispanophones, they also have two surnames: the father's surname followed by the mother's maiden name. The father's surname—the penultimate name—is the one which is transmitted to the next generation and which is the usual means of identification. Cuba's revolutionary leader, Fidel CASTRO Ruz, is known as "Castro" rather than as "Ruz." In most instances, I have omitted the mother's maiden name. However, it is included in the case of two Chilean presidents, both named "Eduardo Frei." There has to be some means of distinguishing between them, and it seems inappropriate to label them "Eduardo Frei Senior" and "Eduardo Frei Junior." The manuscript also provides the full name of Chilean Nazi leader Jorge González von Marées, because his mother's ethnicity was relevant to his ideological outlook.

PREVIOUS LITERATURE

By 1942, not many countries had managed to remain neutral. Some of these—Spain, Portugal, and Argentina—were not at all democratic. There is a growing literature on the democratic neutrals—Switzerland, Sweden, the Irish Free State, and Chile—but there certainly is room for improvement. With assistance from newly declassified documents, this book will discuss the pressures on Chile to remain neutral and the pressures to take sides in the conflict.

One of the key players was the U.S. ambassador to Chile, Claude G. Bowers. Bowers has written his memoirs, although Bowers was hardly fair to himself. His correspondence at the FDR archives in Hyde Park reveals him as far less naïve than one would assume from his memoirs.[8] Like the documents at the Chilean Foreign Office, Bowers's letters at Hyde Park demonstrate that Chilean Foreign Minister Ernesto Barros collaborated with the Axis diplomats. Yet, Bowers's memoirs refer to Barros's "undoubted hostility to Nazis and Japs."[9] Indeed, Ambassador Bowers—as depicted in his own memoirs, but not in his correspondence—appears to have been much too optimistic about a number of factors and people. To him, Chile's delay in closing the Axis missions was largely a result of Chilean democracy. While dictators could make and implement decisions swiftly, politicians who depended on an electorate could not, and Chile was one of the few democracies in Latin America.[10] Bowers wrote favourably about almost everyone he met in Santiago—Foreign Minister Barros,[11] past-President Arturo Alessandri,[12] even German Ambassador Baron Wilhelm von Schön and Italian Ambassador Raffaele Boscarelli, whom he considered career diplomats forced to defend the policies of governments with which they personally were unsympathetic.[13] German records reveal von Schön as a willing collaborator of Germany's National Socialist Party (NSDAP). Bowers described Chilean General Francisco Javier Díaz as an "outstanding officer, usually very tactful and gentlemanly."[14] An investigative reporter from the United States, Kurt D. Singer, revealed him as a principal director of a pro-Nazi organization.[15]

Given the information now available, other sources also have their shortcomings. For decades, *Foreign Relations of the United States* (FRUS) has been available to give insights into the State Department's thoughts on the Río conference, and the U.S. government's efforts to bring Chile into line with the other republics. However, the State Department officials writing in *FRUS* could not have known what became known after capture of the German documents. Except to label Chile's President Juan Antonio Ríos (1942-1946) as "pro-Fascist," Frederick Pike ignores US-Chilean tensions of 1942.[16] Jean-Pierre Blancpain's mammoth 1974 opus, *Les Allemands au Chile (1816-1945)*, devotes less than three full pages out of 883 to the rupture.[17] The Spanish-language version, considerably shorter than the French, conveniently omits *any* reference to events between 1933 and 1945.[18] George F.W. Young's *The Germans in Chile*, also published in 1974, devotes less than two paragraphs to events after 1914.[19] In 1976, Arthur Preston Whitaker devoted less than four pages out of 430 to the subject; most sources which he had were American.[20] Writing in 1977, Michael J. Francis used captured German documents, but none of the Canadian intercepts of Japanese communications and no Chilean sources.[21] After an exhaustive search through German sources, David Kahn wrote *Hitler's Spies* in 1978,[22] but

Kahn did not have access to Chilean documents. Also written in 1978, Robert Alexander's *The Tragedy of Chile*—whose primary concern is the coup of 1973—dismissed events of 1942 in one paragraph.[23] César Caviedes, provides an excellent summary of Chilean politics before 1973, but omits the rupture.[24] Using British documents plus some Chilean documents, R.A. Humphreys wrote a magnificent résumé of Chilean politics and diplomacy during World War II.[25] More documents are now available than when he wrote in 1981-1982. Karl Ilq's book about Germans in Chile traces their activities since the sixteenth [*sic*] century and provides many names and dates, but although written in 1982, it stops short of the Third Reich.[26] One of the rare American books to use a Chilean source was William F. Sater's *Chile and the United States*,[27] which used the memoirs of Foreign Minister Ernesto Barros, but as might be expected, Barros' memoirs are self-serving and omit a number of important points.[28] MAGIC intercepts at the National Archives and Records Administration of the USA are more complete from 1943 onward than for earlier years. The otherwise extensive memoirs of Tobias Barros, Chile's ambassador in Berlin from 1940 until 1943, contain only six pages which deal with the most critical period, April through October 1942, apart from a couple of chapters of interesting trivia about the wives of high Nazi officials and his meeting with Pope Pius XII.[29] Mario Barros van Buren, himself a Chilean diplomat, has written an extensive diplomatic history of Chile from colonial days to 1938. Unfortunately, Barros van Buren considered events since 1938 so controversial that he thought any serious study of them would have to await the twenty-first century, when most of the participants would be dead. Although he did not provide footnotes or endnotes for *any* of his material, he dealt with the period from 1939 to 1958 in a most cursory fashion.[30] The fact that two of the critical participants were, like himself, members of the Barros family may have had some bearing on Barros van Buren's decision not to comment. As recently as 1990, Chilean historian Gonzalo Izquierdo had to base his account of Chilean foreign policy in 1942 upon *Foreign Relations of the United States*, Ernesto Barros' memoirs, and newspaper reports.[31] Luis Galdames's *Historia de Chile*, written in 1995, says that the government of Chilean President Juan Antonino Ríos eventually broke with the Axis for the sake of harmonious relations with the United States, but gives no details.[32] Osvaldo Silva Galdames managed to summarize the entire Ríos presidency in three paragraphs, two dealing with foreign policy. What there is is good, but there is more to say on the subject.[33] Books written in English have tended to avoid the issue of the rupture—or non-rupture. Leslie Bethell's collection of essays, *Chile Since Independence*, published between 1985 and 1993, allows only four sentence to this matter.[34] Sergio Villalobos R., who wrote *A Short History of Chile* for the benefit of English-speaking readers, allows less than a sentence for the presidency of Juan Antonio Ríos. The Villalobos book was published in 1996.With benefit of information which earlier writers could not have, this manuscript deals with events in which the present author played no role. At points it confirms what previous authors have written. At others it offers modifications and challenges. It is of interest that Ronald C. Newton[35] and Jorge Camarasa[36] have written detailed accounts of Nazi activities in Argentina—before, during, and after World War II. Christian Leitz has examined the neutrality of Switzerland, Sweden, Turkey, Spain, and Portugal,[37] as have T.Ryle Dwyer and Robert Fisk that of Ireland.[38] There is a shortage of such literature on Chile. Finally, the two State Department treatises of 1997-1998 which deal with the behaviour of World War II neutrals do not include a section on Chile.[39]

Another word on sources is appropriate. Individuals could make mistakes of fact, but when one compares what the various sources have said, the similarities are more striking than the differences. Independently of each other and quite unwittingly, German, Chilean and U.S. officials in Santiago—all, presumably, knowledgeable people—confirm the essence of each other's reports. Canadians who intercepted Japanese diplomatic traffic might have been expected to know a minimum about Chilean political personalities and Japanese agents in Chile in 1942, but their reports coincide with those of better informed people. One would not expect the highest moral standards from Axis diplomats, but it is unlikely that they would try deceive their own governments. Despite the bad reputation of J. Edgar

Hoover and his FBI in recent years, the FBI report which he presented to the Roosevelt White House in 1943 is so well documented—and so compatible with the other sources—that it must be reasonably trustworthy. It does include rumour and innuendo, often identified as such, and the report's authors undoubtedly went out of their way to look for trouble. Nevertheless, on balance it is a highly credible piece of work which can plug gaps from other sources.

NOTES

1. Ruhl Bartlett, *The Record of American Diplomacy: Documents and Readings in the History of American Foreign Relations* (New York: Knopf, 1964) p. 558.
2. Bartlett, p. 559.
3. Ladislas Farago, *The Game of the Foxes: The Untold Story of German Espionage in the United States and Great Britain during World War II* (New York: David McKay, 1971).
4. FBI, *Chile Today*, Group 24, Papers: Harry L. Hopkins, Box 141, File: FBI Reports, Chile, Franklin D. Roosevelt Archives, Hyde Park, p. 1. Cited hereafter as FBI. Information about the division of the world between the FBI and the OSS is available from Ronald C. Newton, *El Cuarto Lado del Triángulo: La 'amenaza nazi' en la Argentina, 1931-1947* (Buenos Aires: Editorial Sudamericana, 1995), p. 416.
5. Graeme S. Mount, *Canada's Enemies: Spies and Spying in the Peaceable Kingdom* (Toronto: Dundurn Press, 1993).
6. Part of the Department of National Defence Collection (R.G. 24) at the National Archives of Canada (NAC) in Ottawa, two volumes were available at the time: vol. 20306, which dealt with German intercepts in 1941-1942, and vol. 20307, which dealt with Japanese intercepts at the same time.
7. Kathryn Brown, "Intelligence and the Decision to Collect It: Churchill's Wartime American Diplomatic Signals Intelligence," *Intelligence and National Security*, X, 3 (July 1995), p. 449.
8. Claude G. Bowers, *Chile through Embassy Windows, 1939-1953* (New York: 1958).
9. Bowers to Cordell Hull, 17 June, FRUS, *1942*, VI, p. 26.
10. Bowers, pp. v-vi, 121-122.
11. Bowers, pp. 97-113.
12. Bowers, pp. 143-157.
13. Bowers, pp. 68, 87-88. Bowers' assessment of von Schön coincides with that of Tobias Barros, II, p. 283.
14. Bowers to Hull, 17 March, FRUS, *1942*, VI, p. 16.
15. Kurt D. Singer, "Germany's Secret Service in South America," *Background: The Key to Current Events*, vol. III, as printed in vol. 1970, Archivos del Departamento de Relaciones Exteriores, Santiago. Cited hereafter as ADRE.
16. Frederick Pike, *Chile and the United States, 1880-1962* (Notre Dame: University of Notre Dame Press, 1963), p. 247.
17. Jean-Pierre Blancpain, *Les Allemands au Chile (1816-1945)* (Böhlau Verlag: Cologne, 1974), pp. 876-878.
18. Jean-Pierre Blancpain, *Los Alemanes en Chile (1816-1945)* (Santiago: Ediciones Pedagogicas Chilenas, S.A., 1985).

19. George F.W. Young, *The Germans in Chile: Immigration and Colonization, 1849-1914* (New York: Center for Migration Studies, 1974).

20. Arthur Preston Whitaker, *The United States and the Southern Cone: Argentina, Chile, and Uruguay* (Cambridge, Mass.: Harvard University Press, 1976), pp. 155, 291, 380-381.

21. Michael J. Francis, *The Limits of Hegemony: United States Relations with Argentina and Chile during World War II* (Notre Dame: University of Notre Dame, 1977).

22. David Kahn, *Hitler's Spies: German Military Intelligence in World War II* (New York: Macmillan, 1978).

23. Robert A. Alexander, *The Tragedy of Chile* (Westport, Conn.: Greenwood Press, 1978), p. 30.

24. César Caviedes, *The Politics of Chile: A Sociogeographical Assessment* (Boulder, Colorado: Westview, 1979), pp. 173-176.

25. R.A. Humphreys, *Latin America and the Second World War* (London: Athlone, vol. I, 1981; vol. II, 1982), I, pp. 22-25, 64-66, 69, 159-163, 169-170; II, 106-119.

26. Karl Ilq, *Das Deutschtum in Chile* (Vienna: Österreichische Landsmannschaft, 1982).

27. William F. Sater, *Chile and the United States* (Athens: University of Georgia Press, 1990), pp. 114-115.

28. Ernesto Barros Jarpa, "Historia para olvidar: ruptura con el Eje (1942-1943)," in Neville Blanc Renard (ed.), *Homenaje al Profesor Guillermo Feliú Cruz* (Santiago: Editorial Andrés Bello, 1973), pp. 31-96.

29. Tobias Barros Ortiz, *Recogiendo los Pasos: Testigo Militar y Político del Siglo XX* (Santiago: Planeta Chilena, vol. I, 1984; vol. II, 1988), II, pp. 416-422.

30. Mario Barros van Buren, *Historia Diplomática de Chile, 1541-1938* (Santiago: Andrés Bello, 1971), p. 190. Barros van Buren notes the need to wait until the twenty-first century on p. xix, and he deals with the entire 1939-1958 period on pp. 813-870.

31. Gonzalo Izquierdo, *Historia de Chile* (Santiago: Andrés Bello, 1990), III, pp. 197-200.

32. Luis Galdames, *Historia de Chile* (Santiago: Universitaria, 1995).

33. Osvaldo Silva Galdames, *Historia Contemporánea de Chile* (Mexico: Fondo de Cultura Económica, 1995), pp. 304-305.

34. Leslie Bethell (ed.), *Chile Since Independence* (Cambridge, England: Cambridge University Press, 1993), p. 116. The essays in this book appeared first in voloumes III, V, and VIII of the *Cambridge History of Latin America*, published by Cambridge University Press in 1985, 1986, and 1991.

35. Ronald C. Newton, *El Cuarto Lado del Triángulo: La 'amenaza nazi en la Argentina, 1931-1947* (Buenos Aires: Editorial Sudamericana, 1995).

36. Jorge Camarasa, *Odessa al Sur: La Argentina Como Refugio de Nazis y Criminales de Guerra* (Buenos Aires: Espejo de Argentina, 1995).

37. Christian Leitz, *Nazi Germany and Neutral Europe during the Second World War* (Manchester: Manchester University Press: 2000).

38. T.Ryle Dwyer, *Strained Relations: Ireland at Peace and the USA at War* (Dublin: Gill and Macmillan. 1988); Robert Fisk, *In Time of War: Ireland, Ulster and the Price of Neutrality* (London: André Deutsch, 1983).

39. Stuart E. Eizenstat (co-ordinator), *U.S. and Allied Efforts to Recover and Restore Gold and Other Assets Stolen or Hidden by Germany during World War II (Preliminary Study)* (Washington: State Department, 1997); *U.S. and Allied Wartime and Postwar Relations and Negotiations with Argentina, Portugal, Spain, Sweden, and Turkey on Looted Gold and German External Assets and U.S. Concerns about the Fate of the Wartime Ustasha Treasury* (Washington: State Department, 1998).

CHAPTER 1

BACKGROUND

LONG-TERM THEMES IN CHILEAN FOREIGN RELATIONS

Relations with Argentina

The most important of Chile's bilateral relationships with other countries were those with her own immediate neighbours, with the United States, and with the largest nations of Western Europe.

Chile and Argentina share a common history and a common geography. Both were Spanish colonies, first part of the Viceroyalty of Peru and then, after the reforms of King Charles III (1759-1788), part of the Viceroyalty of La Plata. Since independence, the two countries have experienced an ambivalent but ongoing love-hate relationship. Argentina's liberator, José de San Martín, crossed the Andes to assist his Chilean counterpart, Bernardo O'Higgins. In 1855, authorities from both countries agreed in principle that their boundaries would be those of 1810 and that any disagreements over the location of the 1810 boundary must be settled peacefully. There have been no wars, but tensions—even war scares—have arisen at intervals, and boundary disputes continue to this day.

More than patriotism—a strong enough factor—has been involved, because overland transportation routes from the national heartlands to the southern extremities remain limited. Regarding access routes to and through the Strait of Magellan and Tierra del Fuego, Chile and Argentina have to co-operate. No traveller can reach the southernmost population centre of either country without entering the territory of the other. A longstanding territorial dispute over ownership of islands in the Beagle Channel ended only in 1985.[1] As the century ended, there was a dispute over ownership of the icefields some 3000 kilometres south of Santiago. In 1997, a writer in a serious Chilean magazine, *Ercilla*, could argue that the ongoing Anglo-Argentine dispute over ownership of the Falkland Islands affected Chile's national security in a significant way. It helped to offset the enormous military disparity between Chile and its larger Argentine neighbour.[2]

Yet, it would be an exaggeration to suggest that Argentine-Chilean relations have been a record of unbroken tension and hostility. One Chilean who devoted his professional life to harmonious Chilean-Argentine relations was Conrado Ríos, Chile's ambassador to Argentina during World War II. For him, harmony and co-operation between the two neighbours was a passion.[3] Certainly no Chilean government has been able to ignore its powerful neighbour.

The War of the Pacific
Since Chileans fought their War of Independence (1810-1826), they have been involved in other conflicts. From 1836-1839, they fought and won their first war against neighbouring Peru and Bolivia. When Spain's Queen Isabel II (1833-1868) attempted in 1866 to seize Peruvian islands as compensation for money allegedly owing to Spain, Chileans went to Peru's assistance. The alliance fell apart after the conflict.

From 1879 until 1884, Chile again fought and defeated Peru and Bolivia. Colonial boundaries were not clear, but in 1874, Chile accepted the twenty-fourth parallel as its boundary with Bolivia provided that the

Bolivians freeze rates of taxation on Chilean nitrate operations north of that line for a minimum of twenty-five years. Four years later, the Bolivian government repudiated that agreement. Peru had a military commitment to Bolivia, and in 1879 Chile declared war on both countries. Argentina might well have assisted the other two except that its leaders feared what another of Argentina's neighbours, Brazil, might do. As a result of its victory, Chile annexed territory taken from both Peru and Bolivia, depriving the former of mineral-rich land and turning the latter into a landlocked state. There were no peace treaties for decades—until 1904 in the case of Bolivia, 1929 in the case of Peru. Chileans feared imminent warfare against Peru and Bolivia as recently as 1920.[4]

Chileans face daily reminders of this war. Streets named for their naval hero, Arturo Prat, are ubiquitous, as are monuments of his head and shoulders. Chile's permanent naval base on King George Island, established early in 1947 to strengthen Chile's Antarctic claims, is Base Prat. The *Huáscar*—the Peruvian warship which cost Prat his life but which the Chilean navy subsequently captured and retained—is a national shrine at the Talcahuano naval base near Concepción, now Chile's second largest city. Bolivian irredentism has been a dominant factor in Chilean foreign and military policy, a reason why General Augusto Pinochet—commander of Chile's armed forces—told a reporter from the French magazine *Le Figaro* in 1993 that Chile needs a powerful army.[5] In February 1997, Chilean soccer players about to play in La Paz, the Bolivian capital, requested that the national anthem not be played before the game. They feared, because of what had happened weeks earlier in Lima, that spectators mindful of the War of the Pacific might show disrespect.[6] Bolivian demands for a port on the Pacific became an issue in that country's 1997 presidential election campaign.[7]

Relations with Germany
Germany's relations with independent Chile began in 1846 with the arrival of German settlers at Valdivia. When Chile won its independence from

Spain in the first quarter of the nineteenth century, its boundaries were considerably smaller than they subsequently became. Until the mid-nineteenth century, there were few European settlements south of the Bío-Bío River at Concepción, because Araucanian Indians had managed to maintain control of the land. Chilean army victories changed that situation, and Presidents Manuel Bulnes (1841-1851) and Manuel Montt (1851-1861) actively recruited German immigrants. Germans, they assumed, had all the positive characteristics of other Western Europeans and, given the divided state of their homeland, they lacked a strong central government which might attempt to exert pressure on Chile.[8]

In 1848, the Bulnes government sent Bernardo Eunom Philippi, himself a Prussian-born immigrant,[9] back to Germany to find people who would populate what has become the mainland of Chile's Tenth Region—from Valdivia in the north to Puerto Montt in the south, now 840-1024 kilometres south of Santiago via highway. The new arrivals gave a German face to Valdivia and Osorno and created new communities: Puerto Varas, 1852 (named for Antonio Varas, Minister of the Interior, Philippi's immediate superior); Puerto Montt, 1853 (named for the president); Frutillar, 1856. German settlers established farms around the shores of Lake Llanquihue, until then surrounded by virgin forests. In many respects even today, Puerto Varas and Frutillar on the shores of Lake Llanquihue appear more German than Latin American. The same is true, in many respects, of Valdivia. Subsequent waves of German immigration populated Puerto Octay, east of Osorno, and the Island of Chiloé. Some went to Concepción, Valparaíso, Santiago, and the nitrate-rich areas taken from Peru. Farmers, fishermen, and loggers came from areas near Berlin and Stuttgart in the 1890s. Although Araucanian resistance lasted into the 1870s, Indian warfare was not part of the collective experience of Chile's German community.

Germans migrated for reasons, ideological and practical, which would have consequences in the 1940s. Some were liberals, dismayed and disillusioned by the failure of German liberals to establish a more democratic society in 1848. Foremost among the liberals has to be Karl (or Carlos)

Anwandter, one of eighty-five who went to Valdivia in 1850. A street and the Deutsche Schule (German school) in that city bear his name, and many of his descendants continue to reside there. Fifty years of age when he left Germany, Anwandter, a pharmacist, travelled with farmers, merchants, carpenters and others in the construction industry, textile workers, a shoemaker, two doctors, another pharmacist, and a pastor.[10] In a letter to Chilean authorities the following May, Anwandter praised Chile's republican form of government as he and his fellow arrivals applied for Chilean citizenship. Their letter said:

> We left Europe and came to the bosom of this new nation for a happier future, more equitable laws, and liberty, without which progress is impossible.

President Montt's government granted their request for citizenship.[11]

Philippi's correspondence makes repeated references to the unhappy political situation in post-1848 Germany,[12] especially among intellectuals who resented pressures to conform.[13] However, not everyone who wanted to leave was necessarily a liberal. Some saw post-1848 Germany as a powderkeg on the eve of revolution and wanted to escape the forthcoming anarchy and reign of terror.[14] Others were poor people who hoped for better economic opportunity in a new country, where they would own their own lands.[15] Undoubtedly different people moved from Germany to Chile for different reasons, one group as late as 1929.[16]

Historian George F.W. Young, who estimates that Chile received only a trickle of those Germans who migrated, finds those Germans who went to Chile influential far beyond their numbers. Despite its disadvantageous (for Europeans) location on the distant side of a continent which was difficult to circumnavigate, Chile had considerable appeal for those who wished to retain their German culture. Pressures to assimilate would be less than in English-speaking societies, especially as the immigrants' educational level was incomparably higher than that of anyone else currently living between Valdivia and Puerto Montt. (This factor may have attracted some Germans who were more nationalistic than those who emigrated to the United States or Australia.) Indeed, Young has found that the rate of assimilation of those Germans, particularly Protestants, who remained in southern Chile proceeded infinitely more slowly than for those who relocated in Concepción, Valparaíso, or Santiago. There already was a middle class in those cities of central Chile, and German immigrants—especially Roman Catholics—adapted readily to the new society. Farther south, however, Germans were almost the only literate, technically skilled people until the railway reached Puerto Montt in 1913.[17]

The new arrivals created a series of German schools across southern Chile. That in Osorno, established in 1854, was Chile's first, the second (after Buenos Aires in 1843) in South America.[18] Valdivia's Deutsche Schule, named for Karl Anwandter, opened its doors in 1858.[19] In those schools the children of the colonists and their descendants could study science and technology, music, the German language, and, in the words of one participant, "the Teutonic spirit."[20] As late as 1974, when Young wrote his history of the Germans in Chile, children could complete primary and secondary education in schools where the language of instruction was German.[21]

According to his initial instructions, Philippi was supposed to recruit Roman Catholics,[22] but he quickly reported that Protestant applicants outnumbered Roman Catholics by a margin of 20:1.[23] Antonio Varas, Minister of the Interior and Philippi's superior, said that they would be welcome, but that the constitution forbade public worship to any but Roman Catholics.[24] A series of liberal governments in the sixty years after 1871 gradually separated Church and State, and Protestants did establish congregations. Given that Lutheran churches included only Germans, while people from other ethnic backgrounds worshipped in Roman Catholic parishes, Lutheran churches across Chile's Tenth Region remain more identifiably German than do their Roman Catholic counterparts. Yet, as late as 1941, the Roman Catholic Church in Osorno used the German language to advertise the hour of mass in an otherwise Spanish-language newspaper, Osorno's *La Prensa*.[25] Some of the early settlers were Jewish. Aboard the *Susana* when she left Hamburg for Valdivia in 1850 were A.C. Goldberg and C.B. Israel.[26]

The census of 1855 was Chile's first to indicate the number of foreigners (19,669) then in Chile. Of these, 10,551 were Argentines. German immigration had begun only in 1846, but already Chile's German community numbered 1,822 and was, after Argentina's, the largest in the country. Then came the English (1,663), the French (1,650), the Spanish (915), Americans (680), Peruvians (599), Italians (399), Scots (213), and Portuguese (168).[27] After 1855, the German community remained the largest European one in Chile and the most identifiable. By 1865, there were 3,800 Germans, 2,800 English, 2,400 French, and 1,000 Italians.[28] Chilean census takers cite the descendants of these people as "Chileans," without regard to ethnicity. In 1941, Ambassador von Schön estimated the number of German nationals in Chile at some five to six thousand.[29] Historian R.A. Humphreys estimated Chileans of German extraction at no more than 35,000.[30] The FBI reported to the White House:

> It is reliably estimated that there are one hundred thousand individuals of German descent resident in Chile and twenty-nine thousand German Nationals. Of this latter figure, it is indicated that nine thousand are Jewish refugees.[31]

It is possible that somebody miscalculated; it is also possible that there were different definitions of the term "German national." Were Jewish refugees (and perhaps others) from the Fatherland Germans or not?

These figures may be somewhat misleading in that the German settlers had influence disproportionate to their numbers. They were much better educated than most native-born Chileans. Relations between Chile and Germany, at least before 1914, were excellent, as many educated Chileans saw Germany as a counterweight to the United States and the United Kingdom, the dominant commercial powers of the South Pacific. Germans arrived as educators and came to dominate not only the German schools for children but adult education as well—medical studies, the training of army officers, the teaching of teachers. Emil Körmer, an adviser to the Chilean army since 1886, played a significant role on the side of Congress against President José Manuel Balmaceda (1886-1891), who had initially engaged him.[32] So little pressure did Chilean authorities place upon the highly regarded German arrivals to assimilate that by 1950, an estimated 25,000-30,000 of them continued to speak German. In southern Chile, an estimated 13,000 spoke German in 1938.[33] Nor was southern Chile the only part of the nation with a strong German identity. Valparaíso, the principal port and then second largest city, had the earliest *Deutscher Verein* (German Club) in Chile, a German-language newspaper (*Westkuesten Beobachter*), and a German population of merchants and shippers whose ties with the Fatherland were stronger than those of the farmers and artisans who lived between Valdivia and Puerto Montt or on the island of Chiloé. (The first Germans reached Chiloé in 1895.) By 1916, Santiago had an estimated 2,000 German-speaking people as compared to Valparaíso's 1500.[34]

Relations with the United States

U.S. support during the War of Independence had been minimal. Despite the Monroe Doctrine of 1823, whereby U.S. President James Monroe had warned Europeans not to establish new colonies in the Western Hemisphere, the United States had not helped Chile and Peru in the war against Isabel II—even after her navy bombarded Valparaíso. (The United States was only beginning to recover from its own Civil War of 1861-1865 and had no interest in such a fight.)[35] The United States had sympathized with Peru and Bolivia during the War of the Pacific, although from a U.S. standpoint, the U.S. position made sense. Chile, the victor, wanted to—and actually did—annex the nitrate-rich southernmost part of Peru as well as Bolivian territory along the Pacific coast (Tarapacá). Secretary of State James G. Blaine was well aware that German annexation of Alsace-Lorraine after the defeat of France in the Franco-Prussian War of 1870 had destabilized Europe. The loser of the military campaign had irredentist ambitions.

Blaine, and his successor, Frederick Frelinghuysen, had similar fears for the stability of South America.[36] At one point, Blaine actually threatened to suspend diplomatic relations with Chile.[37] In 1891, when Blaine was once again Secretary of State, the Baltimore incident did not help the cause of U.S.-Chilean friendship. The U.S. government appeared at first to support what turned out to be the losing side in a Chilean civil war, and then over-reacted when sailors of the USS Baltimore received rough treatment during shore leave in Valparaíso. Two died and others were injured, but Chileans thought that they deserved greater understanding than Blaine was willing to give. What appeared as a war threat from Washington forced a reluctant Chilean apology, but from that apology arose the widely believed (although historically untrue) story of Lieutenant Carlos Peña. According to legend, Peña volunteered to lower the Chilean flag as an act of contrition, then immediately committed suicide. The credibility of this legend did nothing to improve the image of the United States in the eyes of Chileans.[38]

WORLD WAR I AND THE INTER-WAR YEARS

Along with Argentina, Paraguay and Mexico, Chile remained neutral throughout World War I. There were several reasons for this. People who had travelled from Europe via Cape Horn or the Strait of Magellan had every right to feel that they had distanced themselves from Europe and its problems. Until the opening of the Panama Canal early in August 1914, virtually everyone except the Amerindians and arrivals from neighbouring South American countries had reached Chile by travelling around the bottom of South America. Moreover, public opinion, such as it was, was divided. Although most Chileans hoped to avoid the conflict, some who took an interest in international affairs sympathized with Great Britain and France, while others sympathized with the Central Powers.

Sympathetic to the cause of the Central Powers were officers of the Chilean army, trained by Germans since 1885. Many devout Roman Catholics shared their sentiments for quite another reason. From the perspective of 1914, the Austro-Hungarian Empire appeared the most faithful daughter of the Church. Great Britain had been Protestant since the sixteenth century, and the United States was overwhelmingly Protestant as well. France had separated Church and State in 1905, and Italy had been involved in an ongoing dispute with the Papacy since Italian nationalists had overrun the papal states in 1870. The other Entente power, Russia, was neither Roman Catholic nor highly regarded.

Nevertheless, the Allies had some trump cards. Chile's intellectual élite admired France and French literary achievements. Most of Chile's Protestants were of German extraction, but there were free-thinkers who admired British, French, and Italian willingness to break with the papacy. A Scot, Lord Thomas Cochrane, had commanded important naval battles during Chile's War of Independence and is widely perceived as founder of the Chilean navy. Statues and streets named for him are not as numerous as those for Arturo Prat, but they are numerous. As Germans trained the leaders of Chile's army, British naval officers provided training for their Chilean colleagues, who reciprocated with partiality for the British cause. Finally, British investment in Chile had been considerable before 1914, and the British economic profile was high.

Neither side was without blemish, but British authorities and naval officers showed considerably more respect for Chilean sensitivities than did their German counterparts over skirmishes in Chilean territorial waters. Whether such respect mattered is, however, unclear. In October 1914, several ships of the German navy went to Easter Island. The crews stayed for a week and installed an observation post. British ships intercepted the German ones as they entered international waters, but the Germans sank two British cruisers, the *Good Hope* and the *Monmouth*. Fresh from their victory, the German ships sailed directly to Valparaíso, where the local German community gave them a triumphant welcome.[39]

Until the United States became a belligerent in 1917, there was almost no pressure on Chile to take sides. When the United States did go to war, there was every reason why Chilean politicians wanted to demonstrate some degree of independence. Most Chileans felt that they owed the United

States no favours. Given the distance between Chile and Europe, the overwhelming desire of Chileans for neutrality, and the divided sentiments of those who really cared, neutrality was the path of least resistance between 1914 and 1918. On this occasion, Chileans were able—like the Dutch, the Danes, and the Swiss—to indulge in the luxury of that neutrality.

Nor did U.S.-Chilean relations appreciably improve in the 1920s and 1930s. British and German ships which had traded with Chile were otherwise occupied during the war, and the United States gained an economic hegemony which has survived to this day.[40] Despite closer economic ties, Chilean authorities suspected that their U.S. counterparts still sympathized with Peru which, unlike Chile, had followed the U.S. lead and declared war on the Central Powers. Such perceptions affected the Chilean-Peruvian negotiations which led to the peace treaty of 1929. The Hawley-Smoot Tariff of 1930 effectively excluded Chilean products from the U.S. market and worsened the unemployment situation within Chile.[41]

When Franklin Delano Roosevelt replaced Herbert Hoover as President of the United States in 1933 and Democrats regained control of the U.S. Congress, trade regulations liberalized and opportunities for trade increased. Adolf Hitler became Chancellor of Germany only weeks before President Roosevelt's inauguration, and the Roosevelt administration quickly came to regard co-operation with the Latin American republics as a vital national interest. In 1936, Secretary of State Cordell Hull travelled to Buenos Aires to discuss the world situation with his Latin American counterparts. That was the year when, in defiance of the Treaty of Versailles, Hitler's government had remilitarized the Rhineland. Mussolini had sent Italian troops to Ethiopia in defiance of the League of Nations, and their ally, Generalíssimo Francisco Franco, had launched a rebellion against Spain's legally constituted republican government. (Three years later, with help from Hitler and Mussolini, Franco would win.) In Buenos Aires, the foreign ministers agreed to consult each other "in the event of an international war outside America which might menace the peace of the American Republics."[42] They also agreed "that it is necessary to consecrate the principle of American solidarity in all non-continental conflicts."[43] The meaning of those words remained open to interpretation.

In 1938, the hemisphere's foreign ministers met in Lima shortly after Hitler had threatened an international war over Czechoslovakia's Sudetenland. The British and French governments had agreed at Munich to betray their Czechoslovak ally and allow Hitler to occupy the Sudetenland, the German-speaking parts of that country. At Lima the Foreign Ministers agreed that "the peace, security, or territorial integrity of any American Republic" was a matter of concern to all twenty-one American republics.[44] There were subsequent conferences in Panama in September 1939, after the outbreak of hostilities in Europe, and in Havana in July 1940, after Hitler's *Blitzkrieg* and occupation of the Netherlands and France.

By 1936, Germany had replaced the United States as Chile's largest trading partner.[45] To facilitate its military build-up, Hitler's Germany purchased copper and nitrate from Chile. It also bought fruit, wine, vegetables and honey. In return, Chile bought tools, railway equipment, and weapons from Germany.[46] Nor was German influence merely economic. German officers continued to train Chileans, and some Chilean officers went to Germany for training, even after Germany's defeat in 1918. One of these was Tobias Barros, who went there from 1926 to 1929. One of his friends, Barros says in his memoirs, was later a defendant at Nuremburg, General Alfred Jodl.[47] Barros would return to Germany as Chile's ambassador from 1940 to 1943. A real Germanophile, as his memoirs and correspondence make clear, Barros considered World War II little more than a clash of conflicting imperialisms. That first the Germans and then the British and Americans would enter partnerships with the odious Soviet Union, he thought, indicated the irrelevance of ideology or morality.[48]

Italians had been migrating to Chile since the late nineteenth century, and in the aftermath of World War I, some had become prominent. Arturo Alessandri, Liberal president of Chile for most of the 1920s and again from 1932 to 1938, whose statue stands outside La Moneda, was of Italian extraction, as was Juan Bautista Rossetti, foreign minister in 1941 and the early months of 1942. The FBI estimated that at least 52,000 people of Italian background lived in Chile by 1942, and of these some 12,000 were Italian nationals.[49]

By contrast, there were not many ethnic Japanese in Chile. Japanese had migrated by the thousands to neighbouring Peru and to Brazil, but not to Chile. The FBI was highly tentative in its estimates:

> At the present time [1943] there exists no exact source of information as to the number of Japanese presently in Chile. It is estimated by reliable sources, however, that at the present time there are approximately one thousand Japanese nationals in this country. Eighty per cent of these individuals are reported as having been in the country more than eight years and many of them have married individuals of Chilean nationality and have apparently located permanently in Chile. By 1940, at the time of the twenty-six hundredth anniversary of the Japanese Empire, it was reported that there were six hundred and eighty-eight Japanese residents in Chile.[50]

Clearly ethnic Japanese could not sway events in Chile by force of numbers.

To suggest that Chile's Germans and Italians determined Chilean foreign policy in 1942 would be simplistic. These groups were not monolithic, and while they might swing the balance of power in a close race, they were not sufficiently numerous to dominate. Not until 1924 did a Chilean of German extraction win a seat in the Chilean Senate. There were some Chileans of German extraction in the mining area of Chile's far north, enough to win an occasional seat in the Chilean Senate. After Julio Buschmann's triumph in Llanquihue (southern Chile's Lake District) that year, there were others: Carlos Werner (from Arauca, Malleco, and Cautín—just south of the Bío-Bío, roughly 600 kilometres south of Santiago), 1926-1930; Carlos Schürmann (who was one of five senators from Valdivia, Llanquihue and Chiloé), 1926-1934; Víctor Körner (also from Arauca, Malleco and Cautín), 1930-1938; Jorge Wachholtz (one of five from Tarapacá and Antofagasta in Chile's far north), 1933-1937; Carlos

Haverbeck (one of five from Valdivia and Chiloé elected in 1933, re-elected in 1937 to serve a larger constituency which stretched from Valdivia to Tierra del Fuego), 1933-1945; Oscar Schnake (one of five from Tarapacá and Antofagasta, elected in 1937 for an eight year term, but who resigned in 1939 to become a cabinet minister). By themselves, these people could not dominate the Senate which, at full strength, had 45 members.[51] German-Chileans elected their first deputy in 1888, and they dominated municipal councils in some parts of southern Chile. In Puerto Varas, the municipal council maintained its records in German until World War I.[52] However, they were neither numerous nor influential at the national level. The disillusioned liberal Germans who went to Chile after 1848 were the antithesis of Nazis, and one observer describes Oscar Schnake—the only cabinet minister with a German surname in 1942—as "the strongest advocate of the Allied cause" during Chile's 1942 presidential election campaign.[53] Conversely, some Chileans of neither German nor Italian extraction were partial to the Axis.

By contrast, even in the absence of a Chilean-Japanese community, the Japanese legation in Santiago managed to wield some influence, in partnership with the German and Italian embassies and through bribery of the appropriate people. The presence of German-Chileans and Italian-Chileans was of some significance, albeit limited, to Chile's political landscape.[54]

THE PRESIDENTIAL ELECTIONS OF 1938 AND 1942

Chile was not an easy country for anyone to govern. The constitution of 1833 provided for a strong presidency and, with amendments, it remained in effect until 1925. However, the last of the "strong" nineteenth century presidents, José Manuel Balmaceda (1886-1891), engaged in full scale civil war against Congress in a struggle for authority. Most of the German-led army, apart from Körmer, sided with Balmaceda, the British-led navy with Congress. Congress won. For more than a generation thereafter, cabinets came and went at the whim of Congress. Congress could express non-confidence in the cabinet, and the President could not respond—as in a Westminster-style parliament—with threats of dissolution and new elections.[55]

Although President Arturo Alessandri—a Liberal—was sufficiently popular that he won two non-consecutive presidential elections (in 1920 and again in 1932), even he had to leave the presidency in a storm of controversy in 1924 and again in 1925). General Carlos Ibáñez seized power through a military coup in 1927 and governed by non-constitutional means, recruiting as ministers people who were honest, competent technicians and administrators. Some forgave his authoritarian ways, regarding them as the price to be paid for stability and economic progress. Nevertheless, when the depression hit Chile, Ibáñez lost credibility, and his government lost power in 1931. One commentator has noted,

> ...that in the eighteen months after the fall of Ibáñez, Chile would experience no fewer than nine governments in office, ranging from moderate conservative to avowedly socialist, two general strikes, a mutiny in the fleet, and several coups, as the country plunged deeper into economic depression.[56]

In 1932, Arturo Alessandri won his second presidential election and began to serve what became the full six-year term designated by the Constitution of 1925. At the same time, Chile had a Communist party. The Partido Obrero Socialista (Socialist Workers' Party), founded in 1912, became the Chilean Communist Party—affiliated with Moscow—in 1922.[57] Communists supported the victorious Radical candidates in the elections of 1938 and 1942. Although they remained a definite minority of the electorate, which until 1925 excluded women and illiterate men, they enjoyed a resurgence in the aftermath of the depression.[58] Nazi activity had significant impact on Chile's presidential election of 25 October 1938. Chile's own Nazi party, Vanguardia Popular Socialista (VPS) led by Jorge González von Marées, had a membership of about 5,000—many of them young, all of them reactionary. Many came from prominent German-Chilean families who lived in Valdivia or Osorno.[59] Many others did not have German names.[60] González von Marées and his party, according to historian Robert Alexander,

> ...had special appeal to the German-descended people of the southern part of central Chile, but [it] also won recruits among other sectors of the population. It had most of the accoutrements of a fascist party, including uniformed storm troopers and various symbols.[61]

Blancpain says that Marcial González, Jorge's father, met Sofia von Marées—of German nobility—during a trip to Berlin before 1914.[62] Inspired by Mussolini, González von Marées established his party in April 1932.[63] When Hitler became Germany's chancellor nine months later and Jewish refugees began to arrive in Chile, González became a blatant anti-Semitic racist. Events played into his hands. Alessandri's government admitted Jewish refugees to Chile on condition that they limit themselves to mining or agriculture, but most preferred to establish businesses around Santiago. This made them vulnerable to charges of breach of contract and disruption of Chilean homogeneity.[64] González and his followers greeted each other with a Nazi salute, "Heil!" or "Heil Chile!" Hitler's portrait and a Swastika hung at party headquarters.[65] In 1937 he became one of eighteen deputies elected to the National Congress from Santiago, a position he retained until 1945.[66]

Chile was not alone in having right-wing fanatics. The United States had the radio evangelist priest, Father Charles E. Coughlin. The United Kingdom had Sir Oswald Mosley and his British Union of Fascists and William Joyce's National Socialist League. Quebec's Fascist leader, Adrien Arcand, admired Hitler, and anti-Semitic French-Canadians founded a weekly newspaper, Le Patriote. Anti-Semitism was a significant factor in the United States, the United Kingdom, and Canada. However, in none of these places was there an event to parallel the attempted Nazi takeover of 5 September 1938 in Chile.

On 5 September 1938, in an attempt to stage a Putsch, young Nazis, members of the VPS, stormed the University of Chile and the upper floors of a downtown Santiago business office. The Liberal government of President

Alessandri responded with such determination that at least fifty-five VPS members died, along with one policeman (Carabinero). Most of the fifty-five did not have German surnames.[67] Alessandri's government jailed González von Marées, as well as Conservative presidential candidate (and former president) Carlos Ibáñez, suspected of sympathy if not collusion with the young Nazis. According to Alexander, Alessandri watched with concern the alliance between González von Marées and his Nazis, on the one hand, and Carlos Ibáñez. Ibáñez had disregarded the constitution, imposed press censorship, and deported opponents; he and the young Nazis appeared to share common values.[68] However, Alessandri did not personally order the attack which killed so many young people. Alessandri's biographer, Fidel Araneda Bravo, agrees.[69] Nevertheless, Alessandri had every reason to fear and oppose Naziism, despite his determination as late as 1943 that Chile should remain neutral.

Events of 5 September 1938 are still commemorated in Chile. There is a monument to the fifty-five Nazi "martyrs" in the Santiago General Cemetery, where each year on 5 September Nazis gather to remember their "sacrifice." A plaque on the exterior of the building of Chile's Ministry of Justice—across the street from La Moneda, the presidential palace—bears their names.

Until 5 September 1938, Liberal candidate Gustavo Ross, Alessandri's finance minister, had been favoured to win the election. However, Radical candidate Pedro Aguirre chose to visit the imprisoned Ibáñez, and shortly thereafter, Ibáñez withdrew from the race and threw his support behind Aguirre, creating the Popular Front. Convinced that he could not win, Ibáñez preferred Aguirre to Ross. With 50.2% of the popular vote, Aguirre then narrowly managed to defeat Ross. The provinces of Valdivia and Osorno, home to many German settlers, voted for Aguirre, who assumed the presidency 24 December 1938.

On 10 June 1941 Aguirre appointed Juan Bautista Rossetti, son of an Italian immigrant,[70] as his foreign minister. Sir Charles Orde, the newly arrived British Ambassador to Chile, found the Aguirre-Rossetti government, and Chileans in general, naïvely indifferent toward the menace which Nazi Germany posed. Orde thought that they suffered from "ignorance, mental laziness and a sense of distance from the focus of disturbance in Europe." Chileans were obsessed with their neutrality and the economic advantages which resulted from that neutrality. The impact of Chile's German community, and, in the aftermath of the Ribbentrop-Molotov Pact, the power of Communist voters, strengthened the pressures for neutrality. (Of course, the Communists changed their minds when Hitler invaded the Soviet Union in June 1941). Fortunately from a British standpoint, thought Orde, Germany was becoming "progressively more unpopular as the Nazi objectives of world domination and the destruction of the liberty of smaller nations [became] apparent."[71]

Despite Orde's reservations, Foreign Minister Rossetti did try to use Chile's diplomatic presence in Europe in a constructive way. For humanitarian reasons, in November 1941 he forwarded an appeal from Chile's Senate and Chamber of Deputies to Ambassador Tobias Barros in Berlin. Barros was to inform German officials "that the Chilean Government would be glad to see the ceasing of the shooting of French hostages by way of reprisals throughout the occupied zone." Nobody, thought Chilean authorities, should "suffer for a crime...committed by somebody else."[72] Unfortunately, Nazi barbarism was to continue.

Enrique Bernstein, a diplomat at Chile's embassy in Río de Janeiro, Brazil's capital at the time, subsequently wrote about Chilean-Brazilian relations during Aguirre's presidency. Brazilian authorities consistently sought close ties with Chile, said Bernstein. Their relationship with Argentina was often strained, and if they could not have full confidence in their neighbour, they certainly wanted the friendship of their neighbour's neighbour. For their part, Bernstein and his colleagues at the embassy were delighted to co-operate. The embassy's goal, said Bernstein, was "to strengthen ties on every front between the governments in Río de Janeiro and Santiago."[73] At first they succeeded. In 1940, Spain's head of state, Generalíssimo Francisco Franco, took offence at speeches made in front of

Aguirre by supporters of the Spanish Republicans, whom he had defeated the previous year after a bloody three-year civil war. Franco's government severed diplomatic relations with Chile, and Brazil became protector of Spanish interests in Chile and Chilean interests in Spain during the brief interruption.[74] (Chile's diplomatic rupture with the Axis might have produced more desirable results had the rupture lasted, but such was not to be.) In 1941, Brazil's foreign minister, Osvaldo Arana, went to Santiago for talks with Rossetti. He wanted assurances that if the United States and Brazil became belligerents, Chile—unlike Argentina—would support the Allied cause. According to Bernstein, Aranha returned home "very satisfied."[75]

Then Aguirre's death late in 1941 forced a new presidential election 1 February 1942. The favourite candidate of the German Embassy was Carlos Ibáñez, the Conservative. Auswärtiges Amt in Berlin and the German Embassy in Santiago observed the election with interest. As early as mid-January 1941, when President Aguirre appeared to have completed less than half his term, Under-Secretary of State Baron Ernst von Weizsäcker had suggested to von Schön that German money should be used to influence Chilean elections. Because of the sensitivity of the matter, von Weizsäcker instructed von Schön to destroy the telegram upon reading it.[76] A copy of the telegram did survive, but von Schön took action. On 4 December, following Aguirre's death, he advised Auswärtiges Amt that an election was imminent. The likeliest candidates, he expected, would be former President Carlos Ibáñez, Radical Juan Antonio Ríos, and Chile's former minister in Vichy, Gabriel González Videla. This last—who did not actually become a candidate until the 1946 presidential election (which he won)—appeared to von Schön as the least friendly to Germany. Germany must appear to be neutral in the presidential contest, advised von Schön, but if it could act on the sly, 130,000 Reichmarks might influence the outcome.[77] On 16 December von Schön requested authority to spend $100,000 U.S. on the Ibáñez campaign. Discretion must be absolute, von Schön warned, but "Ibáñez is a friend and admirer of the German people and shares Nazi values."[78] On 12 January 1942 an Abwehr agent in Santiago also requested authorization to provide $100,000 to $150,000 U.S. to the Ibáñez campaign. Von Schön supported the request, delighted that if the Abwehr were to pay the money the role of the embassy would be more obscure.[79] (U.S. intelligence sources discovered that the Japanese legation contributed more than $16,000 U.S. to the Ibáñez campaign.)[80] The Radical candidate, Juan Antonio Ríos, probably did not know the details of Nazi Germany's support for his opponent, but he did know that *he* did not owe Nazi Germany any favours. Needless to say, Ambassador Bowers preferred Ríos from the governing Radical party to Ibáñez.

Bowers supported Ríos out of necessity—because he was the only alternative to Ibáñez. At first Bowers worked actively, although surreptitiously, on behalf of Oscar Schnake, the Socialist leader, whose views on foreign policy coincided most closely with those of the State Department. "A proposition has been made," said Bowers, "to the Branden Copper Company. A man will ask to buy 5000 tons of copper at the Chilean price...If the sale is made...this will realize 9,000,000 pesos. This would be all that Schnake will need...The Embassy here has nothing to do with it, and does not even know about it—if you know what I mean," concluded Bowers.[81] By mid-January, however, Schnake decided that he could not win, and rather than split the anti-Ibáñez vote he withdrew from the campaign and threw his support behind Ríos.

Bowers had little of a positive nature to say about Ríos but much that was negative about Ibáñez. He had heard rumours that the German Embassy was financing his campaign. At no point did his advertisements call for continental solidarity. Young Nazis who supported González von Marées were working at the Ibáñez headquarters, and Ibáñez had secretly met with González von Marées, "the most pronounced Nazi and the most bitter enemy of the United States in the country." Ibáñez, said Bowers, would probably replace Chile's constitution and create a system of government "based on the theories of Hitler, Mussolini and Franco."[82] Secretary of State Cordell Hull wanted Bowers to stay out of the campaign and let Chileans decide for themselves. Hull thought that donations to any candidate on the part of the U.S. government or, for that matter, of U.S. citizens, would violate treaty obligations undertaken at the Montevideo and Buenos Aires Inter-American conferences of 1933 and 1938.[83] Bowers resolved the problem by taking a vacation.[84]

Yet Bowers remained concerned, and he rejoiced when Ríos won. "Ibáñez," he said, "has a campaign fund without precedent in Chile and it is estimated that he is spending close to a million pesos a day." Bowers regarded as "almost hysterical" the support which the Roman Catholic newspaper El Diario Ilustrado had given Ibáñez. Bowers was justified in this comment. El Diario Ilustrado, which had already endorsed the economic policies of the Ibáñez (Conservative) party in its editorial of 8 January, abandoned any pretence of objectivity after Ibáñez visited its offices the following day.[85] On 12 January it accused Socialist leader Oscar Schnake of treason and warned (correctly) that Ríos had offered him a cabinet position. Its editorial that day bore the title "Tyrants of the proletariat." On 20 January the banner headline read: "The entire country has positioned itself on the side of the national candidate." The "national candidate," was, of course, Ibáñez. Subsequent issues portrayed, through both words and pictures, throngs cheering Ibáñez as he travelled through Osorno, Puerto Varas, Puerto Montt, and Valdivia. Coverage of the Valdivia rally was the most shrill, in part because of what Ibáñez reportedly said, in part because of the huge dark print used to print a portion: "I have in my hand the amoral and destructive programme of the Popular Front, which before our very eyes weakened France and bloodied Spain." In other words, Ibáñez identified Chile's Popular Front with elected Spanish politicians who had opposed Franco's military takeover and French politicians who had "caused" France's military defeat of 1940. At the same time, Ibáñez also accused the Popular Front of replacing Chile's flag with the hammer-and-sickle.[86]

At the opposite end of the continuum from El Diario Ilustrado was another Santiago daily, La Nación. Repeatedly its headlines, editorials, and news items reminded readers that Ibáñez had been a "dictator" who governed by non-constitutional means and that Ríos was the candidate of national unity, social justice, and democracy. Its editorial of 8 January actually labelled Ibáñez as a "Fascist." The issue of 28 January carried a huge Ríos advertisement which denied that Ibáñez was "the only candidate who [would] exterminate Communism."[87]

Bowers also noted with horror that two "outstanding Catholic laymen," Senators Miguel Cruchaga and Maximiano Errázuriz, supported Ibáñez.[88] Cruchaga was one of five senators from Tarapacá and Antofagasta, and served as provisional president of the Senate. Errázuriz was one of five senators from Curicó, Talca, Maule and Linares, between Santiago and the Bío-Bío. By one estimate, three presidents of Chile, one archbishop and some fifty deputies and senators had come from his extended family.[89] There was a longstanding alliance between the Roman Catholic Church and Chile's Conservative party.[90] Bowers estimated that the Ibáñez campaign spent $7 for each vote the former president received.[91]

Former President Alessandri, whose opposition to the diplomatic rupture with the Axis may have contributed to the delay, shared Bowers's lack of enthusiasm for either candidate. Historian Robert Alexander notes that Alessandri had never forgiven Ibáñez for ousting him in the 1927 coup d'état, nor had he,

> ...forgiven Ríos for having been Ibáñez's closest associate during the dictatorship and for having plotted against Alessandri's own régime on at least one occasion. In the end, however, Alessandri threw his support to Ríos in order to prevent the greater evil of the ex-dictator's return to power.[92]

Clearly, the highly respected Alessandri—winner of two presidential elections during the inter-war period, had no reason to support decisions of either Ríos or Ibáñez.

The campaign advertisements from the two candidates indicated that leadership ability rather than foreign policy was the principal issue. References to foreign policy were somewhat oblique and indicated that

Communists were a greater threat than Nazis, Fascists, or Japanese Imperialists. On 12 January, Ibáñez had a full page advertisement in *El Mercurio* which began with the headline: "Neither Communism nor Fascism will prosper in Chile while I am in charge." *El Mercurio*, founded at Valparaíso in 1827, a daily since 1829, and published for decades in Santiago, was both Chile's oldest surviving newspaper and its most highly regarded one.[93] Puerto Montt's *El Llanquihue* printed the same advertisement five days later, and again 20 and 22 January. The pro-Ibáñez *El Diario Ilustrado* also carried it.[94] On 21 January an Ibáñez advertisement in *El Diario Ilustrado* portrayed an hour glass with the stand on top, marked "Communism," filtering to the glass below, labelled "Popular Front." The caption read: "Day by day...hour by hour, Communism invades and controls the Popular Front." An election eve commercial ironically called for "Democracy without charlatans and Communists" as well as "A people united, without hatred.[95] "A full page advertisement for Ríos in the 12 January issue of *El Mercurio* called for "National unity, hemispheric unity, democratic unity—one country, one democracy, one president." The following day, Ibáñez—the Conservative general who had usurped power in 1929!—depicted himself as a populist. His advertisement in *El Mercurio* said: "Ibáñez is the candidate of the people." As for Ríos, his picture covered most of an entire page, apart from a one-sentence quotation: "Citizens are not at all willing to suffer dictatorships, much less one based on the fascist or reactionary far right."

The campaign continued in that spirit. A full page Ibáñez advertisement of 27 January promised: "Ibáñez is accompanied by parties which will help resolve the country's problems and by a public fed up with political infighting. From left and right, one country united in the desire to save itself from social and economic disaster." The next day, a Ríos commercial which filled six of the eight columns for the full length of a page in *El Mercurio*, proclaimed: "Neither fascism, nor dictatorship, nor disorder. Respect for all rights, Forward with production, Order and Discipline, Continental Solidarity. It is democracy that we defend."

As election day, 1 February, approached, Ibáñez continued to depict himself as a competent populist while Ríos proclaimed himself the best hope for democracy. A spread over two pages in the issue of 27 January proclaimed, "The south of Chile favours Ibáñez." Accompanying the caption were pictures of crowds at Puerto Montt, Valdivia, Temuco, Puerto Varas, and elsewhere. The Ríos advertisement of the same day warned, "Peace is not the product of terror but of social cooperation. Dictatorship divides Chileans. Democracy unites them by work and justice. Assure peace for Chile. Vote Ríos." On election day itself, full page advertisements said: "Influence your country for the better. Vote for Ibáñez," and "Vote for Juan Antonio Ríos, candidate of democracy."

If a diplomatic rupture was not an issue in other parts of Chile, the candidates—not surprisingly—chose to say nothing about it in the Valdivia-Osorno-Puerto Montt area, where it would have been particularly sensitive. Neither *El Correo de Valdivia* nor Puerto Montt's *El Llanqihue* would endorse either Ríos or Ibáñez. Indeed, *El Correo de Valdivia* said that they were both worthy candidates.[96] On election day, *El Llanquihue* published an editorial critical of both parties, Conservative and Radical, for being too shrill and divisive.[97] A Ríos advertisement which appeared in *El Llanquihue* 11 January 1942, the day before a scheduled visit to Puerto Montt, stressed Ríos's character, patriotism, and energy, but it was short on specifics. An Ibáñez commercial in the same newspaper four days later promised a fight against Communism—although the Soviet Union was fighting for its survival at the time. "Communism," said the advertisement, "disorganizes national activities, provokes strikes, curtails production, weakens the country's internal unity, disrupts international efforts, destroys democracy." A message in huge print guaranteed that if Ibáñez—who had already operated in defiance of democracy from 1927 to 1931—was elected, communism would disappear. There was no place for class warfare, but youth should be patriotic, and there should be greater respect for authority. A half-page Ibáñez advertisement of 23 January reminded readers that during his earlier presidency, Ibáñez had transformed Chile from a country of straw and mud into another of cement and steel. On the other side of a picture of Ibáñez in uniform was a reminder, "The Popular Front [the Radical coalition] brings misery, backwardness, and Bolshevik politics." A Ríos insert of 29 January promised that a government led by him would bring order, prosperity, and a profound respect for law and the constitution. Neither candidate discussed the Río conference nor its principal recommendation.

Ambassador Bowers thought that Ríos' margin of victory over Ibáñez was decisive: 257,980 to 202,035, with 2,065 blank or spoiled ballots. Most surprisingly, given El Mercurio's 27 January reports of the Ibáñez campaign in south Chile, Ríos did very well in the south. His margin of victory was 9,858: 6,406 in Valdivia; 5,154: 4,086 in Osorno; 21, 069: 9,057 in Concepción. (It may have helped that Mrs. Ríos came from Osorno.) He also carried heavily Croatian Magallanes, which includes Punta Arenas on the Strait of Magellan, 4,397: 1,214. His margin of victory in Santiago itself was tighter: 63,130: 60,007. Ibáñez managed to triumph in Llanquihue, which included Frutillar, Puerto Varas and Puerto Montt: 5,067: 3,367. He narrowly carried the nearby island of Chiloé (1,212: 1,162) and the city of Valparaíso (23,181: 21,006).[98] Evidently the ethnic vote was not monolithic. Ríos triumphed with 55.7% of the popular vote against 43.8% for Ibáñez.

SUMMARY AND CONCLUSIONS

Chilean diplomats and politicians had to take into account the opinions and actions of neighbouring governments in Argentina, Peru, and Bolivia. Chileans also had long-established and friendly ties with Wilhelmine and Weimar Germany, long-established and ambivalent ties with the United States. Ties with Great Britain and France were reasonably friendly. At the same time, Chilean politicians were well aware that some voters were well disposed, for reasons of ethnicity or ideology or both, toward the Axis powers. Those Axis powers were in a position to make their influence felt although not, perhaps, as strongly as the FBI thought.

NOTES

1. James L. Garrett, "The Beagle Channel: Confrontation and Negotiation in the Southern Cone," *Journal of Interamerican Studies and World Affairs*, XXVII, 3 (Fall, 1985), pp. 81-109.

2. José Higuera, "Las islas de la discordia," *Ercilla*, No. 3051 (Jan. 27-Feb. 9, 1997), p. 33.

3. See his letter to the editor of *El Mercurio* (Santiago), 1 Sept. 1964.

4. Harold Blakemore, "From the War of the Pacific to 1930," in Bethell, p. 72.

5. Interview with Guy Sorman, first printed in *Le Figaro* 18 Sept. 1993, reprinted in Raquel Correa and Elizabeth Subercaseaux, *Ego Sum* (Santiago: Planeta, 1993), p. 216.

6. *El Llanquihue* (Puerto Montt), 8 Feb. 1997.

7. See especially *El Mercurio* (Santiago), 26 March 1997.

8. Young, p. 74. Simon Collier, "From Independence to the War of the Pacific," in Bethell, p. 24.

9. Mentioned twice by J. Ignacio García, Intendent of Valdivia, 18 Aug. and 8 Nov. 1842, in Emilio Held Winkler, *Colonización Alemana del Sur de Chile: Documentación de su Orígen* (Valparaíso, 1996), p. 11.

10. Bernardo Philippi al gobierno con lista de emigrados qui viajan en el buque *Herrmann* para avecindarse en Valdivia, Cassel, 12 June 1850, Held, pp. 129-130.

11. Quoted and dated in article "Carlos Anwandter," p. 18; repeated 4 Dec. 1851 in decree granting their citizenship, "Anwandter y otros al gobierno: solicitud de naturalizacion," Held, pp. 277-279.

12. Philippi, Cassel, to government, Santiago, 9 Jan. 1849, Held, p. 71; Philippi to government, 11 June, 1851, Held, p. 242; Philippi to government, 10 Aug. 1851, Held, p. 257.

13. Philippi, Cassel, to government, 12 Dec. 1850, Held, p. 186; Philippi to government, 12 April 1851, Held, pp. 234-236.

14. Philippi to government, 11 Nov. 1848, Held, p. 67; see also Philippi to government, 12 Dec. 1850, p. 186.

15. Philippi to government, 11 Nov. 1848, Held, p. 67; Baron Reichenbach, Vienna, to Philippi, Cassel, 28 March 1850, Held, pp. 117-119. See also Young, pp. 69-74.

16. René A. Peri Fagerstrom, *Reseña de la Colonización en Chile* (Santiago: Andrés Bello, 1989), p. 172. For further information on German immigration, see Peri Fagerstrom, pp. 53-75, 81-82, 93-96, 99-104, 111-116, 127, 169, 181-195.

17. Young, pp. 69-78, 167-170. Harold Blakemore, "From the War of the Pacific to 1935," in Bethell, p. 60.

18. Delia Domínguez Moir, "Colonización alemana: épica y leyenda del paralelo 40," Yáñez, p. 9.

19. Yáñez, p. 17.

20. Enrique Kinzel K. and Bernardo Horn K., *Puerto Varas: 130 Años de Historia, 1852-1983* (Puerto Varas: Horn, 1983), p. 276.

21. Young, p. 153.

22. Salvador Sanfuentes, Santiago, to Philippi, Cassel, 2 Aug. 1848, Held, p. 63.

23. Philippi, Cassel, to government, 11 Sept. 1850, Held, p. 144.

24. Varas, Santiago, to Philippi, Cassel, 28 March 1850, Held, p. 127; also Varas to los SENORES Godefroy e hijo, 24 Dec. 1850, Held, p. 191.

25. *La Prensa* (Osorno), 14 Oct. 1941.

26. "Lista de colonos que se embarcaron en el buque hamburgués *Susana* para colonizar la provincia de Valdivia," Held, p. 145.

27. Barros Van Buren, p. 190.

28. Sergio Villalobos R., Osvaldo Silva G., Fernando Silva V., and Patricio Estelle M., *Historia de Chile* (Santiago: Editorial Universitaria, 1992), p. 590.

29. Von Schön to Auswärtiges Amt, 18 Aug. 1941, R.G. 242, National Archives and Research Administration (NARA), College Park, Md., Series T-120, Reel 183,frame 88328. Cited hereafter as AA.

30. Humphreys, I, p. 25.

31. FBI report, *Chile Today (March 1943)*, Box 141, Group 24, Papers of Harry L. Hopkins, File: FBI Reports, Chile, FDR presidential archives, Hyde Park, New York, p. 67. Cited hereafter as FBI. Information about the FBI/OSS division of the world is available from Newton, p. 416.

32. Blakemore in Bethell, p. 54.

33. Blancpain, *Los Alemanes...*, pp. 67, 69, 93 (regarding the educational achievements of the German immigrants). For Germany as a counterweight to the USA and U.K., see p. 147; re medical studies, pp. 151-2; re officer training, pp. 161-169; re teacher training, pp. 153-160; regarding the numbers who spoke German in the mid-twentieth century, pp. 190 (for the entire country) and 115 (for southern Chile).

34. Blancpain, *Los Alemanes...*, p. 149.

35. Dexter Perkins, *The Monroe Doctrine, 1826-1867* (Gloucester, Mass.: Peter Smith, 1966), pp. 539-545.

36. James G. Blaine, Washington, to Judson Kilpatrick, Santiago, 15 June 1881, *Foreign Relations of the United States, 1881, (FRUS, 1881)*, pp. 131-133; Blaine to William Henry Trescot, Santiago, *FRUS, 1881*, pp. 147-148; Frelinghuysen, Washington, to Trescot, 24 Feb. 1882, *FRUS, 1882*, pp. 75-76.

37. Blaine to Trescot, 1 Dec. 1881, *FRUS, 1881*, p. 146.

38. For a more thorough review of U.S.-Chilean relations, see William F. Sater, *Chile and the United States* (Athens: University of Georgia Press, 1990. See also Philip Marshall Brown, "Frederick Theodore Frelinghuysen," in Samuel Flagg Bemis (ed.), *American Secretaries of State and Their Diplomacy*, VIII (New York: Pageant, 1958), pp. 9-17; and Joseph B. Lockey, "Jamesd Gillespie Blaine," *ibid.*, pp. 146-163.

39. Ricardo Couyoumdjian, ""En torno a la neutralidad de Chile durante la Primera Guerra Mundial," in Walter Sanchez G. and Teresa Pereira L. (eds.), *Cientocincuenta Años de Política Exterior Chilena* (Santiago: Editorial Universitaria, 1977), pp. 180-205.

40. Blakemore in Bethell, pp. 68-71.

41. For more extensive accounts of Chilean foreign relations to 1933, see Barros Van Buren and Sater. See also Ricardo Couyoumdjian, "En torno a la neutralidad de Chile durante la primera guerra mundial," in Walter Sánchez G. and Teresa Pereira L., *Cientocincuenta Años de Política Exterior Chilena* (Santiago: Editorial Universitaria, 1977), pp. 180-222.

42. The Consultative Pact [Convention for the Maintenance, Preservation, and Reestablishment of Peace, signed at Buenos Aires, 23 Dec. 1936, proclaimed 16 Sept. 1937], in Bartlett, p. 553. For a Chilean account of the conferences at Buenos Aires, Lima, Panama, and Havana, see Enrique Bernstein C., "Chile y la política de defensa continental desde la Segunda Guerra Mundial hasta el presente," in Sanchez and Pereira, pp. 211-213.

43. "Declaration of Principles of Inter-American Solidarity and Confederation," Bartlett, p. 554.

44. Quoted from Julius Pratt, A History of United States Foreign Policy (Englewood Cliffs, N.J., 1965), p. 375. Pratt quoted from the communique issued by the foreign ministers.

45. Sater, p. 106.

46. Blancpain, Les Allemands..., pp. 873-874.

47. Tobias Barros, II, pp. 159, 297-298.

48. Tobias Barros, II, p. 351; Tobias Barros to President-elect Ríos, 4 Feb. 1942, s/n, vol. 1969, Archivos del Departamento de Relaciones Exteriores, Santiago. Cited hereafter as ADRE.

49. FBI, p. 232; Peri Fagerstrom, pp. 19, 75, 167-168.

50. FBI, pp. 211-212.

51. Information about Chilean Senators is extracted from Luis Valencia Avaria (ed.), Anales de la República (Santiago: Andrés Bello, c. 1984).

52. Blancpain, Los Alemanes..., p. 197.

53. Sater, p. 114.

54. This is a point made by Tobias Barros, II, p. 418.

55. Blakemore in Bethell, pp. 48-58, 67-68, 73.

56. Blakemore in Bethell, p. 85.

57. Blakemore in Bethell, pp. 64, 66.

58. Drake in Bethell, pp. 93-104.

59. Blancpain, Les Allemands..., p. 867.

60. The names of 55 Nazis killed in the abortive Putsch of 5 Sept. 1938 appear on a plaque outside the Ministry of Justice at the corner of Morenda and Moneda, as well as on a monument in the Santiago General Cemetery. Of those, at least five and at most eight had German surnames.

61. Alexander, p. 22, and confirmed by Sanchez, pp. 66-67.

62. Blancpain, Les Allemands..., p. 862.

63. Blancpain, Les Allemands..., p. 863.

64. Blancpain, Les Allemands..., pp. 865-866.

65. Report of a Peruvian who visited the headquarters of González, Luis Alberto Sánchez, Visto y Vivido en Chile: Bitacura Chilena, 1930-1970 (Lima: Editoriales Unidas, S.A., 1975), pp. 66-67.

66. Valencia Avaria, II, pp. 520, 527, 535, 539, 540.

67. There are 55 names listed on the plaque outside the Ministry of Justice and on the Nazi monument at the Santiago General Cemetery.

68. Silva Galdames, pp. 289-293.

69. Alexander, p. 23; Fidel Araneda Bravo, *Arturo Alessandri Palma* (Santiago: Editorial Nascimento, 19797), p. 153.

70. Bowers, p. 59.

71. Orde to Eden, 16 Sept. 1941, Series A981/1, Item CHIL 10, Canberra.

72. R. Dundas Smith, consul-general of Chile, Sydney, to Herbert V. Evatt, Minister of External Affairs, Canberra, 19 Nov. 1941 (with an English-language translation of Rossetti's message), Series A981/1, Item CHIL 10, Canberra.

73. Enrique Bernstein Crabantes, *Recuerdo de un diplomático haciendo camino, 1933-1957* (Santiago: Andrés Bello, 1984), vol. I, p. 66.

74. Bernstein, p. 67.

75. Bernstein, p. 69.

76. Von Weizsäcker at AA, Berlin, to von Schön, 18 Jan. 1941, frame 88266.

77. Von Schön to AA, 4 Dec. 1941, frame 88419.

78. Von Schön to AA, 16 Dec. 1941, frame 88426.

79. Wörmann memorandum, Berlin, 12 Jan. 1942, frame 88433.

80. MAGIC summary #329, 18 Feb. 1943, Entry 9006, Box 3, R.G. 457, NARA, College Park, Md. Cited hereafter as MAGIC.

81. Bowers to FDR, 5 Jan. 1942, PSF.

82. Bowers to Hull, 5 Jan. 1942, PSF.

83. Hull to FDR, 16 and 19 Jan. 1942, PSF.

84. Bowers, Valparaíso, to FDR, 16 Jan. 1942, PSF.

85. *El Diario Ilustrado* (Santiago), 10 Jan. 1942.

86. *El Diario Ilustrado* (Santiago), 24 January (regarding Osorno, Puerto Varas, and Puerto Montt) and 25 January (regarding Valdivia).

87. *La Nación* (Santiago), 24, 25, 27 Dec. 1941, 1, 8, 12, 28, Jan. 1942.

88. Bowers to FDR, 23 Jan. 1942, PSF.

89. Simon Collier, "From Independence to the War of the Pacific," in Bethell, p. 22.

90. Blakemore in Bethell, p. 58.

91. Bowers to FDR, 2 Feb. 1942, PSF.

92. Alexander, pp. 29-30.

93. Collier in Bethell, p. 25.

94. *El Diario Ilustrado*, 14 and 15 Jan. 1942.

95. *El Diario Ilustrado*, 31 Jan. 1942.

96. See in particular the post-election editorial of 2 Feb. 1942 in *El Correo de Valdivia*.

97. *El Llanquihue* (Puerto Montt), 1 Feb. 1942.

98. Bowers' comments are taken from his letter of 2 Feb. 1942 to FDR; election results appeared in *El Mercurio* of the same day.

CHAPTER 2

INFILTRATION

NAZI GERMANY AND CHILE BEFORE PEARL HARBOR

In January 1935, the German navy cruiser *Karlsruhe* visited Valparaíso. This marked the first occasion when a ship from Hitler's navy had entered a Chilean port. The last German cruiser to call, the *Emden*, had done so eight years earlier, during the Weimar Republic. The British Embassy in Santiago advised Foreign Secretary Sir John Simon that there was no cause for alarm. True it was that Chile's German community and other Chileans had given the *Karlsruhe*'s officers and crew a warm welcome. True it also was that Chile's Germans had taken advantage of Chilean neutrality during World War I to buy German war bonds. However, "All that money was lost," and, thought then-Ambassador Sir John Michell, Chilean Germans probably would not care to repeat that experience if there was another war. Moreover, wrote Michell, most Chilean Germans were "not at heart in sympathy with the Nazi régime, although they seemingly comply with the outward form of it." Michell regarded members of Chile's German community as distinctively German and unassimilated, but he said they were also loyal

Chileans. Others appreciated what they had done to develop the country, and the Germans themselves were grateful for the opportunities and the lifestyle which Chile had given them.[1] Michell's observations are compatible with information which respondents provided the author in the course of interviews early in 1997.

Given the size of Chile, by 1942 Nazi Germany had a colossal diplomatic and consular staff in that country. There were an embassy in Santiago, a consulate-general in Valparaíso, seven consulates (Antofagasta, Concepción, Iquique, Punta Arenas, Santiago, Temuco, and Valdivia), seven vice-consulates (Arica, Caldera, Corral, Coquimbo, Osorno, Puerto Montt and Talcahuano), and a consular agency—in a nation of 5,023,539 people.[2] When the break did take place early in 1943, a grand total of ninety-seven people from the embassy alone—forty-two officials, employees, and their families—sought repatriation to Germany.[3] Most of these posts had opened during the Nazi period, and all the key people at the embassy had arrived between 1936 and 1941. Ambassador von Schön had presented his credentials to President Alessandri 22 April 1936, commercial attaché Walter Böttger 8 April 1938, counsellor Wilhelm von Pochhammer 27 August 1938, air attaché Ludwig von Bohlen 14 July 1941.[4] These were not people inherited from the Weimar Republic.

The FBI reported that the German diplomatic corps engaged in a wide range of questionable activities—from manipulating the media to espionage, and at least one British Embassy source agreed. V. Cavendish-Bentinck at the British Embassy in Santiago had told his superior, Foreign Secretary Anthony Eden, that German companies doing business in Chile purchased advertising in newspapers which published German propaganda. "This naturally encourages the editorial staffs to fill up any vacant spaces they may have with that propaganda," observed Cavendish-Bentinck. Nor was there any shortage of such propaganda. Cavendish-Bentinck noted that "bulky packages" of it arrived at the offices of Chilean newspapers.[5]

The FBI and the British Embassy also thought that Nazis influenced radio programmes and film production in Chile.[6] The British Embassy also noted that German State Railways (GSR) encouraged Chileans to visit Germany. GSR had an office in Santiago and sent posters throughout Chile, with the result that ships sailing from Valparaíso to Hamburg were booked well in advance.[7] According to Marcial Martínez, an investigator from the Chilean Foreign Office, the German embassy provided money and direction for Chilean Nazis. One key person identified by Martínez was Wilhelm Hammerschmidt, an official from Göbbels' Ministry of Enlightenment and Propaganda. Chile's counter-intelligence organization, the Dirección General de Investigaciones (DGI), discovered that before Hammerschmidt's arrival in Chile to influence newspapers, films, and broadcasts, Mexico had deported Hammerschmidt for Nazi activities. The DGI agreed that money and advice from the German embassy enabled Nazis to control and influence a number of Chilean newspapers and radio stations, particularly in southern Chile, which Martínez identified.[8]

The FBI knew that agents of Germany's spy organization Abwehr reported to their superiors in Hamburg from bases in or near Santiago, Río de Janeiro, Montevideo, and Buenos Aires.[9] Of these, Santiago was the only place near the Pacific coast. The principal source of messages from Chile was a radio transmitter identified as radio station PYL, located near Valparaíso, and headed since 1937 by Albert Julius von Appen Oestmann, a.k.a. "Apfel." Born in Germany in 1901, von Appen became a Captain in the German Merchant Marine. From 1937 until 1939, he served as inspector for the Hamburg-American Line in Chile. When the outbreak of war terminated commercial traffic, he became that company's representative. Von Appen's employment with the Hamburg-American Line allowed him to "make numerous trips on the Pacific Coast, travelling as far north as Panama." In 1939 he spent three months in Hamburg. Questioned by Chilean authorities in October 1942, Von Appen said that he had been a card-carrying Nazi since 1933.[10] J. Edgar Hoover, head of the FBI, claimed that his organization "intercepted and decoded" messages between PYL in Valparaíso and its German contact station in Hamburg since April 1941.[11]

The FBI was certain that Ludwig von Bohlen, a.k.a. "Bach," air attaché at the German embassy in Santiago, worked with radio station PYL. On 21 July 1941, it reported, PYL notified Germany that it needed "various secret inks and developers...to facilitate communications and correspondence with Axis agents in the United States." Germany instructed Bach to go to Río to fetch the materials from its agent there, "Alfredo."[12]

Another high profile agent connected with PYL was Johannes Szeraws, a commercial sailor who "deserted" the *Frankfurt*, illegally entered Chile, and became "the operator of PYL." The Chilean government ordered Szeraws' deportation, but so vital was Szeraws to PYL that the German embassy intervened on his behalf and requested Chilean authorities to let him stay.[13] Arnold Barckhahn, born in Valdivia in 1918 and arrested 23 October 1942 for his role in PYL, said that throughout 1941 Szeraws regulary worked with papers and envelopes and sent ciphered messages from the office of the Compañía Transportes Marítimos, whose manager was one Frjiederich von Schultz Hausmann.[14] In July 1942 Szeraws reportedly left Valparaíso for Santiago and disappeared.[15] In 1943, the Chilean government ordered Szeraws to leave Chile because of his espionage activities on Hitler's behalf.[16]

An objective observer might retort that the United States embassy engaged in similar activities. The United States ambassador, Claude Bowers, was certainly willing to influence the Chilean media. Bowers urged Coca Cola to purchase commercials on a radio station which he was trying "to bring...into the fold."[17] He reprimanded the editor of Santiago's *El Mercurio* on his handling of the news.[18] He orchestrated a letter writing campaign by friendly Chileans to the editors of various Chilean newspapers.[19] Bowers urged Washington to provide a hefty grant to the friendly newspaper *La Crítica*, which was in dire financial straits.[20] As will become evident, U.S. authorities were not at all reluctant to monitor Axis telecommunications and even to show some of the intercepts to Chilean authorities. The same detached observer would nevertheless have to admit that Naziism was one of the most immoral causes promoted by "civilized" people in the history of the world.

That the German embassy assisted Nazis in Chile is beyond dispute. In May 1939, the German Embassy did its best to assist Hans Voigt, a German citizen who had lived eleven years in Chile and was publishing anti-Semitic propaganda. When Chilean police arrested him and seized his possessions, the embassy managed to extract a confession of police brutality from the foreign minister, Abraham Ortega, and to negotiate the return of Voigt's possessions—although it decided for tactical reasons not to protest the deportation order against him.[21] Captured German documents include correspondence between Walter Böttger, commercial attaché at the German embassy in Santiago, and a Nazi Gauleiter in Berlin named Bohle about the distribution of Nazi propaganda in Chile.[22] According to the ambassador, Chilean authorities were maintaining Böttger under surveillance. Ambassador von Schön protested the surveillance of Böttger to Rossetti, and suggested to Berlin that should such surveillance continue, Germany should harass the Chilean commercial attaché in Berlin.[23]

Historian Christel Krause Converse has made an intensive study of Nazis in Chile during the Third Reich. She sees two varieties of Nazi—the Chilean-born (most of non-German ethnicity and led by González von Marées) and the NSDAP, the National Socialist German Workers Party. The German embassy sponsored and worked with the NSDAP, most of whose members were German-born Germans. Some Chilean-born people of German ethnicity (Chilean-Germans) played key roles in Chile's NSDAP, but by 1938 many had lost their enthusiasm. They resented domination of the party by people from the other side of the Atlantic.[24]

Converse notes "that the German-Chileans were never unified politically."[25] They included Protestants, Roman Catholics, Jews, and non-believers, and their opinions ranged from the far right to the far left. Some were apolitical. This rainbow of opinion prevailed even in Valdivia, an NSDAP stronghold.

Leader of Valdivia's young NSDAP was the Chilean-born Adolf Schwarzenberg. In the words of Converse, Schwarzenberg—a native of Valdivia born in 1929,

...was a descendant of immigrants from the Kassel-Hessen region of Germany, who entered Chile shortly after 1848 to escape political repression and the failing of liberals.[26]

Schwarzenberg was a disorganized n'er-do-well whose relations with his own family were poor. Politics was one of the reasons for family hostility. After becoming a member of the NSDAP in 1933, he founded and led the Deutsche Jugend Chiles (DJC or German Youth of Chile). The DJC promoted ideas of German "racial" superiority, no matter what the citizenship of the ethnic German, and when two DJC members died, Schwarzenberg asked that the *Horst Wessel* song be sung at their funeral. He appears to have believed that service to Hitler was quite compatible with service to Chile.

Claus Krebs replaced Schwarzenberg as DJC leader in 1937, and he had the confidence of both the NSDAP and the German-Chilean Bund (DCB). Some German-Chileans who were proud of their German heritage resented the demonstrations of loyalty to Adolf Hitler, head of state of a distant country, not because of his ideas but because of his role as head of state of a distant country. The NSDAP and, at least until 1937, the DJC and the DCB argued that one demonstrated good Chilean citizenship by being a good German. In other words, German efficiency, energy, and self-discipline would be good for Chile.[27]

Converse demonstrates that alumni of Valdivia's Karl Anwandter Deutsche Schule (German school) founded a youth group for ethnic Germans in 1924. Members sang, danced, hiked, camped and behaved like young Germans elsewhere. The group spread throughout those parts of Chile where ethnic Germans lived, including Concepción where Protestant clergyman Otto Brien and five Germans from Chile saw "fighting off un-German culture" as one of their goals. Schwarzenberg and Karl Roth, an immigrant from Germany who like Schwarzenberg joined the NSDAP in 1933, provided national leadership. The Protestant Church in Puerto Montt and the Roman Catholic Church in Puerto Varas had more appeal than the

Third Reich for most German-Chileans who lived there. In 1935, some fifty DJC members went to Germany for six months. The NSDAP paid many of the bills. By 1937, the sight of large numbers of uniformed young people trained not to speak Spanish to each other had become so offensive that a Valdivia judge imposed restraints on the DJC.[28]

According to Converse, from 1935 to 1937,

> ...the NSDAP gained control over virtually all German-Chilean institutions....Party membership, however, was relatively small and of those who joined, more seem to have done so for a myriad of emotional reasons based on slogans and nebulous perceptions than a commitment to party principles.[29]

Her statistics indicate that the total NSDAP membership between 1929 and 1940 numbered 1,112 German-born and 114 Chilean-born. German blood was a prerequisite for membership. Most joined between 1932 and 1934, 748 of the German-born and all but eleven of the Chilean-born.[30] To many the NSDAP represented a return to the era of Bismarck and the Kaisers, when Germany had been strong, and an escape from the chaos of the Weimar Republic.[31] To some, the NSDAP was "the bulwark against Marxism."[32] Significantly, Converse portrays Ambassador von Schön as a devout "[Roman] Catholic who never joined the party, [and who] proved to be somewhat of an obstructionist to the NSDAP's efforts."[33]

Nevertheless, the role of the German embassy and of German expatriates is obvious from developments in Valdivia. In August and September, 1941, Chilean authorities arrested four, then an additional nine people, "for anti-democratic activities." Puerto Montt's newspaper, *El Llanquihue*, identified the first four as members of a *Landesgruppe*: Emil Bünnig Schröder, Guillermo Kreutz Acer, Carlos Dahling Dreier, and Herbert Heese Heese.[34] One informant told this author that Bünnig Schröder was a native of Germany who had migrated to Chile in 1931. None of the four had surnames of identifiable old stock families from 1846-1855.[35] With the exception of Schröder, none of those names appears in recent telephone directories of the Tenth Region—that part of Chile which stretches from Valdivia to Chiloé—and Bünig Schröder himself was an immigrant. It would appear that none of these accused Nazis came from a long-established Chilean family.

In response to a query from Under-Secretary of State Ernst Wörmann in Berlin about five Nazis arrested in Valdivia as security threats in Chile,[36] von Schön said that the embassy was hiring a lawyer on their behalf. Von Schön admitted that Nazis had been active in the southern provinces, but he warned Foreign Minister Rossetti that actions against the Nazis would not go unnoticed. He and the NSDAP kept that particular promise. Once the Valdivia five went on trial, the Gestapo began to arrest Chileans in Germany and occupied France and did not release them until the Valdivia court acquitted everyone "for lack of evidence."[37] Von Schön made clear to Rossetti his belief that if the Communist party could operate legally, as it did, the Nazi party should also be a legal entity,[38] and he discussed contingency plans with a Gauleiter in Berlin for the survival of the NSDAP in Chile should Chilean authorities outlaw it.[39]

Then followed Chilean police action in Osorno, where Nazi activists maintained too high a profile for Chilean authorities to ignore. Over the Christmas season of 1941, Chilean police had invaded the German vice-consulate in Osorno, arrested vice-consul Richard von Conta, and seized some of the holdings of the vice-consulate's archives. Suspicious of Nazi activities taking place in and around the vice-consulate, Osorno judge Enrique Correa had asked von Conta for permission to search and investigate. Von Conta denied the request, and the police acted anyway. Rossetti returned the archival material to von Schön but denied that the police had acted in an unreasonable manner.[40] Legally or illegally, Osorno's police had been effective. Weeks later, von Schön lamented that continued media attention had delayed the re-establishment of the NSDAP in that south Chilean city.[41]

The FBI thought that certain German businessmen engaged in questionable political activities and with the full knowledge of the German embassy in Santiago. Apfel (von Appen) was one such person; Werner Siering was another.

> Werner Siering, the Nazi manager of the Bayer-Westkott drug organization...collects information as to the political and economic situation in Chile, as to the activities of Chile's various leaders, as to the production of minerals in Chile and Bolivia, as to general conditions in industry and commerce, as to maritime movements, and as to the military situation in the three branches of Chile's Armed Forces. It is said that since 1935 Siering has been transmitting information to Germany and has maintained files with maps, plans, guarded in the German Embassy in Santiago.[42]

The DGI agreed that one Werner Siering of Bayer (the pharmaceutical company) headed Germany's "espionage system...in close collaboration with the German Embassy and the consulates."[43] Siering died in February, 1943, shortly after the diplomatic rupture, probably through suicide.[44]

Late in 1939, the German battleship *Graf Spee* self-destructed in the estuary of the Río de la Plata to avoid capture by the British navy. The crew then surrendered to neutral Argentina, expected to be the most sympathetic nation within easy reach. According to the FBI, at least thirteen sailors managed to escape custody, travel across Argentina under assumed names, and make their way to Bariloche in the Argentine Andes. From there they crossed through the pass and arrived at the Chilean city of Osorno, then travelled north to the port city of Valparaíso. Paul Barandon, Germany's consul-general in that city, provided them with phoney passports under assumed names so that they could leave Chile, make their way back to Germany or occupied Europe, and rejoin the German navy.[45] There was no secret about this. Because of the phoney passports, the Chilean government demanded the recall of Consul-general Barandon from Valparaíso, and Counsellor Wilhelm von Pochhammer moved from the German embassy in Santiago to replace him. The controversy lasted several months.[46]

CHILE'S PRESS, SCHOOLS, AND CHURCHES

Early in 1943, the FBI levelled serious charges at three cultural institutions which affected the thinking of Chileans who lived in southern Chile, particularly those of German extraction. Nazis, it reported, had infiltrated newspapers, schools, and churches. Marcial Martínez supported many of those claims.[47] To what extent were the charges justified? To what extent were they an unintentional exaggeration, written by people rightly concerned about the Nazi menace and paid to go looking for trouble? Were residents of southern Chile in general and German-Chileans in particular brainwashed into thinking that Nazis and the Axis powers were respectable and that the United States was a greater cause for concern than Germany, Japan, and Italy in combination?

Historian George F.W. Young believes that Chile's German clubs, German-language press, and German Churches had become nationalistic, if not chauvinistic, after Germany's defeat in 1918 and the 1919 Treaty of Versailles. Germany's Chilean offspring did not believe that their European homeland deserved its bad reputation and the punishment which the victors were inflicting.[48]

Admiral Wilhelm Franz Canaris, head of the *Abwehr*—Germany's spy agency—from 1935 to 1944, was not a Nazi and found many Nazi atrocities morally repulsive. However, as a patriotic German, he appeared to believe that he had an obligation to support his country's current government.[49] Apparently some German expatriates living in Chile felt the same way.

More than half a century after World War II, it is easier to judge the press than the schools or churches. What the newspapers said is available in print. What teachers said in the classroom and what the clergy said in sermons or in private conversations is more difficult to determine. Many who heard them are now dead, and memories of some of the survivors are unreliable. Either they were too young at the time to have appreciated the subtleties, or they are now too old to remember with the necessary degree of accuracy. Hearsay knowledge is unreliable. Fortunately there is information which allows for judgment on all three fronts, particularly in the case of the newspapers. The evidence is that there was legitimate cause for concern but that the situation was not as bad as it appeared.

The Press

The Germans who arrived in nineteenth century Chile established German-language newspapers. Valparaíso's Deutsche Nachtichten für Sudamerika, founded in 1870, lasted until 1909. The year following its demise, Germans in Valparaíso established the Deutsche Zeitung für Chile, which moved to Santiago in 1914. Santiago already had a liberal German newspaper, the Deutsche Presse, but its life was brief (1912-1920). The Deutsche Zeitung acquired it in the aftermath of World War I and survived until 1943, when Chile suspended diplomatic relations with Nazi Germany. From 1838, when Valparaíso's Germans formed the first of many German Clubs in Chile—which offered, and continue to offer, opportunities for socializing—German Chileans imported newspapers and books in a systematic way. The first German-language newspaper of southern Chile began at La Unión in 1886. Others followed at Valdivia, Puerto Montt, and Temuco. None could compete with the Deutsche Zeitung für Chile, especially after its relocation to Santiago in 1914. Santiago was (and remains) the northern terminus of the railway which carried people and freight (including newspapers) rapidly to Osorno, Frutillar, Puerto Varas, and Puerto Montt.[50] Deutsche Zeitung's only competition was Der Sonntag, founded in 1919 and still active a decade later.[51]

Deutsche Zeitung deserves special attention. Since its establishment in 1910, it had become a highly respected, highly credible newspaper. The Nazi takeover was so gradual as to be almost imperceptible. In 1933 it agreed to allot one page each Saturday to Nazi propaganda, but its principal source of overseas news was Germany's Transocean News Agency and, wittingly or unwittingly, its editors denied or minimized Nazi persecution of Jews. Chilean-Germans distrusted other newspapers and had good reason for doing so. Throughout World War I, many had reprinted as news British propaganda against non-existent or exaggerated German atrocities. Once deceived, readers preferred their own community's newspaper to any other source of news.[52]

There were three Spanish-language daily newspapers in German populated southern Chile, *El Correo de Valdivia*, *La Prensa* (Osorno), and *El Llanquihue* (Puerto Montt). All were well established newspapers, not specifically created propaganda sheets. *El Llanquihue* dated from 1885, *El Correo de Valdivia* from 1895, *La Prensa* from 1917. The FBI identified all three as "owned or controlled by Germans."[53] Martínez advised Chile's foreign office that Chile's counter-intelligence organization, the Dirección General de Investigaciones (DGI), had confirmed the German embassy's involvement with certain Chilean newspapers, including specifically *El Llanquihue*. According to Martínez, the DGI said that money and advice from the German embassy enabled Nazis to control and influence a number of Chilean radio stations and newspapers, including *El Llanquihue*. The embassy's contact person with the newspapers and radio stations it was trying to influence, reported Martínez, was Wilhelm Hammerschmidt, and official from Göbbels's Ministry of Enlightenment and Propaganda.[54] What is evident today is that Nazis received a very limited return on any investment.

The worst single item of anti-American propaganda must surely be the column "Cartas de Santiago" written by one Joaquín Edwards Bello and published in *La Prensa* 7 October 1941, two months to the day before Pearl Harbor. Significantly, Edwards did not have a German surname, and it is most unlikely that one could successfully hide behind a *nom de plume* in a community as small as Osorno. Edwards said:

> In Chile, we all know that there is neither a Nazi problem nor a Nazi threat. The man in the street knows it. The government knows it. Everybody knows it. The Germans intervene less in Chilean affairs than the Americans and the British. It is natural that the Germans have their own priorities, their circles, their own sports associations. Nevertheless, the U.S. government wants a Nazi danger to Chile so

that it can have a pretext to intervene on the Strait of Magellan, on Juan Fernández and other parts of our territory with a maximum of support from the people of the United States. That is what has happened in the past to other nations.

Perhaps Joaquín Edwards Bello was a paid Nazi propagandist. Perhaps he did not know what the German embassy and consulates were doing in Chile, even in Valdivia and Osorno. At any rate, his column appeared but once, and it was unique. The most respectable newspapers occasionally print controversial views of opinionated columnists.

The FBI was certainly correct in its report that all three of the above newspapers printed overseas news from Germany's Transocean News Agency (TO) before (but not after) the diplomatic rupture. That assertion is accurate, but misleading. In all three cases, most of the overseas news—indeed, most of the non-local news—came from United Press, a U.S.-based newsgathering agency. TO was but the icing on the cake, or even the parsley on the meat, and it disappeared from the pages of the three newspapers a full year before Chile cut its ties with the Axis powers. The silencing of TO in the print media of southern Chile was an accomplished fact before the diplomatic tug-of-war of 1942 took place.

Some of TO's stories were blatant Axis propaganda. On 8 August 1941, almost four months before Pearl Harbor, even before President Roosevelt and Prime Minister Winston Churchill issued the Atlantic Charter, El Llanquihue carried a front page TO report from Berlin that the United States was feeding forged documents to Latin American governments. The Americans' intent, said TO, was to persuade the Latin Americans to abandon their neutrality and join the crusade against the Axis. "Never before in history" had anything like this happened, according to TO, and Latin Americans had many more reasons for bitterness over the U.S. track record in their part of the world than over anything Germany had done. On 5 October 1941, a TO story from Madrid was full of praise for a young aviator from Spain's Blue Division, Luis Alcocer, who had died in action on the Soviet front assisting Nazi Germany. TO referred to Alcocer's "heroic death...fighting against Bolshevism." It also noted that in 1936, when the Spanish Civil War was beginning, he had joined Franco's cause, and that he had died at the age of twenty. On 28 December 1941 *El Correo de Valdivia* printed a picture of happy German soldiers, with the caption: "War against the Soviets: German forces throw their thousandth hand-grenade against the Bolsheviks."

Nevertheless, most of TO's stories were fairly straightforward or inconsequential, certainly no more harmful to the Allied cause than some of the UP stories might have been. On 3 August 1941, *El Llanquihue* carried two TO reports of the previous day, one from Rome that the Queen of Bulgaria was visiting the Italian capital and one from Washington that President Roosevelt had named New Dealer Rexford Tugwell as Governor of Puerto Rico. After all, until Hitler declared war on the United States in December 1941, TO had correspondents in that country. In October 1941, *La Prensa* carried accurate TO reports about the termination of negotiations between the U.S. and Japanese governments and the resignation of Prince Konoye as Japanese Prime Minister.[55] On 29 December 1941, *El Correo de Valdivia* printed a TO story about the landing of Japanese parachutists in Sumatra. On 15 January 1942, it reported a story about a dog in Trieste who, having inherited half a million dinars, appeared to be the world's richest dog. Another TO story that same day, from Brussels, indicated that the Olympics Committee would be inactive for the duration of the war. Surely none of this was as harmful to U.S. interests as a United Press story from New York 30 October 1941, printed in *La Prensa* the following day: "[Aviator Charles] Lindbergh accused Roosevelt of wanting to practise a dictatorship in the United States." United Press also reported Allied military setbacks both in Europe and the Pacific.

If the FBI exaggerated the impact of TO in southern Chile, it was less than impartial about the editorial positions of the three newspapers. They were less unfriendly, perhaps more self-serving, than the FBI realized. *La Prensa* editorialized that the United States was a victim of Japanese aggression at Pearl Harbor and that Americans were a "profoundly peaceful" people.[56] The approach in El Correo de Valdivia was more self-centred but understandable—a fear that it was only a matter of time until Chile became involved in hostilities. All foreign stories in that 8 December 1941 issue of El Correo de Valdivia, even those from Berlin and Vichy, came from United Press.

Rossetti had newspaper support for his reservations about a diplomatic rupture, but the newspapers had credible Chilean reasons for their positions. Not one of them rejoiced in the difficulties faced by the United States. Any compromise in Chilean neutrality would be "dangerous," said El Llanquihue in its editorial of 23 January 1942. Chile was in no position to fight a war at that time. El Correo de Valdivia agreed fully. Chile lacked the coastal defences and the economic base to fight a world war.

Neutrality keeps the war from our coasts, protects [our] cities, makes commerce possible, protects our sovereignty, leaves in place our tradition of dignity...It will allow us to organize against what threatens us. Let us look after our own problems.[57]

There was not a word about the merits of the Axis cause or the benevolence of the Axis nations.

On 4 July 1942, La Prensa's editorial hailed the United States as "a firm bulwark of freedom of thought and a respectful guardian of the rule of law." Within the month, there were similar editorials honouring the national holidays of Spain and Switzerland, two countries which although geographically close to the conflict had managed to maintain their neutrality.[58] This was not what Ambassador Bowers wanted, but it was hardly Nazi propaganda.

Some editorials in the three southern Chilean newspapers were very friendly to the United States and to U.S. interests. In mid-August 1942, when President Ríos accepted an invitation to visit Washington, El Llanquihue editorialized enthusiastically about "traditional US-Chilean friendship, the many ties between the two countries, and the mutual respect they had for one another."[59] *El Correo de Valdivia* began to have doubts about the wisdom of Chilean neutrality as early as March 1942, when German submarines sank the Chilean merchant ship *Toltén*, apparently by mistake, off the coast of the United States. Its editorial of 18 March 1942 suggested that neutrality was no protection against Axis aggression after all. (*El Llanquihue* suspended judgment and said that it wanted more facts.[60])

Opinions varied when Brazil declared war on Germany and Italy (not Japan) 22 August 1942 in response to German submarine attacks on Brazilian merchant ships, but the differences were legitimate and logical. *La Prensa*'s editorial the next day blamed the Río conference for Brazil's misfortune. After the Río conference, Brazil had broken diplomatic relations with the Axis belligerents and been less than neutral. *El Llanquihue* noted that Chile was bending the rules on neutrality to assist Brazil but considered that neutrality remained the wisest policy for Chile.[61] These positions, surely, are debateable, but hardly persuasive evidence of partiality toward the Axis.

Again, when Chile did make its diplomatic rupture 20 January 1943, there were mixed reactions. *El Correo de Valdivia* praised the "patriotism, inspiration, and rectitude" of President Ríos. The time had come to align Chile with the democracies and the rest of the Western Hemisphere.[62] *La Prensa* expressed resignation over what it had come to regard as inevitable and seemed pleased that the period of uncertainty had ended. President Ríos should remember, thought *La Prensa*, that Germany, Italy, and Japan had been "traditional friends of Chile and that this friendship has produced both cultural and material [results]."[63]

Whatever one's thoughts on the three newspapers and their contents, they were not consistently blatant Nazi propaganda organs. They did not praise the Axis powers, and, for a time at least, they wanted to keep Chile out of the war. This was an understandable editorial position. Perhaps Nazi atrocities and Japanese militarism should have shocked the editors more than they apparently did, but atrocities committed elsewhere were not what bought other belligerents into the conflict. Nor is it surprising that many

Chileans, including editorial writers, thought that they would have more to lose should Chile abandon neutrality. The newspapers advocated policies which were not necessarily heroic or admirable, but such policies are explicable in terms of Chilean realities—without reference to German or Japanese bribes.

Schools

What happened in the German Schools of southern Chile is not as conveniently documented as what the newspapers said. Originally, said the FBI report of March 1943, German settlers had established schools because other quality schools were not available. However, since 1933,

> ...the German Government has taken increasing interest in the operation of the German school systems and has sent many instructors to the German schools solely for the purpose of spreading the National Socialist ideology and augmenting growth of Naziism. In this way the German School system has been a forceful method for German penetration into the Chilean life.

The British Embassy in Santiago provided additional information. In 1937, Cavendish-Bentinck counted an "excellent" German school in Valparaíso, two schools in Santiago, one at Concepción, others throughout southern Chile with the largest in Osorno. Hitler's government provided books, financial subsidies, and teachers. Any teacher who would go to Chile for three years could have six years of credit toward his pension, said Cavendish-Bentinck. Hitler's government also paid for Chilean students to study in Germany, thirty of whom it invited early in 1937.[64]

The FBI estimated that 5,300 children, some but not all of whom were of German extraction, were attending forty-six German schools. At the Colegio Alemán of Santiago, twenty-nine of forty-seven teachers were German nationals; at Osorno's Colegio Alemán "the teachers are said to be 80% German."[65] Marcial Martínez also thought the German schools a threat to Chilean sovereignty and survival. Martínez warned about German schools in southern Chile, where Nazis set the curriculum and forbade the teaching of the Spanish language and Chilean history. Significantly, nine months later when the Chilean government ordered the closure of Germany's embassy and consular posts, seven teachers from Valdivia, fifteen from Osorno, and three from Puerto Montt asked to be repatriated.[66]

It is highly probable that some—perhaps most—of those teachers felt a degree of commitment to Nazi Germany. Not all of them were likely to have aging parents in need of immediate attention. Given the nature of the Hitler régime, vocal opponents would not have won the necessary financial sponsorship to go to Chile to teach. A 1935 photograph of the Deutsche Schule in Bariloche, Argentina shows both the Argentine flag and the Swastika flying outside the school as children and adults (presumably parents and teachers) stand or sit on the grass. Most of the adults have smiles on their faces. The caption reads: "The German School receives visitors from a German School in the South of Chile."[67] At the very least, teachers and parents at the unidentified Chilean German School lacked strong moral objections to the political convictions of the Bariloche school, or they would not have agreed to such a visit.

One anonymous defender of the German Schools, writing in La Prensa 25 October 1941, confirmed the FBI's enrolment figures. The writer's estimate was that 5,268 students attended Chile's forty-six such schools, that about 4,000 were of German extraction, a few of Scandinavian, Dutch or Swiss background, and the rest Chileans. He (or she) also said that of 322 teachers, 58 came from Germany.

The anonymous letter writer wrote his (her?) column to refute charges about the German schools, the very charges which the FBI and Martínez would repeat seventeen months later. Over the decades, said the writer, the schools had made a significant and positive contribution to Chilean life. The schools encouraged young people to learn German as well as Spanish, not instead of Spanish, and curriculum content conformed to the requirements of Chilean law. Other schools taught English or French as well as Spanish. The German schools were non-political, not agencies of Nazi propaganda.

The writer's credibility might be stronger if he (or she) had identified himself (herself). After all, the column makes some strong statements about the schools' critics. It refers to the "cunning and insidious press campaign which has fabricated charges that the schools promote Nazi propaganda." The critics, it says, have made accusations that are "puerile and cowardly, profoundly odious." Certainly, anyone who uses such language in a public forum like a newspaper should not, as a matter of principle, do so behind a mask of anonymity. Chilean law notwithstanding, Valdivia, Osorno, Puerto Varas and Puerto Montt are some 800 to 1016 kilometres south of the national capital—a fair distance then as now, given the transportation system. It is probable that inspectors from Santiago did not visit the schools with great frequency to ascertain that they were complying with all aspects of Chilean law. Given Nazi proclivity toward telling lies, it is impossible to have confidence in the anonymous writer.

More credible is an article by Julio Plencovich, director of the Deutsche Schule in Puerto Varas from 1976 to 1979. Plencovich points out that there were three directors during the Third Reich: one surnamed Gödicke (whose first name Plencovich did not know) who came in 1931, during the Weimar Republic; Walter Heitzelmann, who served from 1935 to 1938; and Kurt Reinke, whose term began in 1939 and lasted until 1951. Plencovich found a tug-of-war between the democratic traditions of Chile's German community and "the imperialist ideas" of Nazi Germany, with which Gödicke and Heitzelmann had to cope. Reinke married a Chilean and, after the war, went to Germany only for visits.[68] Significantly, no teacher from Puerto Varas was on the list of those seeking repatriation to Germany in 1943.[69] It would appear that Reinke was innocent of strong, Nazi convictions.

It is reasonable to assume that some schools promoted Nazi propaganda and that others were less blatant, even perhaps less ideological. Similarly, some teachers were Nazi sympathizers, even partisans, while others were less outspoken. Membership in the NSDAP was obligatory for German teachers who wanted to work abroad, but presumably some purchased memberships for reasons of convenience rather than conviction.[70] Still, given the ubiquity of Swastikas, portraits of Hitler, and members of the NSDAP, and the exclusion of the Spanish language and of Chilean literature and history from some schools, the FBI and Martínez had valid reasons for concern.

The Churches

The churches, like the schools, had a track record that was less than pure. Ambassador Bowers regarded the Roman Catholic newspaper, El Diario Ilustrado, as an Axis organ.[71] This was simplistic but understandable. El Diario Ilustrado had unusual priorities, whose merits Bowers was unable to appreciate. It was a highly ideological newspaper, Roman Catholic to the core. As far as it was concerned, Communism was the major threat to humanity, and Carlos Ibáñez was the candidate most likely to be tough with the Communists. Notwithstanding the German invasion of the Soviet Union and that country's desperate struggle for survival, Communism, thought El Diario Ilustrado, endangered Chile. (Naziism, Fascism, and Japanese Imperialism evidently did not.) There should be a negotiated end to the war against the Axis at the earliest possible opportunity, for humanitarian reasons. Neutral countries such as Chile should remain aloof from the conflict. Marshal Pétain, who had brought "peace" to France, was a hero. Generalíssimo Francisco Franco, who had brought order out of chaos in Spain, was another hero. Argentina's President, General Ramón Castillo, whose military government favoured ongoing diplomatic ties with the Axis, was also worthy of praise. After all, his policy was promotion of peace. To be condemned were the Popular Front governments of France and Spain which had allowed their countries to drift into anarchy and wars which the Popular Front governments could not win. General Ibáñez promoted the idea that Chile's Popular Front coalition was promoting the self-destruction of Chile and a Communist takeover, and editorials and news coverage in El Diario Ilustrado promoted those dire warnings. It reprinted a 1937 warning from the late Pope Pius XI about the Communist danger. To be fair, however, it did report that Marshal Pétain's police were sending Jews to Germany. It regarded such actions as "atrocities" and quoted the French Bishop of Toulouse as saying that France was not responsible for such crimes. By implication, the responsibility rested with Nazi Germany.[72]

Diario Ilustrado necessarily had greater influence outside Chile's German community than within it. Roman Catholics were but a distinct minority of Chile's German community, and Protestants, Jews, and non-believers were unlikely to read it. On the other hand, it undoubtedly influenced other Chileans.

Bowers noted that Senator Miguel Cruchaga was both a prominent Roman Catholic and honourary president of the Asociación de los Amigos de Alemania (AAA). Bowers noted that another prominent Roman Catholic, Senator Maximiano Errázuriz, was honourary president of its Japanese equivalent. In both cases, Bowers lamented, their Roman Catholicism added respectability to their extracurricular activities.[73] The FBI thought that the Gestapo and other Nazis had intimidated "numerous German, Japanese and Italian priests of the Roman Catholic Church":

> This has been true of Bishop [Guido] Beck in the southern section of Chile and in the case of Monsignor Munita, the Bishop of Puerto Montt. He is reported as having replaced over twenty-four Chilean curates in his diocese by German and Italian priests who are active Fascist propagandists. It is reported that most of the native Chilean lower group are pro-Ally, but since they do not dictate the Church's policy or have an official influence their influence is of relatively little importance.[74]

Intimidated or not, the pro-Fascist clergy named by French social historian Jean-Pierre Blancpain—Bishops Fuenzalida of Concepción and Rucker of Chillán, Archbishop Crescente Errázuriz of Santiago, one Father Viviani Contreras—do include people with Spanish surnames.[75]

The FBI considered "dangerous" German and Spanish activities in certain Roman Catholic schools and schools supported by Roman Catholics. One Father Bram was rumoured "to have introduced the

Swastika flag at meetings held" in Santiago's Liceo Alemán, identified as a "Nazi-subsidized school" operated by the German Government. Father Bram's assistant, Father José Schmidt, was another alleged Nazi. The FBI identified Mrs. Theresa Ebel de Hidalgo, a Chilean of German descent, as a Nazi propagandist who collaborated with Father Alfonso Grieger of the German School at Calle Moneda 1661 in central Santiago. A brother of Mrs. Hidalgo, a Jesuit, was "also a National Socialist sympathizer." Said the FBI:

> The National Socialists have used first-line German or German Chilean Catholics who are completely under the influence of the Nazi command in Chile. The Germans have been very successful in this field in the southern regions, particularly in the territory of Valdivia.[76]

The German Embassy also utilized the services of an ethnic Italian, a Roman Catholic seminarian named Tullio Franchini. In 1941, Abwehr operators in Hamburg instructed agent Bach (air attaché Ludwig von Bohlen),

> ...to pick up documents which had been forwarded through a pro-Nazi Catholic priest in Quito Ecuador, Padre Viane, to a Catholic theological student in Santiago, Tullio Franchini. In Santiago, Franchini resided at the Catholic College, Grande Avenida 8250...These documents were described as intelligence reports and were secured from Franchini by Ludwig von Bohlen who turned them over to Walter Boettger [Böttger], a Commercial Attaché of the German Embassy in Santiago and the national leader for the National Socialist German Workers Party in Chile.[77]

Converse believes that the German-Protestant Churches of Chile were more susceptible to Naziism than were the Roman Catholic.

She has written:

> While a number of Catholics became supporters of the Reich and joined the NSDAP on an individual basis, the German-Chilean

Evangelical congregations actually became subject to the authority of
the Foreign Office for Church Affairs of the Reich.[78]

There were good reasons for this. Even today, more than half a century since
World War II, German Protestant Churches throughout the Tenth Region
remain among the few institutions to use German as well as Spanish as a
means of communication. German Protestants have had their churches to
themselves, while their Roman Catholic compatriots, in the words of
Blancpain, constituted a "double minority"—a minority within Chile's
German community and a minority of Chile's Roman Catholics. According
to Blancpain, there were tensions between Chile's German Protestants and
German Roman Catholics. They did not always think alike. At all times, the
Protestants were less assimilated than the Roman Catholics.[79] Thus, it is
hardly surprising that the FBI would monitor Protestants and Protestant
activities.

The FBI indicated that according to its sources, Martin Kannegiesser
—pastor of the Lutheran Church in Valparaíso (founded in 1867)—was "an
active Nazi chief." In *Deutsche Zeitung*, Converse discovered that in 1937
Kannegiesser had given a series of lectures on the Old Testament. The Old
Testament "proves," he said, "that a people chosen by God erred and is now
damned."[80] The FBI also forwarded unsubstantiated but evidently credible
reports that Kannegiesser had "an assistant named Reimers who is said to be
engaging in Nazi espionage in Frutillar, and it is reported that he has an
assistant who is also a Lutheran pastor, named Schuenemann."[81]

Another Protestant clergyman whom the FBI distrusted was the
Reverend Karl Steybe (whom it identifies as "Carl Steibe") of Osorno. He led
Chile's oldest Lutheran congregation, established in 1863. According to the
FBI,

Carl Steibe...arrived in Chile in 1935. He is president of the German
Protestant Church in Osorno and is said to be a dangerous German
fanatic. He is said to be very active in this territory and to work
closely with contacts in the German Embassy in Santiago. It is stated

that Steibe receives and correlates Intelligence from various southern points which he forwards to leaders in Santiago.[82]

The FBI's case against Steybe is strong. He was one of at least two German pastors—along with Víctor Otto of Puerto Montt—who sought repatriation after the diplomatic rupture.[83] (Víctor Otto had been in Chile since 1928,[84] and he did not attract the FBI's attention.) According to Converse, in 1935—the year of his arrival—Steybe joined Pastor Otto Brien of Concepción at NSDAP meetings and religious services throughout small communities. There they lectured on such topics as "Faith Creates Nationalist Ideology: Hindenburg, Bismarck and Hitler as Examples" and "Racial Theory."[85] Steybe "thanked the NSDAP for infusing a new spirit and pride in the homeland."[86] Steybe was leader of Chile's Evangelical Church, as well as pastor of a congregation with 511 members and almost four times as many adherents in 1938.[87] Amazingly, Steybe did not return to Germany but remained with his congregation until shortly before the formidable earthquake of 22 May 1960 destroyed the church building. After a brief interlude, Steybe became pastor at Puerto Montt, whose congregation —founded in 1865—was second only to Osorno's in longevity. It was during his tenure that construction of that city's beautiful and prominent Lutheran Church building, erected between 1960 and 1963, took place.[88] As in the case of Reinke, it is unclear whether his post-war respectability indicated shared values with the people in his congregation rather than innocence. Puerto Montt residents of pioneer German extraction have told the author that there was overwhelming sympathy for Germany between 1939 and 1945 within their families, not because the families were Nazis but because they had been German. Hitler was but a passing phenomenon. Germany was more than Hitler.

Converse's indictment of Protestants continues. Valparaíso's Pastor Dr. Hans Stokl told an NSDAP gathering that Christianity was the basis of the New Germany. Osorno's Protestants elected two NSDAP members to their board in 1934, and two NSDAP members elected to similar office in

Puerto Varas included the local leader. Otto Brien of Concepción spoke regularly at NSDAP functions and, on at least one occasion, included the *Horst Wessel* song in a baptismal ceremony. Pastor Friedrich Karle of Santiago, a party member, attributed an increase in church attendance among young people to the NSDAP. The Protestant publication, *Der Missionsbote*, regularly praised the Third Reich and reflected its values.[89]

The FBI had another reason for concern about the work of Protestant clergy in Chile. German pastors headed what looked like innocent organizations in South American port cities to render humanitarian assistance to sailors from Germany and German-occupied countries. By such means, the so-called "Harbor Service" could maintain surveillance of shipping between Chile and Allied countries, and arrange the homeward transportation of sailors who might otherwise have agreed to work on Allied ships.[90]

SUMMARY OF FBI SURVEILLANCE OF CHILE'S PRESS, CHURCHES, AND SCHOOLS

To summarize, the FBI did its duty in keeping south Chile's newspapers, German Schools, and churches under surveillance. Nazi Germany was a menace, and media, teachers, and clergy who enhanced its credibility or promoted its cause in any way were potential threats to the security of the United States. However, FBI allegations against the press were exaggerated. What it said about the schools and the churches would appear to contain sufficient specific information to provide legitimate cause for concern.

GERMANY'S ALLIES AND CHILE TO 1942

Without question, as far as the United States and Great Britain were concerned, Germany was the principal adversary in Chile. However, Japan, Italy, Spain, and even France provided cause for worry.

Japanese migration came late to Chile. Japanese who went to South America tended to settle in Peru or Brazil, both of which still have substantial ethnic Japanese communities. In 1936, Peru limited the numbers of Japanese who could migrate there, and a few hundred joined the several hundred already in Chile.[91] A few more years of peace might have led to more migration, but it was not to be. By 1937, the Japanese government had begun to promote propaganda in Chile, although in the words of British diplomat Cavendish-Bentinck, "Japan is a newcomer in the field of propaganda in Chile." By then, Japan was inviting Chilean businessmen and students to go to Japan, largely at the expense of the Japanese government.[92] Yet, the government of Imperial Japan did not necessarily intend to exploit South America's Japanese settlers as a Fifth Column. At the outbreak of hostilities, the Home Office in Tokyo advised:

> If, as a resident in an enemy country, a report is spread that some persons are receiving unjust treatment, exercise self-restraint and do not try to devise means for revenge. Display the necessary and true spirit of our nation. Have [special] consideration for those persons in any enemy country whose views and manners [are of a high order]. Always act in a manner that will guarantee and safeguard life and property.[93]

That message was to have as wide a circulation as possible, in as many countries as possible.

Even if Chile's ethnic Japanese communities did not inspire terror, staff changes at the Japanese legation in Santiago might have. The staff was small, only nine people, but seven of those nine—all except two civil attachés—had joined the legation in 1941, most of them in the second half of the year. Keyoshi Yamagata, the minister, presented his credentials to President Aguirre 21 October 1941, ten weeks later than Secretary Naoya Nagamina (4 August 1941) and three weeks later than the military attaché, Lieutenant Colonel Haruo Teshima. A third civil attaché, Kosaburo Tada, had arrived 7 October 1941. Most ominous was the presence of *three* naval attachés. Rear Admiral Katsumi Yukishita actually lived in Buenos Aires, but as of 7 October 1941 he was also accredited to Chile. An assistant naval attaché, Lieutenant Commander Tadasi Kameda, also a resident of Buenos Aires, had presented his credentials much earlier in the year, 15 February 1941. A naval attaché who would actually live full time in Santiago, Sadayoski Nakayama, presented his credentials 23 December 1941—two weeks and two days after the attack on Pearl Harbor.[94] Official Washington well might wonder why so many highly placed Japanese officials, especially naval officers, were establishing residence in Argentina and Chile.

Chile's ethnic Italians tended to settle in the principal cities of Santiago and Valparaíso, but there were clusters from Arica near the Peruvian border south to Puerto Montt. The FBI and the British Embassy thought that most of those born in Chile had assimilated and thought of themselves as Chileans, not Italians. Hence, the FBI discounted rumours that former president Arturo Alessandri "had been a contact man for the Italian Ambassador in Santiago and has furnished confidential political information to this individual." The FBI attributed Alessandri's reluctance to break relations with the Axis "to...the fact that he sincerely believed that policy to be Chile's best course."[95] Nor did the FBI make any negative comment about Foreign Minister Rossetti. Italians born in Italy were another matter, and the FBI thought that some of them had "acted prominently in the furtherance of the Fascist ideal."[96] The British Embassy agreed, and doubted whether Italian efforts at propaganda would have much impact.[97]

The Spanish community included both Republican refugees whose side had lost the Civil War (1936-1939) and diplomats appointed by the victor, Generalíssimo Francisco Franco. Franco had triumphed in large measure because of military assistance from Hitler and Mussolini, and his foreign minister from 1940-1942, Ramón Serrano, was an enthusiastic partisan of the Axis. Before Pearl Harbor, however, the Germans, Italians, and Japanese could protect their own interests. The Spanish would prove useful at a later date, because Canaris organized an effective intelligence-sharing arrangement between the *Abwehr* and its Spanish counterpart, *Sirene*.[98] During the Civil War, both Republicans and Franco's partisans published newspapers in Chile, but neither sponsored radio programmes.[99]

Like the Spanish, Chile's French had divided loyalties. The FBI thought that only ten per cent supported the Vichy-based government of Marshal Philippe Pétain, who favoured collaboration with Nazi Germany. That ten per cent would favour the people who allowed Hitler to occupy sixty per cent of France and shoot at those who were trying to liberate French territory must be the result of one of three factors, thought the FBI.

(1) They are representatives of French concerns who receive their financial support through Vichy;

(2) They are persons who have members of their families residing in occupied France and consequently fear reprisals;

(3) They are persons who have property in France and wish to prevent its confiscation.

Needless to say, whatever their motivation, Vichyites might help the Axis cause. The FBI was particularly concerned about Paul d'Hyboubille, who took command of the French legation in 1941. D'Hyboubille was reportedly "a close friend" of Pierre Laval, the most notorious collaborator in Pétain's government who would face a firing squad for treason in 1945. D'Hyboubille himself was "considered as a German collaborator and has maintained close contact with the German Embassy in Santiago," said the FBI.[100] However, Cavendish-Bentinck pointed out that even before the collapse of France, "French prestige does not rank high in Chile, and even those Chileans who have lived for years in France are seldom really pro-French."[101] If Cavendish-Bentinck was as accurate on this point as he was on others, the Allies had little to fear from Vichyite propaganda.

Finally, there were the Croatians. Punta Arenas on the Strait of Magellan, then as now, had a substantial Croatian population. If through bombing or sabotage the Axis had managed to close the Panama Canal, the Strait of Magellan would have been a vital artery to the Allied cause. As it was, ships of any nationality which passed between Atlantic and Pacific might stop at Punta Arenas, the largest community on the strait, for supplies. From the birth of the Kingdom of Yugoslavia in December 1918 there had been tensions, often violent, between the two largest Yugoslav communities, the Serbs and the Croats. When Hitler's army invaded Yugoslavia in May 1941 the Nazis exploited that tension and collaborated with Croatian nationalists. Between them they proclaimed the independence of the Kingdom of Croatia whose king was an Italian prince. The FBI reported that certain Croatians in Punta Arenas communicated regularly with Germans. In the event of a diplomatic rupture, the FBI noted, residents of Punta Arenas might conduct a campaign of sabotage throughout the Strait of Magellan.[102] The Kingdom of Croatia had no diplomats of its own accredited to or resident in Chile.

SUMMARY AND CONCLUSIONS

Hitler's Germany was well aware of its opportunities in Chile and took full advantage of them. Given Chile's size, Germany's diplomatic and consular staff was massive. The Abwehr filed reports, and clandestine radios were active. Nazi propaganda appeared in the media, and friends of the Axis held influencial positions in churches and schools. The United States embassy and the FBI knew of these activities and kept official Washington posted.

NOTES

1. Mitchell, Santiago, to Sir John Simon, London, 21 Jan. 1935, Series A981/1, Item CHIL 6, Australian Archives, Canberra. Cited hereafter as Canberra.

2. Regarding the number of German posts, see FBI, p. 104. Regarding the Chilean population, see the Chilean census of 1940.

3. Report of the Spanish Ambassador in Chile, who represented German interests after the diplomatic rupture, to Foreign Minister Joaquín Fernandez, 8 Feb. 1943, #16, vol. 2093, ADRE. Cited hereafter as Spanish Ambassador's report.

4. FBI, pp. 103-104.

5. Cavendish-Bentinck, Santiago, to Eden, London, 11 April 1937, Series A981/1, Item CHIL 15, Canberra.

6. FBI, pp. 115-116. Cavendish-Bentinck to Eden, 11 April 1937, Series A981/1, Item CHIL 15, Canberra.

7. Cavendish-Bentinck to Eden, 11 April 1937, Series A981/1, Item CHIL 15, Canberra.

8. The report of Marcial Martínez appears in vol. 1970, Archivos del Departmento de Relaciones Exteriores (ADRE), Santiago de Chile. Martínez cites the DGI as a source.

9. FBI, pp. 139-140.

10. FBI, pp. 143-141.

11. Hoover to Harry L. Hopkins, Ambassador at Large, the White House, 2 Oct. 1942, R.G. 24, Papers of Harry L. Hopkins, FBI Reports, Chile, FDR Archives, Hyde Park. Cited hereafter as Hopkins.

12. FBI, p. 157.

13. Bowers to Barros, 9 July, with Bowers' Memorandum "German Espionage Agents in Chile" plus selected intercepts, vol. 2012, ADRE.

14. FBI, p. 168.

15. FBI, p. 171.

16. FBI, p. 173.

17. Bowers to Welles, 16 March 1942, Personal Secretary's File, Chile folder, FDR Archives. Cited hereafter as PSF.

18. Bowers to FDR, 2 April 1942, PSF.

19. Bowers to FDR, 29 April 1942, PSF.

20. Bowers to Welles, 1 Aug. 1942, PSF.

21. See in particular the correspondence from Pochhammer, counsellor at the German Embassy in Santiago, to AA, 15, 17, and 20 May, 1939, RG 242, NARA Series T-120 Reel 183, frames 88201, 88202, and 88204. Cited hereafter as AA.

22. Böttger and Leisewitz, Santiago, to Gauleiter Bohle, Berlin, 20 Feb. 1942, frame 88471.

23. Von Schön to AA, 18 and 23 Aug. 1941, frames 88328 and 88333.

24. Christel Krause Converse, "The Rise and Fall of Nazi Influence among the German-Chileans" (Ph.D. thesis, Georgetown University, 1990), especially the abstract, pp. ii-iii.

25. Converse, p. 23.

26. Converse, p. 32.

27. Converse, pp. 31-67.

28. Converse, pp. 68-123.

29. Converse, p. 125.

30. Converse, p. 128 (statistics) and p. 143 (German blood requirement).

31. Converse, p. 129.

32. Converse, p. 131.

33. Converse, p. 185.

34. El Llanquihue (Puerto Montt), 14 Aug. 1941.

35. Lists of immigrants, ship by ship, as reported by Held, pp. 83, 89-90, 129-130, 145-147, 159, 165, 194, 248, 261, 312-313.

36. Wörmann memorandum, 14 Aug. 1941, frame 88326.

37. See von Schön to Berlin, 12 Sept. 1941 (frame 88353), 13 Sept. 1941 (frames 88354-88356), 16 Sept. 1941 (frame 88357), 7 Oct. 1941 (frames 88400-88401). See also Wörmann memoranda of 23 Sept. 1941 (frames 88380-88381) and 26 Sept. (frames 88383-88387).

38. Von Schön to AA, 20 Aug. 1941, frames 88329-88330.

39. Von Schön to Gauleiter, 7 Oct. 1941, frames 88400-88401.

40. Von Schön to Rossetti, 23 Dec. 1941; Judge Humberto Mewes, Valdivia, to Rossetti, 19 Jan. 1942; Rossetti to von Schön, 9 March 1942; Von Schön to Rossetti, 11 March 1942; all in ADRE, boveda 14, vol. 13.

41. Von Schön to AA, 16 Jan. 1942, frame 88437.

42. FBI, p. 174.

43. Vol. 1970, ADRE.

44. The quotation and the report of Siering's death come from FBI, p. 174. There are further references to Siering on pp. 102, 122, 123, 124, 128, 177, and 194.

45. FBI, pp. 100-102. An Argentine source confirms that two veterans of the *Graf Spee*, Helmut Ruge and Heinz Geef, had escaped from one of the detention sites and might well have gone to Chile: Report of Salomon Nehme, Jefe de Investigaciones, 19 Aug, 1942, Serie Miscelaneas I. Caja 61, Expedientes de tripulantes del buque de guerra aleman Almirante Graf Von Spee (1940-1944), Documento 15, Número de Expediente 3705, Archivo Historico de San Juan, Argentina.

46. Humphreys, I, p. 48. See also Edward P. von der Porter, *The German Navy in World War II* (New York: Thomas Y. Crowell, 1969), pp, 31, 42-55; Donald MacIntyre, *The Naval War against Hitler* (London: B.T. Batsford, 1971), pp. 12-15; Dan van der Vat, *The Atlantic Campaign: World War II's Great Struggle at Sea* (New York: Harper and Row, 1988), pp. 93-96.

    Captured German correspondence also deals with the escapees from the *Graf Spee*. See von Schön to AA, 19 Dec. 1939 (frame 88226), 12 Oct. 1940 (frames 88254-88255), 31 Jan. 1941 (frames 88269-88270), 17 Feb. 1941 (frame 88275), 13 March 1941 (frame 88288), 16 April 1941 (frame 88297), 30 April 1941 (frame 88298), 20 May 1941 (frame 88300), 19 June 1941 (frames 88307-88308), 4 July 1941 (frames 88310-1), 11 July 1941 (frame 88312), 22 July 1941 (frame 88313), 23 July 1941 (frame 88314), 24 July 1941 (frames 88316-88317); Weizsäcker memorandum, 2 Jan. 1941 (frames 88258-88259); Wörmann's summary of discussions with Tobias Barros about Barandon, 5 Feb. 1941 (frames 88273-88274); Wörmann memorandum 19 Feb. 1941 (frames 88276-88277).

47. For more about Martínez, see the following chapter.

48. Young, pp. 169-170.

49. Farago, pp. 203, 607-609. Another author has suggested that despite his position, Canaris's dislike of the Nazis was so intense that he deliberately undermined their war effort; Anthony Cave Brown, *Bodyguard of Lies* (New York: Harper and Row, 1975), pp. 151-252, 277, 339-3341, 348. However, this was not obvious at the time.

50. Young, pp. 163-164.

51. The author saw a 1939 issue of *Der Sonntag* at the German Colonial Museum in Frutillar when he toured it in February and March, 1997.

52. Converse, pp. 26-27, 140-141, 201, 405-412. The present author, unable to find *Deutsche Zeitung für Chile* in any public depository in Santiago or the Tenth Region, has had to rely on Converse for its contents. When she visited Chile in the mid-1970s, she managed to find a private individual who had kept the back issues.

53. The FBI's commentary on the media comes from FBI, pp. 105-119. The quotation comes from p. 112.

54. The report of Marcial Martínez appears in vol. 1970, Archivos del Departmento de Relaciones Exteriores (ADRE), Santiago de Chile. Martínez cites the DGI as a source.

55. *La Prensa* (Osorno), 11, 12, 17 Oct. 1941.

56. *La Prensa* (Osorno), 8 Dec. 1941.

57. *El Correo de Valdivia*, 21 Jan. 1942.

58. *La Prensa* (Osorno), 18 July 1942 (Spain) and 1 Aug. 1942 (Switzerland).

59. *El Llanquihue* (Puerto Montt), 16 Aug. 1942.

60. *El Llanquihue* (Puerto Montt), 19 March 1942.

61. *El Llanquihue* (Puerto Montt), 24 Aug. 1942.

62. *El Correo de Valdivia*, 21 Jan. 1943.

63. *La Prensa* (Osorno), 21 Jan. 1943.

64. Cavendish-Bentinck to Eden, 11 April 1937, Series A981/1. Item CHIL 15, Canberra.

65. FBI, p. 93.

66. Spanish Ambassador's report.

67. Ricardo Vallmitjana, *Bariloche, Mi Pueblo* (Buenos Aires: Antorchas, 1995), p. 110.

68. Julio Plencovich, "La historia del colegio Alemán de Puerto Varas," in Kinzel and Horn, pp. 278-283.

69. Report of the Spanish Ambassador in Chile, who represented German interests after the diplomatic rupture, to Foreign Minister Joaquín Fernández, 8 Feb. 1943, #16, vol. 2093, ADRE. Cited hereafter as Spanish Ambassador's report.

70. Converse, pp. 211-212. For Converse's detailed account of Nazi influences in the German schools, see pp. 206-245.

71. Bowers to Welles, 4 Feb. 1942, 29 April 1942, PSF.

72. *El Diario Ilustrado*, issues throughout 1942 and January 1943, especially those of 3, 4, 9, 11, 12 January 1942, 11, 12, and 14 July 1942, 3 and 5 Sept. 1942, 1 Jan. 1943.

73. Bowers to Welles, 16 March 1942, PSF.

74. FBI, p. 119.

75. Blancpain, *Les Allemands...*, p. 861.

76. FBI, pp. 119-120. The quotations come from p. 120.

77. FBI, p. 157.

78. Converse, p. 247.

79. Blancpain, *Los Alemanes...*, pp. 95, 189, 193-195.

80. Converse, p. 265. Taken from *Deutsche Zeitung*, 19 April 1937.

81. FBI, p. 188. Young provides the dates of the founding of Chile's Lutheran Churches, p. 162.

82. FBI, p. 195.

83. Spanish Ambassador's Report.

84. Pastor Helmuth Schünemann, "Las iglesias y escuelas luteranas alemanas en la Región del Lago Llanquihue hasta el ANO 1942," Kinzel and Horn, p. 272.

85. Converse, p. 260. Converse's source was *Deutsche Zeitung*.

86. Converse, p. 261.

87. Converse, pp. 259, 261.

88. Schünemann, p. 270.

89. Converse, pp. 252-260, 303.

90. Report of Kurt Singer, vol. 1970, ADRE.

91. FBI, 211-212.

92. Cavendish-Bentinck to Eden, 11 April 1937, Series A981/1, Item CHIL 15, Canberra.

93. Foreign Office, Tokyo, to Japanese embassy, Buenos Aires, 11 Dec. 1941, intercept #107, R.G. 24, vol. 20307, National Archives of Canada (NAC), Ottawa.

94. FBI, p. 213.

95. FBI, p. 52.

96. FBI, p. 232.

97. Cavendish-Bentinck to Eden, 11 April 1937, Series A981/1, Item CHIL 15, Canberra.

98. Farago, pp. 512-513, 514-515, 545, 560, 599, 600, 607, 610-612.

99. Cavendish-Bentinck to Eden, 11 April 1937, Series A981/1, Item CHIL 15, Canberra.

100. FBI, p. 258.

101. Cavendish-Bentinck to Eden, 11 April 1937, Series A981/1, Item CHIL 15, Canberra.

102. FBI, p. 204.

CHAPTER 3

CONFRONTATION

THE INTER-AMERICAN CONFERENCE AT RÍO DE JANEIRO
It was during the final weeks of the presidential election campaign when
Rossetti had to travel to the Río Conference. There he and other
hemispheric foreign ministers would decide what to do in the aftermath of
Pearl Harbor and Germany's subsequent declaration of war upon the
United States. According to Bernstein, officials at the Chilean embassy in
the Brazilian capital and Brazilian Foreign Minister Aranha fully expected
Rossetti to side with the pro-Allied majority rather than with Argentina. To
their dismay, he did not. Bernstein said that Rossetti had been a superb
deputy in Chile's House of Representatives, where he and Jorge González
von Marées had been two of eighteen successful candidates in Santiago's
first district during the congressional election of 1937. Bernstein regarded
him, nevertheless, as a less than competent diplomat. Still, said Bernstein,
he could be witty. When Rossetti expressed fear that Japan might react to a
diplomatic rupture by bombarding Chile's lengthy coastline, Sumner Welles
assured him that Chile could depend upon massive support from the United

States fleet. Rossetti responded, "What fleet? The one sunk at Pearl Harbor?"[1]

Anxious not to alienate voters in Chile's German community, Rossetti sided with his colleagues from Argentina against almost everyone else. More than 400,000 people (by no means all of them voters) lived in south Chile's Germanic provinces of Valdivia (191,642), Osorno (107,341), and Llanquihue (117,225)[2] at that time. Understandably, the governing Radicals could not take those provinces for granted.[3] Rather than support a resolution which would have *required* the republics of the Western Hemisphere to end diplomatic relations with the Axis, the Argentine and Chilean delegations sought and won a milder resolution, which merely *recommended* the severance of diplomatic relations.

El Mercurio provided extensive coverage of the Río conference, initially indicating that Chile would stand solidly alongside the rest of the hemisphere against the Axis. The headline of 14 January read, "Foreign Minister Rossetti will propose in Río de Janeiro full Inter-American naval and military collaboration." An editorial the following day—the day the conference opened—indicated Chilean support for "continental solidarity." The 16 January issue reported the opening of the conference the previous day and said that as far as Rossetti was concerned, its greatest achievement would be creation of a new inter-American economic order. On 17 January, a lengthy editorial praised the address by Sumner Welles, Under-Secretary of State and chief delegate from the United States. One columnist indicated Chilean willingness to sell useful war materials to the United States. Then came the first indication of disagreement. Colombia, Mexico and Venezuela were proposing a rupture of diplomatic relations between the republics of the Western hemisphere and the Axis belligerents. Argentina, Chile, Paraguay, and Peru opposed the motion. Yet, on 19 January, the banner headline read, "Brazilian circles predict unanimous approval of the rupture of diplomatic relations with Axis countries." The banner headline the following day indicated that the Foreign Ministers had reached agreement on the diplomatic rupture. None of the stories of 19 or 20 January indicated that Argentina and Chile were in any way out of step with everybody else.

Reports became less clear 22 January when *El Mercurio* reported: "Argentina accepted officially and Chile 'technically' the rupture of relations with the Axis countries." On 23 January *El Mercurio* admitted to some confusion as to who had agreed to what. Under the banner headline, "Chile and Argentina prevent unanimity on the rupture," the story indicated that Chile had a long, indefensible coastline. Yet, maintenance of normal diplomatic relations was not necessarily a panacea, noted *El Mercurio*. Despite strict neutrality, many European countries had suffered attack. At any rate, *El Mercurio* reported that the decision taken at Río would be submitted to Congress for ratification. On 24 January, *El Mercurio* printed the four articles which the foreign ministers had agreed upon at Río.

As the Río conference drew to a close, Aranha announced to enthusiastic applause that Brazil was terminating diplomatic relations with Germany, Italy, and Japan. The only delegates to remain seated and silent, according to Bernstein, were those from Chile and Argentina.[4]

The editorial of 25 January in Chile's most prestigious newspaper was an indication of controversy to come. *El Mercurio* noted some ambiguity in the recommendation about rupture and said that the breaking of diplomatic relations with the Axis was a congressional responsibility under the constitution, especially as the three Axis powers had said that they recognized no difference between diplomatic rupture and a declaration of war. Again *El Mercurio* noted Chile's long, vulnerable coastline. Nevertheless, it quoted Rossetti as saying that Chile had made a substantial contribution to inter-American unity. Rossetti apparently wanted to run with the hares and chase with the hounds. He would have some explaining to Bowers immediately after the presidential election. Despite their differences over which presidential candidate voters should support, both *El Diario Ilustrado* and *La Nación* agreed that a diplomatic rupture was undesirable. The 25 January editorial in *El Diario Ilustrado* was pleased both that the hemisphere's foreign ministers had been able to approve a resolution unanimously and that each country could decide for itself whether or when to make the break. *La Nación* had already expressed reservations when Colombia severed its ties with the Axis in December, 1941. That unneutral action on the part of Eduardo Santos's government, it feared, had brought the war closer to South America.[5] Ongoing diplomatic communications, said an editorial of 16 January, might avoid conflict. Chile had its long, vulnerable coastline, and its economy depended upon extensive, equally vulnerable, foreign commerce. *La Nación* rejoiced that Argentina's government shared similar convictions.[6]

In brief, Chileans had their reasons for maintaining diplomatic relations with the Axis powers. Chilean nationalism was not always compatible with the will of official Washington. Chilean governments needed to consider the reactions of voters, especially as presidential elections approached, and German and perhaps Italian voters might not approve a diplomatic rupture with their families' countries of origin. Most Chileans lived near the Pacific coast, and some feared that the Japanese forces which had attacked the U.S. fleet at Pearl Harbor might bombard Chile's coast. Yet Foreign Minister Rossetti wanted to demonstrate friendship for the United States and to support inter-American solidarity as he promoted what he saw as Chile's best interests. Attempts to square the circle would absorb his attention and that of Ambassador Bowers after the election.

THE ROSSETTI INTERLUDE

Rossetti and Bowers met 2 February 1942, the day after the Radical party's victory in the presidential election. At this point, according to Enrique Bernstein, Rossetti missed a golden opportunity. An outgoing government, thought Bernstein, ought to have taken a controversial decision and spare its successor any embarrassment. Bernstein noted with approval that in 1964, outgoing President Jorge Alessandri (1958-1964) broke diplomatic relations with Fidel Castro and spared his successor, Eduardo Frei Montalva (1964-1970), considerable agony.[7]

While Bowers sought, and expected, compliance with the Río resolution—a termination of diplomatic relations between Chile and the Axis powers[8]—Rossetti had considerations of his own. Chile had a long and vulnerable coastline, and her shipping links to foreign markets and suppliers as well as to distant Easter Island were also vulnerable. Chile's armed forces lacked the resources to protect the coastline and the shipping lines from Axis submarine attacks, and given what had happened at Pearl Harbor, there was reason to doubt the United States' ability to assist.

From Santiago, Bowers forwarded Chilean fears and desires for weapons to the point that Secretary of State Cordell Hull thought that Bowers was being unreasonable. In view of the global demands upon the United States early in 1942, said the Secretary of State, there were limits as to what it could do for Chile. While Ambassador Bowers and Chile's housing minister, Guillermo del Pedregal (who had talked to Bowers while Rossetti was attending the Río conference), agreed that ongoing diplomatic relations offered Chile no guarantee against a Japanese submarine attack, del Pedregal did not want to offer the slightest provocation. A rupture in diplomatic relations might appear to the Axis countries as a provocation, he thought.[9]

The Axis powers were also aware of Chilean vulnerability and Chilean concern about that vulnerability. During the Río conference, Rossetti had expressed his fears to the Spanish Ambassador in the Brazilian capital, who forwarded information to von Schön.[10] Immediately after the Río conference, Italian Foreign Minister Count Galeazzo Ciano discussed the matter with Chilean Ambassador Ramón Briones and forwarded a summary of the conversation to German diplomats in Rome.[11] For its part, the Japanese government gave assurances to Conservative Senator Maximiano Errázuriz that as long as Chile remained "neutral," Chilean shipping would be safe.[12] (That was the same Senator Errázuriz who was head of the Japan-Chile friendship society.[13]) Much of the captured German correspondence of 1942 deals with the safety (or otherwise) of Chilean shipping.

Rossetti spent the remainder of his term as foreign minister trying to avoid provocations of every description. When he had passed through Buenos Aires on his way to the Río conference, he agreed with the Argentines that it would be unnecessary and unwise to sever diplomatic relations with the Axis powers, let alone declare war. At the same time, he did not want to emphasize policy differences, and at a banquet he delivered a speech on hemispheric solidarity that even the United States ambassador, Norman Armour, could approve.[14] At Río, he again squared the circle. According to the Buenos Aires newspaper, La Nación, Rossetti referred to the Western Hemisphere as "an indivisible front" but stated that there were "special situations"—presumably Chile's long, vulnerable coastline and her shipping lanes—which required each nation to face its own realities.[15]

Back in Santiago, he continued to straddle the fence. He certainly gave Bowers the impression that he personally favoured a diplomatic rupture. However, as El Mercurio had indicated in its editorial of 25 January, this was a matter to be decided by Congress, not by him personally. Responsibility for any delay rested with Congress, Rossetti managed to convince Bowers. Nor was it wise, thought Rossetti, to rush the matter in Congress after a heated, partisan election campaign. Bowers pleaded for patience in Washington.[16] If the United States could make an offer of soldiers to protect Chile's mines and power plants before the Chilean Congress met late in February, the chances of success would improve.[17] As the days passed, Bowers became increasingly optimistic.

> [Rossetti] now has a card in his hand he has not had before—he is in position to inform Congress in secret session of the war material we are sending for the protection of the coast...He is clever and powerful in debate.

> No one opposing breaking relations doubts that this is inevitable and may come at any moment, and most agree that Chile will be in the war soon. But many take the position that Chile's friendship and support of the United States should follow the line of our government

in the case of England until attacked. These, of course, overlook the fact that Chile has agreed that an attack on one of the American Republics is an attack on each and all.[18]

When results failed to materialize, Bowers became defensive about official Washington's thoughts on Chileans in general and Rossetti in particular. Both, he thought, were admirable. Both needed more time.[19]

Rossetti had first hand evidence from Osorno that activities sponsored by the German embassy and its consular network were not always traditional diplomatic or consular activities. (See page 37.) Rossetti did not know for certain what von Schön was writing to his superiors in Berlin about the forced entry of Chilean police into the German vice-consulate in that city, but he had enough documentation to justify a rupture if he cared to use it.

Yet, Rossetti was under minimal pressure and could stall for time with a minimum of controversy. First, although El Mercurio favoured the Allied cause and gave extensive coverage to war news, throughout February and March it said little about the diplomatic rupture one way or the other. Media pressure on Rossetti was not a factor. Nor was diplomatic pressure from Allied diplomats—other than that from Bowers—significant. Indeed, Bowers lamented the lack of support he was receiving. While the British Embassy deserved praise, thought Bowers, for effective propaganda, "Sir Charles Orde, the Ambassador, is not well, and his methods lack the brute force of the Axis diplomats." The Dutch chargé d'affaires was "wholly ineffective." The Polish Minister did "little beyond giving masses for the Polish martyrs." The Danish minister did "nothing that I can discover," and the Belgian minister was little better. The Chinese minister was "young and inexperienced." The Canadian minister, whose arrival in Santiago featured prominently in the 4 March edition of El Mercurio, was not even worthy of mention. Apart from the Argentine minister, whose government opposed the rupture, most of the Latin American diplomats were irrelevant. Of all the other Allied heads of mission, only the Yugoslav minister maintained a high profile at the Foreign Office:

The Yugoslav Minister, Dr. Kolombatovic, is intensely and effectively active. After the Germans, the Yugoslavs have the largest and most prosperous colony here. They are ardently devoted to their country and are intensively organized. They follow Kolombatovic blindly, contributing money whenever asked. They have the brute force that matches that of the Germans, and the Germans cannot pound the table any louder than Kolombatovic. He is an educated man, speaking English, French, Spanish, Yugoslav, Russian and German, and he saw service in the Army and understands espionage. He talks bluntly to the Foreign Office.[20]

(Bowers' optimism about the effectiveness of Dr. Kolombatovic among Chile's Yugoslav—largely Croatian—community contrasts with the concern of the FBI, as mentioned in the previous chapter. Perhaps the FBI, like any police force, had to be on the lookout for trouble, but Bowers did tend to err on the side of optimism.)

Given the lack of pressure from people other than Bowers to break with the Axis, Rossetti managed to stall for time. Certain issues lacked complexity. Rossetti tolerated the presence of accredited Axis diplomats, but he did not want additional ones to join them. In mid-February, when the Chilean embassy in the Argentine capital asked whether to give a visa to a Japanese diplomat from Buenos Aires who wanted to spend a week in Santiago, Rossetti replied in the negative. The situation was too delicate, he said.[21] Later that same month, Rossetti formally protested the sinking of Venezuelan and Brazilian merchant ships. On the one hand, Rossetti went out of his way to hear what the Argentines thought of his policies.[22] On the other hand, he was willing to work with United States technical experts in hunting for clandestine Axis radio transmitters located in Chile.[23] In March, Argentine Foreign Minister F.M. Enrique Ruiz Guinazú visited Santiago. Rossetti appeared to find the occasion embarrassing and managed to keep it low key.[24]

ACHIEVEMENTS OF CHILEAN DIPLOMATS UNDER ROSSETTI

Makers of Chilean foreign policy had necessarily to consider the implications of that foreign policy upon Chileans themselves. While it was important to consider what the neighbours, from the United States to Argentina, might think, and while it would have been irresponsible to ignore what the Axis powers might do, leaders of a democracy had to consider the implications of a rupture upon Chileans themselves. In view of the fact that few Chileans lived far from the Pacific coast, the possibility of submarine attacks was an important matter, but there were also other issues. The record shows that Chile's diplomats could—and did—assist Chileans in distress. They also reveal that that assistance was, to say the least, limited.

Chilean diplomats assisted Chileans in Germany and German-occupied France during the Valdivia trials of Nazi activists. German Under-Secretary of State Ernst Wörmann estimated that there were only 100 Chileans in Germany—mainly students, artists, or small businessmen—but German authorities found them and their compatriots in Paris vulnerable and useful. If President Aguirre's government would arrest and try Nazis from Germany, Hitler's government would arrest Chileans. Ambassador Tobias Barros in Berlin urged Secretary of State Ernst von Weizsäcker to be patient. He was convinced that the Germans would have a fair trial in Valdivia and win acquittal for lack of evidence. Arbitrary arrests of innocent Chileans would not help Germany's image in Chile, he warned. From Santiago, von Schön also warned that German statements about the arrested Chileans lacked credibility. With the release of the Valdivia defendants, German authorities released all but one of the Chileans, and that one had been arrested months before the Valdivia reprisals on grounds of being a Communist.[25]

In this case, Chilean intervention proved useful. However, it is possible that without a German Embassy and German consular posts there would have been fewer Nazis in Chile to create the Valdivia problem in the first place. Hence, Nazi officials would not have been tempted to take Chileans as hostages. While it is probable that those Chileans imprisoned in reprisal for what had happened to the Nazis appreciated the efforts of Tobias Barros on their behalf, it is at least possible that in the absence of diplomatic relations, there would have been fewer of them, and the problem would have been smaller. Nevertheless, any arrested Chileans would have had little prospect of immediate release. Given that some were Jewish, this would have been a deadly serious matter.

Dangerous as he already knew the Axis powers to be, Rossetti could take some comfort from the thought that Chilean diplomats in Italy really were doing something worthwhile. Chile had responsibility for protection of Polish interests in Italy, and Ambassador Ramón Briones and Counsellor Jorge Barriga served as intermediaries between Polish diplomats at the Vatican and Poles in Italy—both the Polish Red Cross and Polish individuals who needed assistance with passports and finances.[26] They also helped Jews. Nowhere were their services more useful than in connection with Chile's consulate in Zagreb. The facts that the crisis in Zagreb coincided with the Río conference and that the German government mediated the dispute must have served as deterrents against an immediate diplomatic rupture.

As Chile had a substantial population of Croatian extraction,[27] during the interwar years Chile had not only a legation in Belgrade, Yugoslavia's capital, but a consulate in Zagreb, capital of Croatia. When Hitler attacked Yugoslavia in the spring of 1941 and Croatia seceded to become a collaborationist ally of Nazi Germany and Fascist Italy, Chile left the Belgrade legation as a legation and the Zagreb consulate as a consulate. Anti-Semitism in Croatia and the Croatian government's policy of interning Jews had been a front page story in the Puerto Montt newspaper *El Llanquihue* as early as 14 August 1941.

On 14 January 1942, shortly before the Río conference, Croatian police invaded Chile's consulate in Zagreb, arrested and imprisoned the consul, Emilio Sever, and seized both his personal assets and the contents of the consulate. According to Croatian authorities, Chile's failure to upgrade the consulate to a legation was evidence that Chile did not recognize Croatian independence, and because of that non-recognition, Chile and Chilean officials therefore forfeited any rights to diplomatic immunity. An added complication was that Sever was not clearly and unquestionably a Chilean citizen. When Croatia had achieved its "independence" from Yugoslavia, Sever was a Croatian businessman who was also, to his misfortune, a Jew. As far as Croatian authorities were concerned, Sever was still a Jew who ought to be treated like other Jews under the current laws of Croatia.

Under the circumstances, Barriga raced to Zagreb. There, with German and Italian assistance, he managed to negotiate Sever's release from prison and permission for Sever and his family to leave Croatia altogether. Barriga's attempts to persuade Croatian authorities to return Sever's property were unsuccessful, although Germany promised some compensation, and Barriga did recover most of the contents of the consulate itself. Barriga and Briones considered Croatia a wild and dangerous place where some 700,000 Jews—an exaggeration—had already been killed. Both knew that without the help of the German legation, whose Minister was dean of Zagreb's diplomatic corps, and of Chile's embassy in Berlin, Barriga's trip to Zagreb would probably have been an exercise in futility.[28] Full diplomatic relations with the Axis powers did provide some benefits.

Yet, did not the ongoing business-as-usual approach leave other Chilean officials as possible targets for hostage taking or arrest, as Sever had been? One vulnerable official was Armando Labra, Minister at Chile's legation in Tokyo. Even before Rossetti left office, it was becoming apparent that Labra feared for his personal safety and was little better than a hostage. Before the Río conference, Labra had been in a position to report that the Japanese government wanted to buy cotton from Peru and saltpetre from Chile,[29] and after Río, he could confirm arrival of a shipment of Chilean wine.[30] Soon, however, the messages were of a different nature. Via diplomatic channels to which Rossetti had access, Labra appealed to President-elect Ríos to remember him and his staff before undertaking any change of policy. Any evacuation must precede a declaration of war, he warned. Once the war started, evacuation would be impossible.[31] On 25

March, Labra wrote Ernesto Barros—by that time Ríos's nominee for the position of Foreign Minister—to warn that war in Asia would be very different from war in Europe. In Asia, said Labra, there was hatred against white people, but in Europe there was respect for diplomatic immunity. If the Soviet Union were to attack Japan, Japan would become a hell of fire, hunger, misery, and hatred.[32] Rossetti had every opportunity to see Labra's letter to the incoming Foreign Minister as Rossetti still held the office when Labra sent it.

Rossetti must have realized that, unlike Briones and Barriga in Rome and Labra in Tokyo, Chile's ambassador in Berlin—Tobias Barros—was an Axis propagandist and lobbyist, not a reporter. At one point, he actually told someone at the German Foreign Office that "contrary to the instructions of his government" he had not intervened on behalf of Chilean Jews imprisoned in occupied France.[33]

Tobias Barros believed strongly that Chile ought to remain neutral, and as far as he was concerned, neutrals maintained diplomatic relations with everyone. As the Río conference was beginning, Ambassador Barros wired the Chilean foreign office to say that the interests of Chile and Argentina were very different from those of countries closer to the United States.[34] Barros praised the role of the German foreign office in arranging the liberation of Consul Sever in Zagreb.[35] On 19 January, he forwarded a report that British warships had attacked German merchant ships inside Spanish territorial waters near Fernando Poo (an island in the Atlantic off the African coast). The British had no respect for the rights of neutrals, charged Tobias Barros, and Anglo-Saxons had little respect for Spanish people.[36] Tobias Barros did not limit his opinions to what was happening in Nazi Germany and German-occupied Europe.

Ambassador Barros continued with this type of despatch. He said that the German government regarded Chile's role at Río as constructive in that Chile wanted the rupture with the Axis to be optional, not mandatory. He also warned that according to "usually reliable sources" in Berlin, any country which dared to sever diplomatic relations might quickly find itself on the receiving end of a Japanese attack. Given what had happened at Pearl Harbor, Barros said that the United States was in no position to guarantee Chilean security. On the contrary, neutrality and the diplomatic status quo would be the safest, wisest course of action for Chile. Nor did he think that Chile need feel guilty about pursuit of its self-interest. For more than two years after the British declaration of war against Germany, the United States had sent diplomats to the German capital, and there was no reason why Chile could not do likewise now that the United States had become a belligerent. Moreover, Chile needed whatever overseas markets there were, and a closure of diplomatic posts would limit the possibilities for sales. Nor was Barros unaware that following a rupture, diplomats such as himself would be virtual prisoners until the Axis governments received guarantees of the safe return of their embassy and consular officials.[37] When Juan Antonio Ríos won the presidential election, Tobias Barros asked Rossetti to forward many of those same arguments to the president-elect and to warn him about "Anglo-American propaganda." Chilean neutrality, Barros informed Ríos, was truly an indication of national maturity.[38]

As long as Rossetti was Foreign Minister, Tobias Barros used his embassy as a platform for discussion of global issues and Chilean foreign policy, not merely as a provider of information about Germany and German-occupied Europe. From Berlin he continued to lobby for his version of neutrality,[39] and nobody in Santiago appears to have reprimanded him for exceeding his authority.[40] He could help Chileans[41] and Poles[42] in distress, forward messages on behalf of diplomats from other Latin American countries,[43] and relay Rossetti's protest over the sinking of Venezuelan and Brazilian merchant ships to the German Foreign Office.[44] However, when Rossetti requested clarification of press reports about German setbacks on the Russian front,[45] Ambassador Barros replied—inaccurately—that "news" of Soviet victories and German setbacks had been greatly exaggerated.[46] Ambassador Barros passed along Axis propaganda that the Royal Air Force had conducted a massive bombardment of Paris, killing 600, wounding 1000.[47]

Rossetti's final challenge was the mid-March sinking of the Chilean merchant ship *Toltén* near Atlantic City, New Jersey. A torpedo from a German submarine had hit the *Toltén*, and, as instructed, Ambassador Barros did express Rossetti's concern to the German Foreign Office. German authorities, the Ambassador told Rossetti, were full of good will, but it was not clear to the Navy that the *Toltén* was a Chilean rather than an American ship. (Under instructions from the U.S. Coast Guard, the *Toltén* had dimmed her lights, whereas neutrals normally displayed all their lights.) In future, Chileans ought to be more careful.[48] Perhaps of some value to the safety of Chilean shipping, Rossetti was able, through Ambassador Barros, to deny rumours that United States forces had landed on Chilean soil.[49]

With benefit of hindsight it is clear that the usefulness of Ambassador Barros was limited. Probably unwittingly, he passed along misinformation, and, despite his efforts, Chilean ships—not to mention those from other Latin American countries—continued to face dangers. Yet, notwithstanding any personal reservations, Rossetti chose not to change the direction of Chilean foreign policy. He knew that his days in office were about to end, and he did not wish to commit his successors to changes which might have major repercussions. His successor could weigh the value of Chile's diplomatic efforts in Germany, Italy, and Japan, and make his own decisions.

THE TRANSITION

In his memoirs, Ambassador Bowers said that when the news that President-elect Ríos had chosen Ernesto Barros as his foreign minister became public, people telephoned the U.S. embassy to offer congratulations. Barros had served as president of the Chile-America cultural institute, and as a lawyer he had represented a number of American interests. Sixteen years later, when Bowers wrote about Barros, he described him as a friend with whom he had had a difference of opinion on one issue—whether or not Chile should continue to host diplomats from Axis countries.[50] Chilean documents now indicate that Bowers's expressed confidence in Barros was completely unwarranted, and Bowers's own correspondence reveals that the ambassador was aware of Barros's perfidy.

Bowers was one of the first to learn that Ernesto Barros, cousin of Ambassador Tobias Barros, was the choice of President-elect Ríos for the position of foreign minister. As early as 20 February, Bowers informed President Roosevelt that Barros was one of two candidates on the short list and, because of the state of the other's health, the more likely to get the position.[51] On 25 February, Bowers confirmed the appointment to President Roosevelt.[52] Not until 22 March did El Mercurio identify members of the new cabinet.

Bowers's initial impressions of Ernesto Barros were highly positive. On 4 February, he had identified him as a "warm friend of the United States," despite the fact that Barros opposed a rupture with the Axis for fear that Chile's coastline was vulnerable to attack.[53] When announcing his position on Ríos' short list to President Roosevelt, Bowers described Barros as "militantly, openly, a champion of the United States and a close friend of mine."[54] When confirming Barros' appointment, Bowers said, "I do not know a single Chilean whom I would rather trust as far as we are concerned." That Barros continued to favour ongoing diplomatic relations with the Axis appeared but a minor consideration. Chances of an attack on Chilean commercial shipping, thought Barros, would increase after a diplomatic rupture, and given the importance of Chilean minerals to the American war effort, such attacks would jeopardize U.S. as well as Chilean interests.[55] This happened before the sinking of the Toltén.

While Bowers celebrated, German authorities had mixed feelings about Chile and Chileans during the early months of 1942. Ambassador von Schön had preferred an Ibáñez victory to a Ríos one because he thought Ríos the more dependent of the two on leftist support. However, he noted, neither candidate had taken a firm position on the war,[56] and when Ríos won, von Schön took comfort that Ríos had a German wife and was not an outspoken critic of Germany.[57] Von Schön evidently did not know that Ríos and his wife no longer loved each other. The Chilean ambassador in Madrid told his German counterpart in the Spanish capital that he had been a childhood friend of the president-elect and had received assurances that Ríos would not change the direction of Chile's policy of neutrality.[58] From the German Embassy in Rome came the official Italian profile of Ernesto Barros, President-elect Ríos's choice as foreign minister:

> The new Chilean foreign minister, Ernesto Barros Jarpa, a man in his fifties [GSM: actually he was 48, born in 1894[59]], belongs to the Liberal party and comes from a good family...He has an outgoing personality and is a man of the right. The Chilean ambassador in Rome, who has known him for a long time, believes that Barros Jarpa will continue Rossetti's policy of neutrality.[60]

In Santiago, Ambassador von Schön even had high hopes for the incoming Interior Minister, Raúl Morales, who would turn out to be the most ardent advocate of a rupture between Chile and the Axis. Morales, said von Schön, was "for neutrality."[61] The only serious sour note came from the German ambassador in Buenos Aires who pronounced, "The new Chilean foreign minister, Barros Jarpa, has a reputation as a friend of the United States."[62]

Unlike Bowers and von Schön, Winston Churchill had a preview of what the foreign policy of Ernesto Barros would be. On 19 April 1942, the British Prime Minister received an intercept which Yamagata had sent to his superiors in Tokyo days earlier. Yamagata was reporting on a conversation which he had had with former President Alessandri. Noting that Barros had been his foreign minister during his own first term as President of Chile, Alessandri told Yamagata that Ríos had consulted him about a reappointment of Barros to that same portfolio. According to Yamagata, Alessandri indicated to Ríos that Barros would be a good man for the job, "conditionally on the maintenance of Chilean independence." Barros and Ríos agreed with that condition.

Alessandri also confirmed for Yamagata a rumour that Ríos had offered to appoint him as Chile's ambassador to the United States. However, said Yamagata, the former president had refused the honour in order that he might retain "freedom of action."[63] There is no indication that Churchill did anything with this information.

Any initial respect which Bowers had had for the foreign minister's boss, President Ríos, quickly evaporated, and Ambassador Bowers' friendship with Ernesto Barros turned to hostility. From the start, Bowers had low expectations towards President-elect Ríos. The U.S. ambassador told his immediate superior, Under-Secretary of State Sumner Welles:

> Juan Antonio Rios is a handsome man who "looks like a President" and is friendly to the United States. He is not a great man and he has neither the humanitarian traits nor the idealism of Aguirre Cerda, nor the brilliance and color of Alessandri. He is a lawyer whose practice has largely been in the corporation field and he has been connected professionally with the American businesses here and for a time was on the board of the Telephone Company. I am sure we shall have nothing to fear from him in the matter of protecting American interests here. The danger is that he will think this all we should ask him in the way of pro-Americanism. He is apt to confuse Big Business with the United States and I suspect that he is certain that "Dollar Diplomacy" and not the "Good Neighbor Policy" reflects the United States...In the campaign he took a square position for democracy and against totalitarianism indirectly but he refrained from any comments that totalitarians would resent. Reared in the South among the Germans...he got a surprisingly large vote in the German centers of Valdivia and Osorno, but this was probably personal. His wife is a German and I hear that she is very pro-German and that there have been family quarrels on the war. It is said a divorce was pending because of a mistress when he was nominated for President, then his wife concluded she could tolerate the mistress for residence in the Moneda.

Bowers predicted accurately that Ríos would not rush to sever diplomatic relations with the Axis.[64] He was also right about the president's philandering, and this proved useful to the U.S. cause. Late in July 1942, while Mrs. Ríos was visiting the United States for an indeterminate period of time, a "luscious" beauty, Pila Subercaseaux, dined with Ríos. He asked her to play the piano for him, and she agreed, provided "he would do anything she asked him." When he promised that he would, she asked him to sever diplomatic relations with the Axis powers and harangued him for his failure to do so to that point.[65] Evidently *her* opinions were not those expected of Mrs. Ríos.

An early hint that Chile's foreign minister might not be as friendly as previously thought appears in a letter of 18 June to President Roosevelt. There Bowers described Barros's lobbying on behalf of the diplomatic status quo as "inexplicable."[66] On 14 July he went further:

> There is no doubt in my mind that Barros...is tricky, given to brazen misrepresentations and suppressions, and is dishonest. This is shocking to me, and the American colony has been shocked by his attitude in view of his reputation for years as a strong pro-American. I suspect that he is trying to make his policy conform to the selfish interests of the Chilean shipping company and other Chileans who are now making money hand over fist. Very confidentially I am told by the Electric Company that after he became Minister he was offered a retainer of 30,000 pesos...and that he took it without a blink.[67]

Yet, dishonesty and an apparent willingness to accept bribes were not the only considerations. Bowers had become convinced that former president Arturo Alessandri had great influence upon Barros. Bowers had also become aware of the influence and input of Ambassador Tobias Barros:

> The Foreign Minister's cousin, a complete Nazi tool, is Chilean Ambassador in Berlin and is reporting, even by telephone...all the propaganda handed him by Goebbels [Göbbels]; and this is hurried to Rios.[68]

On 11 August, Bowers reported that Foreign Minister Barros was deliberately misleading President Ríos with regard to U.S. expectations of

Chile.[69] For that reason as well as his thought that Ríos might be more willing than his foreign minister to accept the rupture, Bowers hoped that he could bypass Barros and deal directly with the president.[70]

In mid-August Brazil declared war on Germany after German submarines torpedoed five Brazilian merchant ships off the South American coast. To Bowers, President Ríos missed a golden opportunity. That would probably have been a politically acceptable occasion to sever diplomatic relations with the Axis. Unfortunately, he explained:

> Rios is not a strong man. He has no imagination. No flare. No initiative. Little moral courage. And he is easily swayed.

> Our situation is this: Barros...who is resorting to everything in an effort to prevent the breaking of relations is in [a] position to see Rios daily and tell him whatever he wishes in secret. No one else has that privilege. That puts us at a disadvantage.[71]

Whether Bowers was fair to Ríos is questionable. The sinking of the Brazilian ships could be (and was) an argument for continued Chilean neutrality. If Brazil had not been as committed as it was to the Allied cause, then perhaps the Germans would not have sunk the Brazilian ship.[72] Historian Osvaldo Silva Galdames certainly does not see Ríos as a weakling. He describes him as being "of authoritarian character."[73] Either Bowers or Silva Galdames must be at least partially wrong.

On 21 September Bowers advised President Roosevelt: "[Ríos] is a man without an ideology, without ideals, without strong convictions or principles. He is a second rate politician, an opportunist...He has very little moral courage." On a happier note, Bowers was able to confirm of Ríos, "He is not a Nazi." To Nelson Rockefeller, a future vice-president of the United States who in the service of the State Department visited Chile that month, Bowers described Ríos as "the Warren G. Harding of Chilean politics." Republican though he was, said Bowers, Rockefeller had to agree that Ríos was comparable to the handsome but ineffective 29th president of the United States.[74]

ERNESTO BARROS AS FOREIGN MINISTER

For several weeks Barros managed to convince Bowers that he remained a closet friend of the United States. No, he would not visit that country, he told the U.S. ambassador, until Chile had severed diplomatic relations with the Axis. However, said Bowers:

> He wants to remove the pro-Nazi Ambassador [Conrado Ríos] in Argentina and send Luis Subercaseaux [a Conservative who supported the rupture]; he wants to suppress the Nazi paper here, the *Alemán*; and he wants to go after all the pro-Axis activities here, the agents, spies, propagandists, and all organizations [which are] enemies of the United States and wipe them out.[75]

Barros' track record as foreign minister reveals that what Barros did was the very antithesis of what Bowers expected him to do. Nor did he change ambassadors in Buenos Aires, despite the fact that he had good reason for doing so. During the unconstitutional Ibáñez presidency (1927-1931), Conrado Ríos had served Ibáñez as foreign minister and then as Chile's ambassador to Peru. Like Tobias Barros, Conrado Ríos had been an officer in the Chilean army.[76]

From his office in Santiago, Ernesto Barros could not know everything that was happening in the world. He did know what his diplomats were telling him about war on the Russian front,[77] the political situation in Vichy France,[78] a possible Italian invasion of Corsica,[79] Germany's relations with Italy[80] and European neutral and lesser Axis countries,[81] or the 30 April elections to the Japanese Diet.[82] However, he had no guarantee that his diplomats were well informed. It is also possible that he did not know that a Chilean army officer friendly to Germany used his radio transmitter late every Monday afternoon to forward sensitive information to Hamburg.[83]

He could be more confident about reports on the reactions of Axis governments to events elsewhere—official German reaction to a speech of Churchill's,[84] German approval of Chilean neutrality,[85] German concern about the investigative commission appointed by the Chamber of Deputies to study the behaviour of German diplomats in Chile,[86] the angry reaction of the English-language *Japan Times* to the Río conference,[87] the Japanese cabinet's favourable reaction to Argentine and Chilean foreign policy,[88] or Japanese concern over President Ríos's proposed visit to Washington.[89] At times Ernesto Barros could feel that his diplomats were doing something practical—taking steps in connection with the repatriation of Chileans from war zones,[90] looking for trade opportunities,[91] straightening out problems of citizenship. When did an Italian cease to be an Italian and become a Chilean, with no obligation to Italian military service?[92] He could also have useful conversations with Axis diplomats about the safety of Chilean vessels and his unwillingness to tolerate Axis naval attacks on targets south of the Panama Canal.[93] He did admit to von Schön that important as the Panama Canal was to Chile, Chile had no obligation of any sort to sever relations, let alone go to war, should an Axis attack close it.[94]

Unlike Barros, a shrewd foreign minister might have observed a few clues. Why did the Berlin Embassy, headed by a senior military officer who knew something about defence strategy, remain silent on the Battle of Midway but comment on the Japanese capture of two tiny, remote, fogbound islands in the Aleutians? Why did the Tokyo Legation mention neither Midway nor Guadalcanal? Why was Ambassador Tobias Barros indignant at British and American air raids on German cities,[95] but full of praise because his cousin the Foreign Minister refused to condemn German atrocities on the Soviet front?[96] Nor did Ernesto Barros react when the German government honoured Ambassador Barros for what he had done in the promotion of German-Chilean friendship by making him a recipient of the Order of the German Eagle.[97] (Other recipients included Romania's dictator Ion Antonescu and the commander-in-chief of Sweden's armed forces, General Olof Thörnell, a Germanophile.[98]) Barros appears to have been equally at ease when Labra's daughter sought to marry the Italian Embassy official who had written Fascist propaganda for Mussolini's Ethiopian campaign as well as books about Italian Fascism. Both fathers approved the marriage, but Labra wondered whether the Chilean Embassy in Rome might try to persuade Mussolini to let the couple marry.[99] It is obvious that pressure for a diplomatic rupture did not come from Chilean diplomats in the principal Axis capitals—Berlin and Tokyo.

The Chilean government's investigative agency, the Dirección General de Investigaciones (DGI), confirmed that German diplomats and consular officials engaged in questionable activities. The matter came to a head when a New York magazine, *Background: The Key to Current Events*, devoted its third issue to an article by Kurt D. Singer, "Germany's Secret Service in South America." The first two chapters dealt with Chile, and the Chilean Foreign Office was sufficiently concerned that it asked one of its officers, Marcial Martínez, to write a report. On 12 May 1942, Martínez submitted a confidential report to Foreign Minister Ernesto Barros.[100]

According to the DGI, the Hitler party held gatherings at which the Swastika and the Chilean flag flew side by side on German patriotic days and other special occasions. Following the singing of Chile's national anthem, everyone would sing German "hymns," and until it became illegal under Chilean law, many wore Nazi-style uniforms to the meetings. Martínez named names as he outlined the Hitler party's structure and discussed the support which it received from diplomats at the German Embassy and from consular officials. Walter Böttger, commercial attaché at the German embassy in Santiago, was *de facto* director of Nazi activities in Chile, and Ambassador von Schön was the titular head. Martínez included photographic evidence of von Schön at a gathering of Chilean Nazis, as well as pictures of uniformed Nazis, arms outstretched in the direction of the Swastika or Hitler's portrait, at meetings in Frutillar and Puerto Montt.

Nazis formed private armies and played secret war games around Lake Llanquihue and elsewhere. The "soldiers" had extensive military equipment, although they fired blanks. The DGI was able to confirm that war games took place in March 1939 when Ambassador von Schön visited the agricultural colony of Penaflor. The FBI attributed Chilean "tolerance" of such activities to a fear of antagonizing Böttger, Germany's top Nazi agent in Chile.[101]

Singer had written that Chilean Nazis had formed an organization named the Association of the Friends of Germany (*Asociacion de Amigos de Alemania*, or AAA). One Chilean army general, Arturo Ahumada, was president of the AAA, and two other generals—Francisco Javier Díaz and Carlos Vergara—were directors. These men shared a traditional Chilean distrust of the United States and a conviction that Hitler offered stability to the world. The DGI confirmed the role of the three generals in the AAA. The AAA, said Martínez, wanted to strengthen the bonds between Germany and Chile, and to promote Nazi values within Chile by working with "respectable" Chileans. Members of the governing Radical party attended AAA meetings and joined the generals in toasts to Hitler.

Singer had found the German embassy in Santiago very influential. Money and advice from the German embassy, he said, enabled Nazis to control and influence a number of Chilean newspapers and radio stations, particularly in southern Chile, which he identified. The DGI agreed. It also agreed with Singer—and the FBI—that one Werner Siering of Bayer headed Germany's "espionage system...in close collaboration with the German Embassy and the consulates." Indeed, wrote Martínez, the consulates provided phoney passports to its agents so that they could fulfil their missions and extricate themselves from delicate situations. Among the recipients of such "passports" were crew members from the *Graf Spee*.

Singer had scrutinized the clergy and their so-called "Harbor Service." He said that photostats of documents collected by German spies in Chile—not all of them people of German extraction—were still finding their way to Germany inside the German embassy's diplomatic pouch. The DGI was unable to confirm or deny these charges, but they were, to say the least, plausible.

Singer had accused Nazis of forming private armies and playing secret war games around Lake Llanquihue and elsewhere. The "soldiers" had extensive military equipment, although they fired blanks. The DGI was able to confirm that war games did take place in March 1939 when Ambassador von Schön visited the agricultural colony of Penaflor.

In brief, the DGI confirmed the embassy's support for Nazi cells in southern Chile. The very presence of the German embassy rendered Naziism respectable to Chileans of German extraction, to army generals, even to Radical politicians. The DGI confirmed the role of German officials in influencing Chile's media, in espionage, and in providing phoney passports.

The FBI distrusted the pro-German lobby group AAA.[102] Again, there was good reason. Colonel Friedrich Wolf, military attaché at the German Embassy since July 4, 1940, had formed a partnership with various retired officers of the Chilean army who were active in the AAA.[103] As long as Germany and Chile maintained diplomatic relations, the AAA was evidently a "respectable" organization. This information evidently made little impression on Ernesto Barros.

Foreign Minister Barros explained his determination to maintain Chile's diplomatic ties with the Axis privately to his cousin Tobias Barros and publicly, long after the war, in his memoirs. His memoirs portray the foreign minister as a Chilean nationalist. The U.S., he argued, had no qualms about neutrality between 1914 and 1917, nor again between 1939 and 1941. The Axis nations were as evil before the United States went to war in December 1941 as thereafter, yet the United States had remained neutral. As nobody had attacked Chile, Chile had as much right to remain neutral and maintain full diplomatic relations with all belligerents as had the United States before it went to war.[104] To his cousin, the Foreign Minister expressed and elaborated upon those opinions. On 4 April, Ernesto Barros wrote Tobias that he agreed 100 per cent with him regarding Chile's international attitude.[105] Whether this meant that Ernesto shared Tobias's distrust of the British and Americans or simply believed that Chile and the Axis powers should continue to exchange diplomats is not altogether clear.

The Chilean government did not control Chile's newspapers, but when diplomats issued complaints about the what was appearing in them, Ernesto Barros apologized rather than boast about Chile's free press. When *Diario Alemán para Chile* provoked the Brazilian ambassador with a vitriolic attack against Brazil and its foreign minister, Oswaldo Aranha, Barros told von Schön that *Diario Alemán* had abused the concept of freedom of the press.[106] However, Barros apologized to von Schön when the Communist newspaper, *El Siglo*, first accused German and Japanese diplomats of financing a rubber-smuggling operation,[107] and then carried a cartoon which portrayed Hitler as a vicious dog.[108] Pleasing von Schön was a high priority for the Chilean foreign minister.

On 18 August, Ambassador Barros expressed concern about a speech by Interior Minister Raúl Morales in the presence of President Ríos. From German sources, the Ambassador had learned that Morales thought that Chile could no longer consider itself a neutral country. Tobias Barros wondered whether a diplomatic rupture was imminent.[109] The Foreign Minister replied that Chile's neutrality was "absolute" and said that the German sources had taken Morales' speech out of context. Ambassador von Schön, Ernesto Barros said, was pleased with Chile's "independent" Foreign Policy, and in Washington President Ríos would explain Chile's policy of "independence."[110] This happened weeks after Barros had convinced Bowers that he had "been talking very aggressively to Baron von Schön."[111]

Nevertheless, Bowers did score one success with the Ríos-Barros administration. In July 1942, he intervened to prevent a change of personnel at the Danish legation in Santiago, sought by the government in occupied Copenhagen.[112] While he might have to contend with unsavoury diplomats from Germany, Japan, Italy, Spain, and Vichy France, he at least need not worry about Danes of questionable loyalty.

ERNESTO BARROS'S INDIFFERENCE TO GERMAN ESPIONAGE AND SUBVERSION

It is well established that in time of war, enemies can learn about each other in neutral countries. Spain maintained intelligence operations inside Canada during the Spanish-American War of 1898.[113] Switzerland and Portugal served as information centers during the world wars,[114] and at the German legation in Dublin, diplomat Eduard Hempel received reports on the Luftwaffe's bombing raids of England during the Battle of Britain.[115] On 15 December 1942, the Foreign Office in Tokyo sent its diplomats in Bern and Lisbon lists of British and American newspapers which it wanted them to purchase.[116] Ernesto Barros either did not believe or did not care that the Axis powers could use Chile in any less than appropriate way.

Foreign Minister Barros was indifferent to the subversive role of German Embassy and consular officials in the subversion described in the Martínez report. As Martínez's report was "personal and confidential," few were aware of it. Nevertheless, on 26 May the Chamber of Deputies voted to establish a commission to investigate illegal Nazi activities. The government could not intervene to prevent this, the foreign minister apologetically told his cousin, for fear of creating a controversy. In his words, the commission's mandate would be limited to investigation of "illegal activities—if there are any."[117]

On 17 June the German ambassador met President Ríos and Foreign Minister Barros for a discussion of shipping, and their meeting received widespread publicity in Chilean newspapers.[118] However, such publicity did not persuade Ernesto Barros that the time for a diplomatic break with the Axis had come. About the same time, Ernesto Barros and Yamagata actually speculated that information from Chile which led to the sinking of ships was coming from members of Chile's German community who were contacting German spies in the United States.[119] Nevertheless, diplomatic relations continued, as though the spies were without contact with the embassy.

There was a flurry of excitement in June when Oscar Schnake, by this time Minister of Industrial Development, addressed a Socialist Party gathering. He wondered aloud how any decent person could remain neutral before the reality of a Fascist threat to the world. Why, if the Axis won, there would be "a Chilean Quisling." Fascists might favour neutrality, said Schnake, but most Chileans certainly did not. Chile ought to support the Allied cause with all the means at its disposal. World War II was not simply a struggle between distant and rival nations; it was an ideological struggle which threatened democracy throughout the world. Neutrality was out of the question. Santiago's *La Nación*, which had supported President Ríos during the election campaign, accused Schnake of "demagoguery" and called upon readers to support the President's policy of neutrality.[120] After a briefing from Barros, on 25 June Chilean Senators voted overwhelmingly in favour of the diplomatic status quo.[121]

On 30 June 1942, U.S. Ambassador Bowers told Foreign Minister Barros that the Federal Communications Commission had confirmed the existence of an unauthorized station in Valparaíso, discovered that Axis spies were using it to send messages to Hamburg, and learned how to crack the cipher and "read" what the senders were saying. Radios were sensitive because of the speed with which they could send messages—certainly faster than the post office. The intercepts, said Bowers, included seven types of information:

1. Boat arrivals to and departures from ports on the west coast of South America;

2. Information on the activities of the United States Government in connection with the military and other aid furnished to countries on the west coast of South America;

3. Information relating to the exports of the United States;

4. Information on the defence measures taken by Latin American countries;

5. General information from the United States;

6. Political information, chiefly pertaining to Chile;

7. Administrative details, pertaining to the functioning of the station and its agents.

The Valparaíso transmitter, said Bowers, forwarded information collected by Axis spies in Chile, Argentina, Peru, Colombia, Ecuador, Guatemala, Mexico, and the United States.

Bowers thought that if he provided enough details—naming names and citing events, dates, and addresses—Barros might be moved. Perhaps he could verify some facts for himself. Perhaps he would conclude that such a detailed account could not possibly be fiction. Surely, thought Bowers, the involvement of the German Embassy in the clandestine broadcasts provided good reason for closure of the German Embassy.

Bowers presented intercepts taken from PYL, as he called Germany's clandestine station in Valparaíso. The air attaché at the German Embassy in Santiago, Ludwig von Bohlen (known on PYL as "Bach"), had gone to Río de Janeiro to purchase "secret inks and developers" from a German agent there in order to "facilitate communications with agents in the United States." Twice "Bach" also received intelligence reports about U.S. aid to Ecuador and about Ecuadorian politics from the Roman Catholic seminarian in Santiago, Tullio Franchini, whose address Bowers provided. Franchini's source was Father Viane, the Roman Catholic priest in Ecuador who was partial to the Axis. In turn, "Bach" gave the documents to another colleague at the German embassy in Santiago, Commercial Attaché Walter Böttger, who was to forward them to Germany. (This was the same Walter Böttger whom Chile's DGI had already identified as a Nazi agent.) Another time, the Hamburg station asked PYL for the latest edition of a specific Chilean Sea Chart. "Bach" obtained a copy and sent it to Germany through the Spanish diplomatic pouch.

Late in 1941, "Bach" requested and received permission to share information on ship movements with the Japanese Naval Attaché. He then proceeded to do so with Japan's Military Attaché, Haruo Teshima, thought to be Japan's spymaster, and because of the frequent contacts between the German embassy and the Japanese legation, it was a safe assumption that Japanese spies would tell Germans what they knew. Besides "Bach" (von Bohlen) and Böttger, other German officials named as sources and intermediaries by PYL included Germany's military attaché and the German consul-general in Valparaíso—who had been a source of concern to Chile's DGI because of his role as a supplier of phoney passports. According to El Mercurio and the FBI, Ambassador Bowers fully briefed Ernesto Barros about PYL and its activities 30 June 1942. When U.S. sources in

Montevideo, Uruguay provided evidence to the media in November, Barros—who was no longer foreign minister—explained his failure to take action to the absence of a Spanish-language version of the facts. The FBI rejected this statement and said that he had had one since early July.[122]

Ambassador Bowers also informed Ernesto Barros that the German embassy could provide moral and legal support for Axis spies. Bowers told Barros about the case of Johannes Szeraws, the commercial sailor who had "deserted" the *Frankfurt*, illegally entered Chile, and become "the operator of PYL." Bowers reminded Barros that the Chilean government had ordered Szeraws's deportation, but so vital was Szeraws to PYL that the German embassy had intervened on his behalf and requested Chilean authorities to let him stay.[123]

Captured German documents confirm Bowers's assertions. On 16 February 1942 von Schön reported to Berlin that he had found a reliable radio operator, one Pedro del Campo who owned a short wave transmitter and was ready to be useful if Chile and Germany should sever diplomatic relations.[124] Having failed to persuade Ernesto Barros to close the Axis diplomatic and consular posts, on 28 July Bowers provided further documentation on German espionage to the Chilean Foreign Minister. Someone at the Foreign Office, not necessarily Barros himself, provided copies of the intercepts to an agent of the Abwehr (German's spy service) named Brücke. Brücke realized at once that U.S. counter-intelligence had cracked the German cipher and could "read" German radio mail. Brücke lamented that Americans knew about "Bach," a radio operator at Antofagasta named Pedro, a contact person in Valparaíso, and others. Szeraws had disappeared. It was also unfortunate, thought Brücke, that Americans had conclusive evidence that the Spanish diplomatic courier carried sensitive German documents in his pouch. Ambassador von Schön forwarded Brücke's letter to Berlin.[125]

Further revelations confirmed that the Nazi espionage network based in Santiago extended thousands of kilometres beyond Chile's borders. Von Schön mentioned a payment to a spy named Leiser in the Brazilian capital.[126] He also mentioned the arrest of another agent, Luni, in Havana. Von Schön had little doubt that intercepted telegrams were responsible, and Brücke added that following his arrest in September, Luni had been condemned to death.[127] The FBI wrote a detailed report about the case of Enrique Augosto Luni, whose German name was Heinz August Luning. German businessmen in Chile—identified in the FBI report—sent him funds and communicated with him by radio. So overwhelming was the evidence that Chilean authorities made several arrests in October 1942, and on 10 November Luni himself died on the gallows in a Cuban jail.[128] Yet, diplomatic relations between Germany and Chile continued. Moreover, in a letter endorsed by von Schön, Brücke sent the Abwehr a precise map on a scale of 1:25,000 of Ecuador's Santa Elena Peninsula. The map indicated locations for harbours, munitions depots, destroyers, and submarines. The Japanese military attaché in Santiago had managed to obtain the map, and Brücke forwarded it to Berlin with the Spanish courier, deeming it "too sensitive" for ordinary mail. Included with the map was a letter from the Ecuadorian president to his foreign minister.[129]

In all fairness, the historical record does indicate that the Abwehr could—and occasionally did—operate in Chile quite independently of Germany and German consular posts. On 6 August 1942, an Abwehr agent in Berlin noted that United States intelligence officials were intercepting and accurately deciphering messages between an Abwehr radio operator in Valparaíso and another in Hamburg. Auswärtiges Amt (German's foreign office), he said, had no connection with any of this. According to the memo, the Abwehr found the Spanish diplomatic pouch a most effective means of conveying secret messages.[130] Bowers had cause for concern all right, but the closure of the German, Italian, and Japanese missions would be only part of the solution. Barros could not have known all these details, but Bowers provided him with sufficient information that he must have known the German embassy's ongoing presence to be incompatible with Allied interests.

JAPANESE ESPIONAGE AND SUBVERSIVE ACTIVITIES

Because Chile was the only Pacific coast nation in the Americas and one of two Latin American countries with which Japan maintained diplomatic relations throughout 1942, it was one of Japan's listening posts. There is no evidence that Ambassador Bowers or anyone else briefed Ernesto Barros very thoroughly on Japanese activity, but that there was activity should have been evident to any foreign minister with imagination. With benefit of hindsight, one may argue that the data collected by Japanese in Chile was not particularly useful, but in 1942, the fact that the Japanese legation was in regular contact with Tokyo and might say something of value was a cause for concern.

Not everything that the Japanese legation did was inappropriate. It is normal for diplomats to be concerned about their own people, and Keyoshi Yamagata, Japan's Minister in Chile, is hardly to be condemned for this. However, it was in the Allied interest to know the extent and the nature of Japan's ties with the Japanese diaspora.

Chile's Japanese population was not large—only 600 according to Yamagata,[131] but neighbouring Peru had a substantial Japanese community, estimated at 32,000 by U.S. journalist John Gunther, who visited Peru in 1940.[132] On the other side of the continent, Brazil also was home to Japanese and their descendants, but the Japanese embassy in Buenos Aires was in a better position than Yamagata to protect the interests of Brazilian Japanese. Elsewhere in the Western Hemisphere, Japanese nationals also had interests which were of some concern to Yamagata.

Yamagata monitored the deportation from Chile of one Miyazaki, manager of Mitsui's branch at Arica, near the Peruvian border. Miyazaki was not a spy, Yamagata insisted in his communications to the Foreign Office in Tokyo and the Japanese Embassy in Buenos Aires, and he should be free to leave Chile "voluntarily," not through deportation.[133] Yamagata considered Miyazaki a victim of a political tug-of-war between Interior Minister Raúl Morales and Ernesto Barros,[134] whom Yamagata found totally sympathetic to Miyazaki and who thought that Miyazaki's departure ought to be "voluntary."[135] On 24 October Yamagata expressed concern over three other Japanese residents of Chile arrested as spies and then acquitted in court but nevertheless sent by the Interior Minister to an isolated island.[136] Yamagata assisted other Japanese in their travel arrangements.[137] There was also the Japan-Chile Association headed by Senator Errázuriz, with whom Yamagata maintained contact.[138] The Japanese Foreign Office also demonstrated interest in the well-being of Chile's Japanese. In return for Japanese respect for ships of Chilean registry on the high seas, Tokyo warned, Chileans should treat Japanese nationals with respect.[139]

More time-consuming than his work on behalf of Japanese in Chile was Yamagata's concern for Japanese Peruvians. Since the closure of Japan's legation after the Río conference, Spain had been Protector of Japanese interests in Peru. However, Spain needed assistance, and Yamagata appears to have shared the highly plausible conviction that nobody would defend Japanese interests as well as Japanese. On 22 April 1942 he informed Tokyo about a ship sailing from Peru with employees from the ex-legation in Lima and other Japanese nationals.[140] The same day he wrote at length about the closure of Japan's mission in Lima.[141]

Other reports on Peru followed: on Peruvian-Chilean relations, Peruvian-U.S. relations, treatment of Japanese in Peru and of Japanese-Peruvians, the role of the Spanish Embassy in the defence of Japanese interests in Peru.[142]

On 5 December 1942 Yamagata forwarded information from one Oashi who said that Peruvian authorities were disconnecting the telephones of Japanese and removing them from their communities.[143] While Yamagata wrote about the Peruvian government's high-handedness toward Lima's Japanese community, Tokyo instructed him what to do about the Japanese in Peru when Carlos Ibáñez should become his country's ambassador to Peru.

Before Ibáñez's departure for Lima, Yamagata was to meet him to discuss "the facts regarding oppression of Japanese residents in Peru.

Please ask him to get the attention of the Peruvian authorities when he arrives in that country and try to dissuade them from inhuman conduct towards Japanese residents.[144]

That, however, never happened as the Chilean Senate refused to confirm the Ibáñez appointment.[145] However, Japan's "contact men" in Lima reported to Yamagata until the Chilean government removed his cipher privileges. At that point, Yamagata thought it wise for them to work through the Japanese Embassy in Buenos Aires.[146]

Yamagata also assumed some responsibility for Japanese who lived elsewhere in the Western Hemisphere. On 11 August he filed a report on the internment and desperate living conditions of ethnic Japanese in the United States.[147] Later that month Tokyo instructed Yamagata to enlist the assistance of the papal legate in looking after Japanese in countries that had severed diplomatic relations with Japan.[148] The Spanish were helping,[149] but evidently there was more to be done. On 18 August Yamagata forwarded to Tokyo a report on Colombia's Japanese which he had received from the Spanish Embassy.[150]

Japanese investments, as distinct from Japanese people, were another consideration. Yamagata filed reports on Japanese investments and property in Chile and arranged ways to protect it until the current crisis had passed.[151] On 25 June 1942, Tokyo warned Yamagata to prepare for the freezing of the assets of Axis nationals in Chile,[152] a not unreasonable precaution.

More potentially serious was Japanese surveillance of the Allied war effort from Santiago. From their legation in Santiago, Japanese officials and agents could monitor war-related developments throughout the Western Hemisphere, protect the interests of Japanese nationals—particularly those in Chile or Peru, collect information on Allied shipping, and attempt to arrange the purchase of strategic materials. For these same reasons, the Allies wanted to eavesdrop upon communications between Chile and Japan. Information on shipping and sales of strategic Chilean commodities to Japan appears to have been minimal, but this may have been in part because the

Allies knew what was happening and could take appropriate counter-measures.

Canada's Wartime Examination Unit (WEU) or electronic eavesdropping agency collected intelligence of use to Canada's British and American allies.[153] On 25 June 1942 it intercepted a message from Yamagata to the Foreign Office in Tokyo which said that while U.S. war preparations were proceeding faster than anticipated, the Soviets and the British were behind schedule.[154] This information appears to have had little impact on the course of the war as Japan was no longer as free as it had been to choose where it would fight. On 4 July Yamagata filed a report about the staffs and the espionage efforts of the German, Italian, British, and U.S. embassies in Santiago.[155] Three days later, Yamagata filed intelligence that had arrived from the United Kingdom via the Chilean ambassador.[156] On 6 August Yamagata forwarded intelligence from the United Kingdom and Germany provided by the Chilean ambassadors in those countries.[157]

Not surprisingly, however, from Santiago Yamagata could observe the Western Hemisphere better than he could watch the United Kingdom—a place more accessible to his colleagues in Bern or Lisbon. On 12 June 1942 Yamagata told Tokyo that "Contact is being made" with a Chilean naval officer who was leaving for the United States.[158] Four days later, he wrote about hiring spies in Chile and Peru.[159] Two of Yamagata's Peruvian spies, Yamamoto and Oashi, had Japanese surnames,[160] but there was also one San Esteban,[161] who presumably would arouse fewer suspicions than an ethnic Japanese if he tried to cross borders or visit a telegraph office. From Santiago Yamagata could report on the arrival of Peng Chun Chang, the Chinese minister,[162] and of Chinese public relations efforts.[163] On 1 August the Japanese Foreign Office told Yamagata that, with assistance from Chilean consulates, spies (presumably Chilean nationals) would soon leave for Brazil, Panama, and the United States.[164] Panama was already a belligerent, and on 22 August, Brazil would declare war on Germany and Italy, although not Japan. Yamagata was able to discuss such topics as the appointment of Chilean diplomats to various countries,[165] censorship in the United States,[166] items in U.S. newspapers and magazines,[167] U.S. arms shipments to Peru,[168] disagreements between Spain and Cuba,[169] wartime conditions in Brazil,[170] the tin supply in the United States,[171] the sugar industry,[172] and the U.S. steel industry.[173]

Yamagata's information was not always first hand. In June 1942, he told Tokyo that he could not confirm a report that Chileans had witnessed a submarine attack on a Dutch ship south of Antofagasta.[174] Also in June, he informed Tokyo that United Press had reported the sailing of a Soviet ship from the Peruvian port of Callao.[175] The USSR and Japan were not at war, although this information might have been useful to Japan's German ally. Nevertheless, Yamagata could hardly be faulted for repeating what he had read in a newspaper. However, on 1 July Yamagata asked the Japanese Ambassador in Buenos Aires, Baron Shu Tomii, to find out whether ships of United States registry travelling via the Panama Canal stopped in Peru (where Yamagata's spies might monitor their ongoing progress). Yamagata also wanted to know whether any ships from the United States had adopted Chilean registry,[176] in the hope that they might thus avoid attack from enemy submarines. On 13 December 1942, by which time the diplomatic rupture between Chile and Japan was imminent, Yamagata wired the Japanese Embassy in Buenos Aires a report on Chile's commercial shipping.[177]

Tokyo made requests to Yamagata. On 9 September 1942, Japanese Prime Minister Tojo wanted Latin American reactions to Franco's dismissal of Ramón Serrano, his pro-Axis foreign minister.[178] Three days later, Tojo wanted a report on the Peru-Ecuador boundary dispute:

> According to reports there is a conspiracy afoot against the government in Ecuador, of which the leaders are people close to the former President. It is supposed that this conspiracy has to do with the border troubles between Ecuador and Peru, and with the present government's having handed over to the United States military bases in the Galapagos and Santa Elena Islands. Please investigate the circumstances and inform us.[179]

On 12 October Tojo wanted a spy (identified only as MO...) in the Canadian intercepts to study shipbuilding in the United States.[180] The FBI identified MO as a Conservative deputy in the Chilean Congress, Rafael Moreno.[181] As Japanese could not travel to the United States in 1942, it was useful to find a sympathetic Chilean. So important was this information to Tojo that Yamagata gave MO... $5000 and told him to ask for more if he found that he needed it "for his living expenses in the U.S. and Canada." U.S. Ambassador Bowers—apparently unaware that MO... was a spy, wrote a letter of introduction so that MO... could meet Under Secretary of State Sumner Welles. Finally, Yamagata instructed MO... not to return directly to Chile should Chile sever diplomatic relations with Japan before he returned but to file his report at the Japanese Embassy in Buenos Aires.[182]

Other Japanese spies and intelligence gatherers who appear to have been Chileans roamed the hemisphere, but their findings were not always first rate. Canadian intercepts reveal that on 24 August 1942, Yamagata provided expense money for "G," who was planning a trip to the United States.[183] Then, because of his wife's illness, "G" decided not to go.[184] After Brazil's declaration of war, spy "M" went to Río with a message from Yamagata,[185] and employees of Japanese firms looked at conditions in North America.[186] The manager of one such firm and some of his employees were the ones to report on the U.S. tin supply.[187] Despite these efforts, on the eve of the Battle of Midway (4-7 June) Yamagata thought support for the war in the United States to be low,[188] and on 10 August, Yamagata forwarded a message that President Roosevelt was close to despair. At a meeting of U.S. and Latin American officials, according to Yamagata's informant(s), Roosevelt "held his head in his hands and groaned that the situation was hopeless."[189] The U.S. government had access to these Canadian intercepts, and given the quality of the information which Tokyo was receiving from Santiago, Washington should have had few immediate worries. However, there was always the danger that Japanese intelligence might not always be of such low quality.

SUMMARY AND CONCLUSIONS

Shortly after the Japanese air force bombed Pearl Harbor and Japan's Axis partners declared war on the United States, U.S. authorities wanted all Latin American republics to sever diplomatic relations with the Axis powers. The presence of Axis diplomats in the Western Hemisphere, argued the State Department, constituted a threat to the Allied war effort. By late January 1942, all republics except Argentina and Chile had complied with Washington's wishes. The U.S. ambassador to Chile, Claude G. Bowers, actively sought to bring Chile into line, and he had good reason for so doing.

Until 2 April 1942, Rossetti continued as Chile's foreign minister, and the hallmark of his tenure was caution which bordered on timidity. If there was a diplomatic rupture, might the Japanese navy attack the Chilean coastline? Might Axis warships deliberately sink Chilean merchant ships? (The *Toltén* incident demonstrated that there were no absolute safeguards.) How would Chileans of German and Italian extraction vote in the presidential election? What would the Argentines think? At the same time, he was aware that Chilean diplomats in Europe had managed to help some people in distress—Chileans, Poles, and Jews who were not necessarily Chilean. Faced with pressure from the U.S. and Yugoslav missions on the one hand, his ambassador in Berlin and neighbouring Argentina on the other, Rossetti could afford to let matters drift. April 2 would arrive, and with the inauguration of a new administration his responsibilities would become somebody else's.

The hallmark of that successor, Ernesto Barros, was dishonesty. For several weeks he managed to convince both U.S. and German ambassadors that he was playing their game. Whether or not he actually took bribes, he was irresponsible in disregarding information about Axis espionage and subversion. He showed little imagination but too much confidence in his Germanophile cousin, Ambassador Tobias Barros. The respect and affection which Ambassador Bowers had for Ernesto Barros turned to hostility and mistrust.

NOTES

1. Sater, p. 114.

2. Census of Chile, 1940.

3. For a summary of Chilean politics from 1920 to 1942, see Izquierdo, pp. 17-65. See also Jose del Pozo, "La periode d'alliances politiques multiclassistes au Chile (1936-1956), *North/South: Canadian Journal of Latin American Studies*, XIII, 25 (1988), pp. 7-27.

4. Bernstein, p. 72.

5. *La Nación (Santiago), 21 Dec. 1941.*

6. *La Nación (16 Jan. 1942).*

7. Bernstein, p. 71.

8. Bowers to FDR, 2 Feb. 1942, PSF.

9. *Foreign Relations of the United States, 1941 (FRUS)* VI, pp. 560-577; *FRUS, 1942,* VI, pp. 1-19, especially Bowers to the Secretary of State, 20 Jan., pp. 1-2, and Hull to President Roosevelt, 24 Jan., pp. 5-6.

10. Von Schön to AA, 15 Feb. 1942, RG 242, NARA, Series T-120, Reel 183, frame 88468.

11. Mackensen, Rome, to AA, 2 Feb. 1942, frame 88451.

12. Wörmann memorandum, 6 March 1942, frame 88493.

13. FBI, 128, 216.

14. Rossetti, Buenos Aires, to the Acting Foreign Minister, Santiago, 9 Jan., # 13 and #15, boveda 14, vol. 10, ADRE.

15. Conrado Ríos, Chilean Ambassador to Argentina, Santiago, to the Acting Foreign Minister, Santiago, 20 Jan., #32, boveda 14, vol. 10, ADRE.

16. Bowers to FDR, 2 Feb. 1942, PSF; Bowers to Welles, 4 Feb. 1942, PSF.

17. Bowers to FDR, 4 Feb. 1942, PSF.

18. Bowers to FDR, 20 Feb. 1942, PSF.

19. Bowers to Welles, 16 March 1942, PSF.

20. Bowers to Welles, 16 March 1942, PSF.

21. Ríos to Rossetti, Santiago, 13 Feb., #58; Sepulveda, Embassy of Chile in Buenos Aires, to Rossetti, 15 and 16 Feb., #s 61 and 65; boveda 14, vol. 10, ADRE. Also Rossetti to the Embassy of Chile in Buenos Aires, 14 Feb., #48 and 16 Feb. #52, ADRE.

22. Rossetti to Embassy of Chile in Buenos Aires, 27 Feb., #48, and 1 March, #67, Boveda 14, vol. 9, ADRE.

23. Memorandum of the U.S. Embassy, Santiago, 13 March, vol. 2012, ADRE.

24. *El Mercurio*, 10 March 1942; Bowers to Welles, 2 April 1942, PSF.

25. Wörmann memoranda, 14 Aug. 1941 (frame 88326), 21 Aug. (frame 88332), 23 Sept. (frames 88380-88381), 26 Sept. (frames 88383-88387); von Schön to AA, 18 Aug. 1941 (frame 88328), 25 Sept. (frame 88382), 8 Oct. (frame 88402); Ermansdorff memoranda Berlin, 29 Sept. (frame 88389), 1 Oct. (frame 88392), 13 Oct. (frames 88403-88405); Schumburg memorandum, Berlin, 19 Sept. 1941 (frame 88360); von Weizsäcker memorandum, Berlin, 20 Sept. 1941 (frames 88361-88364).

26. Vols. 2045, 2046, 2047, ADRE.

27. For information on Croatian migration to Chile, see Peri Fagerstrom, pp. 166-167.

28. This information is available in correspondence of Barriga and Briones, Rome, to the Chilean Foreign Ministry, Santiago, 19 Jan., #5, and 20 Jan. 1942 (s.n.), vol. 2043, ADRE; and in telegrams #1-#5, 3-19 Jan. 1942, vol. 2044, ADRE.

29. Labra to the Chilean Foreign Office, 2 Jan., #2, vol. 2049, ADRE.

30. Labra to the Chilean Foreign Office, 4 Feb., #12, vol. 2049, ADRE.

31. Labra to Rossetti, 19 Feb., #18, vol. 2049, ADRE.

32. Labra to Barros, 25 March, #26, vol. 2049, ADRE.

33. Memorandum by the Director of the Political Department, Berlin, 23 September 1941, *Documents on German Foreign Policy, 1918-1945*, Series D, vol. XIII, pp. 555-6.

34. Tobias Barros to the Acting Foreign Minister, 14 Jan., #15, vol. 1969, ADRE.

35. Tobias Barros to the Acting Foreign Minister, 16 Jan., #18, vol. 1969, ADRE.

36. Tobias Barros to the Acting Foreign Minister, 19 Jan., #25, vol. 1969, ADRE.

37. Tobias Barros to the Acting Foreign Minister, 22 Jan., #28, vol. 1969, ADRE.

38. Tobias Barros to Ríos, 4 Feb., s.n., vol. 1969, ADRE.

39. Tobias Barros to Rossetti, 4 Feb., #41, vol.   1969 , ADRE.

40. Letters from the Foreign Office to Tobias Barros, 3 Jan.-31 March, #1-#59, vol. 1968, ADRE.

41. Tobias Barros to Rossetti, 7 Feb., #44, vol. 1969, ADRE.

42. Rossetti to Tobias Barros, 31 March, #59, vol. 1968, ADRE.

43. Tobias Barros to Rossetti, 9 Feb., #45; 11 Feb., #47; 10 March, s.n., vol. 1969, ADRE.

44. Rossetti to Tobias Barros, 27 Feb., #34, vol. 1968; Tobias Barros to Rossetti, 4 March, #60, vol. 1969, ADRE.

45. Rossetti to Tobias Barros, 8 March, #37, vol. 1968, ADRE.

46. Tobias Barros to Rossetti, 9 March (#63) and 10 March (#65), vol. 1969, ADRE.

47. Tobias Barros to Rossetti, 7 March, #61, vol. 1969, ADRE.

48. Rossetti to Tobias Barros, 15 March, #44; 18 March, #46; 25 March, #49 and #50; 27 March, #52 and #53, vol. 1968. Also, Tobias Barros to Rossetti, 16 March, #70; 21 March, #77; 23 March, #78; 26 March, #81; 27 March, #84, vol. 1969, ADRE.

49. Rossetti to Tobias Barros, 27 March, #54, vol. 1969, ADRE.

50. Bowers, p. 113.

51. Bowers to FDR, 20 Feb. 1942, PSF.

52. Bowers to FDR, 25 Feb. 1942, PSF.

53. Bowers to Welles, 4 Feb. 1942, PSF.

54. Bowers to FDR, 20 Feb. 1942, PSF.

55. Bowers to FDR, 25 Feb. 1942, PSF.

56. Von Schön to AA, 26 Jan. 1942, frame 88444.

57. Von Schön to Berlin, 2 Feb. 1942, frame 88450.

58. Von Stohrer, Madrid, to AA, 20 Feb. 1942, frame 88472.

59. German intelligence report in a Wörmann memorandum, 27 March 1942, frames 88599-88600.

60. Bismarck, Rome, to AA, 24 March 1942, frame 88586.

61. Von Schön to AA, 24 March 1942, frame 88583.

62. Meynen, Buenos Aires, to AA, 18 March 1942, frames 88553-88554.

63. Yamagata, Santiago, to Foreign Minister, Tokyo, 14 April 1942, HW1/512, Public Record Office, Kew Gardens. Cited hereafter as PRO.

64. Bowers to Welles, 16 March 1942, PSF.

65. Covering letter from Bowers to Welles, 4 Aug. 1942, for a memorandum written by C.F. Lyon, dated 31 July 1942; Sumner Welles Papers, Official Correspondence, 1920-1943, Box 46, FDR Archives. Cited hereafter as SW.

66. Bowers to FDR, 18 June 1942, PSF.

67. Bowers to FDR, 14 July 1942, PSF.

68. Bowers to FDR, 25 Aug. 1942.

69. Bowers to Welles, 11 Aug. 1942, PSF.

70. Barros to FDR, 4 Aug. 1942, PSF.

71. Bowers to Welles, 25 Aug. 1942, FDR.

72. Argument in editorial of La Prensa (Osorno), 23 Aug. 1942.

73. Silva Galdames, p. 304.

74. Bowers to FDR, 21 Sept. 1942, PSF. Interestingly, Nelson Rockefeller's archival material at the Rockefeller Family Archives in North Tarrytown, New York, includes little on Chile except the fact that he planned to be there between 13 and 16 Sept. 1942; R.G. 4, Box 145, File "Trips to South America, 1942"; and Box 12, Files "Trips to South America, 1942" and "Sumner Welles, 1941-1942." There is more extensive information on Rockefeller's trips to Brazil, Peru, and Ecuador.

75. Bowers to FDR, 14 May 1942, PSF. Bowers described Luis Subercaseaux as "a Conservative aristocrat wholly with us"; Bowers to FDR, 18 June 1942, PSF.

76. Sánchez, pp. 65-66. Sánchez supports Bowers's assertion that Conrado Ríos sympathized with the Axis.

77. Tobias Barros to Ernesto Barros, 26 July, #186; 5 Aug., #177; 12 Aug, #183; 21 Sept., #218; vol. 1969, ADRE.

78. Tobias Barros to Ernesto Barros, 10 April, #95; 20 April, #109; vol. 1969, ADRE.

79. Briones to Ernesto Barros, 20 May, #36, vol. 2044, ADRE.

80. Tobias Barros to Ernesto Barros, 4 May, #118, vol. 1969.

81. Tobias Barros to Ernesto Barros, 17 April, #104; 28 June, #147, vol. 1969, ADRE.

82. Labra to Ernesto Barros, 21 May, s/n, vol. 2048, ADRE.

83. Von Schön to AA, 10 June 1942, frame 88655.

84. Tobias Barros to Ernesto Barros, 13 May, #122, vol. 1969, ADRE.

85. Tobias Barros to Ernesto Barros, 18 May, #124, vol. 1969, ADRE.

86. Tobias Barros to Ernesto Barros, 5 June, #131, vol. 1969, ADRE.

87. Labra to Ernesto Barros, 8 May, #40, vol. 2048, ADRE.

88. Labra to Ernesto Barros, 1 Aug., #57; 19 Sept., #68, vol. 2048, ADRE.

89. Labra to Ernesto Barros, 3 Sept., #66, vol. 2048, ADRE.

90. Labra to Ernesto Barros, 5 Aug, #59, vol. 2048; Briones to Ernesto Barros, #s 42-61, vol. 2044, ADRE.

91. Tobias Barros to Ernesto Barros, 26 Apr., #112; 5 June, #132; vol. 1969. Also Briones to Ernesto Barros, 31 May, #37, vol. 2044, ADRE.

92. Briones to Ernesto Barros, 25 June, #40, vol. 2044, ADRE.

93. Von Schön to AA, 15 June 1942 (frames 88657-88658) and 23 June (frame 88664).

94. Von Schön to Berlin, 2 July 1942, frame 88674.

95. Tobias Barros to Ernesto Barros, 5 Aug., #177, vol. 1969.

96. Tobias Barros to Ernesto Barros, 17 Aug., #186, vol. 1969, ADRE.

97. Tobias Barros to Ernesto Barros, 31 July, #172, vol. 1969, ADRE. There is no evidence in the appropriate volume, 1968, that the foreign minister responded. See also Weizsäcker to Ribbentrop, 30 July 1942, frame 88697.

98. Peter Tennant, *Touchlines of War* (Hull, England: University of Hull Press, 1992), p. 101.

99. Labra to Ernesto Barros, 13 Aug., #61, vol. 2048, ADRE.

100. Singer's article, both in the English-language original and in Spanish-language translation, and Martínez's report, appear in vol. 1970, ADRE.

101. FBI, p. 97.

102. FBI, pp. 85-89.

103. FBI, p. 102.

104. Barros pp. 31-96.

105. Ernesto Barros to Tobias Barros, 4 April, #60, vol. 1968, ADRE.

106. Ernesto Barros to von Schön, 23 April, s/n, boveda 14, vol. 13, ADRE.

107. Von Schön protested 10 June and Barros apologized three days later; the correspondence is available in Boveda 13, vol. 13, ADRE.

108. The German Embassy protest of 1 October and Barros's reply appear in Boveda 14, vol. 13, ADRE.

109. Tobias Barros to Ernesto Barros, 18 Aug., #187, vol. 1969, ADRE.

110. Ernesto Barros to Tobias Barros, 19 Aug., #129, vol. 1968, ADRE.

111. Bowers to FDR, 2 June 1942, PSF.

112. Bowers to FDR, 23 July 1942, PSF; Bowers to Welles, 1 Aug. 1942, PSF.

113. Graeme S. Mount, *Canada's Enemies: Spies and Spying in the Peaceable Kingdom* (Toronto: Dundurn, 1993), pp. 1-11.

114. Christopher Andrew, *Her Majesty's Secret Service: The Making of the British Intelligence Community* (New York: Viking, 1986), pp. 221-229; Christopher Andrew and Oleg Gordievsky, *KGB: The Inside Story* (New York: Harper Collins, 1990), pp. 239, 277-278, 305-306; Douglas L. Wheeler, "In the Service of Order: The Portuguese Political Police and the British, German, and Spanish Intelligence, 1932-1945," *Journal of Contemporary History*, XVIII (1983), pp. 1-25.

115. Hempel to Abwehr, 6, 15, and 23 Sept. 1940, file 102047, Auswärtiges Amt (Bonn).

116. Tokyo to Bern, Lisbon, 15 Dec., #1320, NAC.

117. Ernesto Barros to Tobias Barros, 27 May, #87, vol. 1968, ADRE.

118. Yamagata to Tokyo, 17 June, #499, NAC.

119. Yamagata to Tokyo, 22 June, #419-422, NAC.

120. La Nación (Santiago) published in its entirety Schnake's speech of 4 June in its 5 June issue. The editorial appeared 7 June.

121. Cited by former President Arturo Alessandri and reprinted in El Diario Ilustrado, 12 Jan. 1943.

122. FBI, p. 154. News of the Valparaíso spy ring appeared on the front page of El Mercurio 4 November 1942.

123. Bowers to Barros, 9 July, with Bowers' Memorandum "German Espionage Agents in Chile" plus selected intercepts, vol. 2012, ADRE.

124. Von Schön to AA, 16 Feb. 1942, frame 88469.

125. Brücke via von Schön to the Supreme Commanders of the Abwehr, Busch and Stiege, Berlin, 5 Aug. 1941, frames 88703-88704.

126. Von Schön to AA, 23 Sept. 1942, frames 88760-88761.

127. Von Schön to Berlin, with a postscript from Brücke, 25 Sept. 1942, frame 88762.

128. FBI, pp. 151-153.

129. The letter from the foreign minister to the president was dated 26 Dec. 1941; letter of Brücke via von Schön to the Abwehr, Berlin, 3 June 1942, frames 88643-88645.

130. Abwehr memo, Berlin, 6 Aug. 1942, frame 88705.

131. Yamagata to Buenos Aires, 10 Nov. and 11 Dec., #s 1098-1100 and 1285, NAC.

132. John Gunther, Inside Latin America (New York: Harper and Brothers, 1941), p. 216.

133. Yamagata to Tokyo, 25 Aug., 29 Aug., 23 Aug., #s 779, 807, 815-817. Yamagata to Buenos Aires, 18 Sept., 31 Aug., 19 Sept., #s 855, 860, 885. Yamagata to Tokyo, 19 Sept., #906, NAC.

134. Yamagata to Tokyo, 25 and 23 Aug., #s 779, 815-817. Yamagata to Buenos Aires, 3 Sept., #847, NAC.

135. Yamagata to Buenos Aires, 29 Aug., #808, NAC.

136. Yamagata to Buenos Aires, 24 Oct., #1009, NAC.

137. Yamagata to Buenos Aires, 2 Oct., #s 912, 962, NAC.

138. Yamagata to Buenos Aires, 14 Nov., #1145, NAC.

139. Tokyo to Yamagata, 17 Sept., #930, NAC.

140. Yamagata to Tokyo, 22 Apr., #190-191, NAC.

141. Yamagata to Tokyo, 22 Apr., #192-193, NAC.

142. Yamagata to Tokyo, 16 May and 2 June, #s 283 and 291-292; Yamagata to Buenos Aires and Tokyo, 15 June, #390; Yamagata to Tokyo, 16 June, 5 July (twice) 25, 15, July, 10 Aug., 31 Aug. (twice), 22 Sept., #s 396, 530, 541, 690-691, 695, 706, 777, 863, 899; Yamagata to Buenos Aires, 21 Oct., #1026, NAC.

143. Yamagata to Buenos Aires, 5 Dec., #1272, NAC. The WEU report says that this was happening in Brazil, but the name of the informant, Oashi, indicates that this was happening in Peru.

144. Tokyo to Yamagata, 20 July, #561, NAC.

145. Yamagata to Tokyo, 15 July, #563-564, NAC.

146. Yamagata to Buenos Aires, 10 Nov., #1080, NAC.

147. Yamagata to Tokyo, 11 Aug., #698, NAC.

148. Tokyo to Yamagata and Buenos Aires, 22 Aug., 773, NAC.

149. Yamagata to Tokyo, 31 Aug., #777, NAC.

150. Yamagata to Buenos Aires, 27 Aug., #801, NAC.

151. Yamagata to Tokyo, 21 and 17 June, #s 409-410, 412; Yamagata to Buenos Aires, 5 Nov. and 11 Dec., #s 1098-1100, 1285, NAC.

152. Tokyo to Yamagata, 25 June, #481, NAC.

153. Bradley F. Smith, *The Ultra-Magic Deals and the Most Secret Special Relationship, 1940-1946* (California: Presidio, 1993), p. 143. See particularly pp. 88-89, 113-114, 119-120, 124, 173-174. See also John Bryden, *Best-Kept Secret: Canadian Intelligence in the Second World War* (Toronto: Lester, 1993).

154. Yamagata to Tokyo, 25 June, #445, NAC.

155. Yamagata to Tokyo, 4 July, #539-540, NAC.

156. Santiago to Tokyo, 7 July, #748, NAC.

157. Yamagata to Tokyo, 6 Aug., #785, NAC.

158. Yamagata to Tokyo, 12 June, #397, NAC.

159. Yamagata to Tokyo, 16 June, #400, NAC.

160. Yamagata to Tokyo, 16 June, #396; 25 July, #690-691; 15 July,# 695; 3 Aug., #777; 31 Aug, #863, NAC.

161. Yamagata to Tokyo, 22 Sept., #899, NAC.

162. Yamagata to Tokyo, 29 July, #594, NAC.

163. Yamagata to Tokyo, 10 and 17 June, #s 492 and 493, NAC.

164. Tokyo to Yamagata, 1 Aug., #634, NAC.

165. Yamagata to Tokyo, 2 Aug, #641, NAC.

166. Yamagata to Tokyo, 5 Aug, #650-652, NAC.

167. Yamagata to Tokyo, 25 Aug., #744-745.

168. Yamagata to Tokyo, 14 Aug., #783-784, NAC.

169. Yamagata to Buenos Aires, 10 Oct., #944, NAC.

170. Yamagata to Tokyo, 7 Oct., #973-974 and #979-980, NAC.

171. Yamagata to Buenos Aires, 14 Nov., #1172, NAC.

172. Yamagata to Buenos Aires, 21 Nov., #1192-1193, NAC.

173. Yamagata to Buenos Aires, 5 Dec., #1260, NAC.

174. Yamagata to Tokyo, 5 June, #s 473 and 474, NAC.

175. Yamagata to Tokyo, 3 June, #475, NAC.

176. Yamagata to Buenos Aires, 1 July, #488, NAC.

177. Yamagata to Buenos Aires, 13 Dec., #1303, NAC.

178. Tokyo to Yamagata, 9 Sept., #828, NAC.

179. Tokyo to Yamagata, 12 Sept., #908, NAC.

180. Tokyo to Buenos Aires, 12 Oct., #965, NAC.

181. FBI, p. 222.

182. Yamagata to Buenos Aires, 10 Nov., #1106, NAC.

183. Yamagata to Tokyo, 26 Aug. and 3 Sept., #s 794, 813, NAC.

184. Yamagata to Tokyo, 22 or 27 Sept. (copy is not clear), #904, NAC.

185. Buenos Aires to Yamagata, 3 Sept., #823, NAC.

186. Yamagata to Buenos Aires, 14 Nov., #1140, NAC.

187. Yamagata to Buenos Aires, 14 Nov., #1172, NAC.

188. Yamagata to Tokyo, 26 May, #287, NAC.

189. Yamagata to Tokyo, 10 Aug., #714-715, NAC.

CHAPTER 4

RESOLUTION

THE TURNING OF THE TIDE

There were several critical battles in 1942. If these did not hasten Chile's rupture with the Axis, they certainly rendered the rupture less risky than it had appeared. Between 4 and 7 June, U.S. forces repelled the Japanese attack on Midway. On 7 August, U.S. Marines landed in the Solomon Islands and captured Guadalcanal. On 8 November, General Eisenhower successfully launched Operation Torch, and within a few days Morocco and Algeria had been liberated. On 12 November, the U.S. Navy won a decisive naval battle in the Solomon Islands. By then, British forces had won the Battle of El Alamein and driven the German army from Egypt. Meanwhile, it was obvious—even to Ernesto Barros[1]—that German forces in Russia were in difficulty. Within Chile, attitudes slowly began to change.

Historians have depicted the Battle of Midway (4-5 June) as a major "turning point" in the war between Japan and the United States.[2] The foreign minister evidently did not, nor did his cousin in Berlin. Despite his military credentials, Tobias Barros appeared more impressed by the

American failure to prevent a Japanese capture of Kiska and Attu in the Aleutians on 7 June. Actually, Kiska and Attu had little strategic importance compared to Midway. Their geology was rough, and they too often experienced fogs and storms to be useful as air or naval bases.[3] Yet, Ambassador Barros had a different interpretation which his cousin, the Foreign Minister, did not challenge. If the United States could not defend its own territory, how could it possibly protect Chile from Japanese wrath should Chileans provoke the Japanese by closing their legation?[4]

Others disagreed. On 4 June, the very day the Battle of Midway began and before its outcome was at all assured, the Minister of Industrial Development, Oscar Schnake, delivered a speech about foreign policy before an audience in Santiago. Schnake questioned the wisdom of continued relations with the Axis belligerents so forcefully that Puerto Montt's El Llanquihue ran an editorial in defence of the diplomatic status quo. That editorial also questioned whether it was appropriate for the Minister of Industrial Development to criticize the government's foreign policy.[5]

The lack of cabinet solidarity was no longer a secret. On 13 June, El Llanquihue's front page carried a United Press report from Washington of the previous day, undoubtedly read by Germany's vice-consul in Puerto Montt, that President Ríos would probably receive an invitation to go to Washington before the end of the year. By late June—that is, after the Battle of Midway—Ernesto Barros's policies were sufficiently controversial that he had to defend them before a secret session of the Chilean Senate. On that occasion he was successful, as one member of the Chamber of Deputies reported to Yamagata,[6] but Yamagata was not totally reassured. On 8 July he transferred some of his legation's money, in cash, to the opposition Conservative party for safekeeping.[7] About the same time, the Japanese government assumed that if its navy attacked Chilean shipping, the Panama Canal, or the Pacific coast of South America, Chile might abandon its policy of neutrality. Yamagata assured Chilean authorities that the Japanese navy would exercise the utmost caution.[8] On 23 August, German submarines commanders received orders that under no circumstances were they to fire at ships of Chilean or Argentine registry.[9] Axis diplomats knew that the heat was on, and that they could not count on Barros to prevail.

On 14 August, President Ríos formally accepted the invitation to visit Washington.[10] *El Llanquihue*, citing a statement from the office of Foreign Minister Barros, said that "cordiality and co-operation" were the hallmarks of US-Chilean relations, and that Chile would undoubtedly make economic gains as a result of the meeting.[11] Osorno's *La Prensa* was not as naïvely optimistic. Its editorial said that ninety per cent of the Chilean people believed that Ríos's trip came at a price—abandonment of neutrality and adoption, at least *de facto*, of belligerency status. Such a change, thought *La Prensa*, was quite unnecessary. As the world's most southerly nation, surely Chile was sufficiently remote from the conflict that it could distance itself from hostilities. Chile's coasts remained vulnerable to submarine attack. As long as Chile remained unprovocative, its mines could supply the "arsenal of democracy," the United States. Closer ties with the United States would endanger the Chilean economy and Chilean democracy.[12]

To prevent that rupture remained the German embassy's highest priority. Von Schön regarded bribery as a weapon for maintaining neutrality. On 9 July, he had asked Berlin for 100,000 Reichmarks in order to keep Chile neutral.[13] At most, his actions delayed the break but did not prevent it.

Little by little, Chilean foreign policy did become less neutral and more favourable to the Allies. In August 1942, the Chilean government publicly protested when Germans submarines sank five Brazilian merchant ships near the South American coastline. Hundreds died. The German action, said Chile, was contrary to "international law and the rules of humanity."[14] Brazil subsequently declared war against Germany and Italy, and Chile further compromised its neutrality. The Chilean government softened the laws of neutrality for Brazil as it already had for the United States and Mexico. Brazilian ships could stay in Chilean ports for more than twenty-four hours and take on supplies. Their cargoes would not be considered contraband of war. They could acquire unlimited quantities of petroleum, not simply what was needed to go to the nearest Allied port.[15]

Yet, Ernesto Barros's policy of continued neutrality strained Chilean relations with Brazil. Less than enthusiastic about President Ríos, whom he regarded as merely the lesser of two evils in a contest with Ibáñez, Bertstein had initially been delighted at the appointment of Barros as foreign minister, but he quickly became disillusioned. Chile's ambassador in the Brazilian capital, future president Gabriel González (1946-1952), then resigned in protest. Ríos and Barros rejected the resignation and reaffirmed confidence in their ambassador.[16]

In late September, there were new revelations of German espionage in Chile.[17] According to James P. Speer II, U.S. vice-consul in Valdivia, those revelations affected the behaviour of Nazis in his community. They became less brazen and more secretive than they had been. The German embassy summoned Valdivia's Nazi leaders to Santiago, reported Speer, and had them swear an oath to obey any order from Hitler, even at the cost of their lives. When they returned home, Valdivia's Nazi leaders had others take the same oath. Then, Valdivia's Nazis returned to their former aggressive patterns of behaviour and called a series of meetings. Speer thought that authorities in Valdivia felt so intimidated that they were leaving the Nazis to do as they pleased, and he feared that if there was a diplomatic rupture, a Nazi uprising might quickly follow. Ambassador Bowers forwarded Speer's letter to Sumner Welles with a covering note of his own. Valdivia was not typical of southern Chile, said Bowers. There were not as many militant Nazis anywhere else.[18]

On 1 October the Chilean Foreign Office threatened to arrest Axis diplomats who continued to transfer large sums of money from Germany to Chile via the Banco Alemán Transatlántico in violation of Chile's foreign exchange laws.[19] Early in October the Chilean government also ordered the deportation of three Germans who confessed to operating clandestine radio transmitters and maintaining contact with Luni, the German spy in Cuba. One of the three, Alfredo Kleiber, had a rather high profile as manager of that same German bank (Banco Alemán Transatlántico) in Chile.[20] Von Schön's correspondence confirms FBI intelligence that Kleiber headed a valuable espionage ring. After all, he had subordinates throughout his bank's Chilean branches who could (and, according to the FBI, did) engage in espionage throughout the country.[21] Unfortunately for the Allied cause, any helpful intentions on the part of the Ríos government proved of minimal value. Because Argentina refused transit rights so that the three Germans could board a ship for Spain, the Chilean government simply interned them at Zapallar, a resort town near Valparaíso. There they had minimal surveillance and extensive personal contact with Germany embassy officials, including the ambassador himself.[22]

That same month, the cumulative effect of the American victory at Midway, Germany's difficulties at Stalingrad, German misdeeds against Brazil, and pressure from the United States bore fruit, first in the government's capitulation on the issue of telecommunications, and then with the forced resignation of Ernesto Barros. All this happened despite a warning from Japan that in the event of a change in Chile's policy of neutrality, Chilean shipping in the Pacific would be vulnerable.[23]

Throughout August, Bowers continued to lobby for the diplomatic rupture, but without British support. In a tone of disgust, Bowers described a group of Britons, the Willingdon Commission, who had visited Santiago. To his dismay, the commissioners appeared more interested in post-war Anglo-Chilean trade than in the war itself.

> [T]he Commission was composed almost exclusively of bankers and industrialists, of the Tory element that was with Chamberlain and his policies, and that all with whom I talked very noticeably moderated their praise of Churchill. At heart this group seemed to me to be of the older appeaser element and not friendly to Churchill.

Nor had Ambassador Sir Charles Orde thrown his support behind Bowers.

> He talks to me personally as though he would like to see relations with the Axis broke [sic], but he appears a bit academic about it, and

he talks to me like an outsider spectator observing a fight that interests him mostly as a spectator. He certainly has made no effort to help at the Foreign Office in this regard. His position seems to be that since breaking of relations with the Axis concerns only the American nations that formulated the agreements of Rio, it would do harm to us...to intervene. I get the distinct impression that he tries to convey the idea to me that the British Embassy is playing our game by staying out.[24]

Orde did not portray himself in such a passive light. He noted that Barandon, Germany's consul-general in Valparaíso declared *persona non grata* after providing the *Graf Spee* escapees with false passports, nevertheless returned to Chile. According to Orde, he and Bowers both lobbied with an indifferent Chilean government to oust him once and for all. Orde admitted that Bowers had taken the lead,[25] but perhaps he saw no need to push the case vigorously when Bowers was doing such a fine job. A year later, Orde wondered whether, given the Ríos administration's apparent commitment to neutrality, additional pressure might prove counter-productive.[26]

Since the United Kingdom's Public Record Office released its HW1 series between November 1993 and April 1994, it is more understandable why Winston Churchill's government did not push Orde to take a stronger stand. That series includes intercepted diplomatic traffic—from enemies, from neutrals, and even from allies—which Churchill read on a day to day basis throughout the war. The record reveals that he did indeed read intercepts from Italian and Japanese diplomats in Santiago, as well as from Tobias Barros in Berlin and Jorge Barriga in Rome. However, little in those reports threatened Allied shipping. Indeed, even if Chile had not been half a world away, most reports were rather inocuous—on labour relations in the United States,[27] on the German military situation,[28] on assurances of ongoing Chilean neutrality,[29] on Brazilian thoughts about Italian Fascism.[30] At times, intercepts from Chilean diplomats in Axis capitals might even be useful. Four days after the Allied landings in North Africa, Barriga reported from Rome that Mussolini was losing his grip on power.[31] When there was something substantial—instructions from Tokyo to Yamagata to spy on Chilean air bases and harbour facilities—Churchill was preoccupied with the pending North African campaign.[32] (Churchill appears to have ignored the presence of a German spy in the Chilean Foreign Office. Thanks to that spy, von Schön had advance knowledge of Churchill's forthcoming trips to Moscow and Cairo.[33]) Moreover, what Churchill read about Axis activity in Chile or about the thoughts of Tobias Barros was minuscule in comparison with what he learned from Japanese, Turkish, and (to a lesser extent) Italian and Portuguese officials in enemy and neutral European capitals.

Moreover, through intercepted Japanese and Italian diplomatic traffic, Churchill was fully aware that Spanish officials were passing sensitive information to the Axis. Spaniards forwarded to Suni, Japan's minister in Madrid, information about the situation in India, long restive under British rule.[34] On 6 April 1942, Suni forwarded a secret intelligence report on Allied plans for the invasion of India.[35] Retention of India was a high priority for Churchill. Churchill was also aware that on 18 May 1942, Spanish sources alerted Italian officials to the forthcoming Anglo-American attack on North Africa, which did materialize in November.[36] On 1 November, Spain's ambassador in London, the Duke of Alba, predicted that invasion, Operation Torch, with a fair degree of accuracy.[37] For these reasons, Churchill had good reason to regard any diplomatic rupture which did not close Spanish listening posts as rather futile. Yet, neither the United Kingdom nor the United States could afford to antagonize Generalissimo Francisco Franco, for fear that he would ally himself even more forcefully with the Axis.[38]

Even less than supportive at one point was, surprisingly, the U.S. War Department. On 1 August, the Acting Secretary of War, Robert T. Patterson, questioned the advantages of a diplomatic rupture between Chile and the Axis. The War Department needed Chilean copper, and Chile was providing it. Chilean shipping was "now immune from Axis attack," but after a rupture it "would be subject to hostile submarine action." These points, thought Patterson, more than outweighed the advantages of the diplomatic rupture: an end to Chilean-Japanese trade, the elimination of Axis influence in Chile, and the setting of a good example for the rest of Latin America.[39] Under-Secretary of State Sumner Welles was dumbfounded. Despite Chilean obstinacy, he wrote President Roosevelt, the United States had sent Chilean authorities "four batteries and a few airplanes" in order that Chile might defend herself from a sudden Japanese attack. Certainly the Chileans wanted more, and the State Department would consider the request after a rupture. However, continued Welles, there had been no commercial trade of any description between Chile and Japan since 7 December 1941, and most of the Chilean copper transported to the United States travelled in ships of Allied belligerents. The Japanese were not sinking those ships because they lacked the capacity to do so, not for reasons of good will. The rupture must come, said Welles to President Roosevelt, because of the Axis diplomats' role in "directing subversive activities" and in espionage, particularly with regard to shipping. Welles was optimistic that Argentina could not long resist if Chile were to break with the Axis.[40]

Because of his conviction that Foreign Minister Barros was misleading President Ríos, Bowers requested—and received—an audience with Ríos early in September. Bowers discovered that indeed Barros had been withholding information from the president, "information regarding the use of telecommunications by the Axis." When Bowers presented his evidence, Ríos, he thought, "seemed stunned." Ríos appeared appalled that Barros had not forwarded the information provided to him by Ambassador Bowers, and Bowers "then showed the President a number of intercepts, in substance, which shocked him." Ríos also displayed amazement "that the German Embassy's telegrams had increased 216 per cent since 1941" when there was no trade between Chile and Germany.

There were other pressures as well. Bowers told Sumner Welles, his immediate superior in Washington, that the Peruvian ambassador had pleaded with Barros to make the break, but that Barros thought it essential that "some South American countries [have] contact with Berlin and Tokyo."[41] Then, in mid-September, Nelson Rockefeller paid a visit to Santiago. Bowers commented:

> Nelson Rockefeller has been valuable, though he has done much that a diplomat would not do. He was received on the assumption that all economic aid to Chile would depend on him. For that reason he has been much sought by officials and the President has seen him three times. They have asked his opinion about things and he has let them have it with a sledge hammer. He asked me how far he could go, and I told him that if he was asked about how Americans feel he could tell them frankly. In this manner the impression has been conveyed that unless Chile lines up with the United Nations she will be in a sorry position.[42]

With his projected trip to Washington in mind, President Ríos told Rockefeller that he could not break with the Axis before visiting the United States "because of internal matters." Rockefeller replied that "in that case [it would] be better if he broke and did not go."[43]

Ambassador Bowers mounted a public relations campaign of his own, taking high profile action to preserve a high profile historic church in Santiago in hope of winning good will for the United States. When the priest had told him that the parish could not afford the taxes and would have to level and sell part of the property, Bowers spoke to Ernesto Barros, "as an individual, not as an Ambassador, as a historian with a reverence for historic things." Barros expressed interest, and the government reduced the taxes to a level which the parish could afford to pay. The foreign minister then released to the media correspondence between himself and Bowers on the subject, and, said Bowers, "the press has been filled with fulsome praise of me." Bowers thought that he had won good will among Chilean Roman Catholics, whom the Spanish ambassador, Luca de la Tena, was lobbying on behalf of the Axis.[44]

On other matters, the U.S. government worried less about its image than about results. It wanted action. The first confrontation came over telecommunications. On 5 September Bowers told Barros that the U.S. government was "deeply disturbed" at Chile's ongoing communications links with the Axis countries. These links, said Bowers, were a threat to shipping, and therefore to human lives.[45] Allied cryptographers, said Bowers, could read but a fraction of the messages, which were numerous. The German government was spending $6000 per month to send telecommunications from Chile, said Bowers, despite the total absence of trade or tourism. To the memo Bowers attached decrypted German messages about shipping and the impact of submarine warfare. One decrypt of 12 June 1942 dealt with a Chile-based German spy and his contact in Rio de Janeiro. Bowers commented to Barros:

> Brazil must be very pleased to find that movements and arrangements for German spies in Rio...are arranged through the German Embassy in Santiago.[46]

One undated decrypt even dealt with the military situation in the United States!

On 24 September, Bowers discussed the issue personally with President Ríos,[47] and on 25 September Bowers repeated some of his points to Barros:

> The German Embassy is spending some twenty-eight times and the Japanese Legation more than thirty times as much for cipher telegraphic communications as they were before the war in spite of the fact that neither of these Governments has commercial, financial, or travel arrangements with Chile. Even if we did not have some absolute proof of the fact that military information damaging to hemispheric defense and the efforts of the United Nations is arriving and being collated in Chile for the transmissions by the Axis missions over the Transradio Chilena, the tremendous increase in the volume of these messages can be explained in no other way.[48]

Even the operator of a clandestine Axis radio station in Cuba, charged Bowers, received ciphered instructions from Transradio Chilena, Chile's telecommunications authority.

Ernesto Barros refused to accept any responsibility. To Conrado Ríos, Chile's Ambassador in Argentina, he pointed out that there had been no sinkings in the Pacific Ocean south of the Panama Canal. To accuse Chile of complicity in problems thousands of miles away was unfair, he said, despite the evidence in the Luni case, and Chile deserved as much respect from belligerents as such other neutrals as Ireland, Switzerland, Portugal, Sweden, and Turkey.[49] Whether these others received the degree of respect which Barros thought they were receiving is another matter.[50]

Nevertheless, the will of the U.S. embassy prevailed, and in short order. On 16 October Barros wrote Bowers that the Chilean government would no longer allow Axis diplomats to send ciphered cables to their capitals. The message from Transradio Chilena (written in English) to von Schön was somewhat less blunt but still to the point:

> Please note that as from now this company refuses to accept for transmission or delivery any message whatsoever in a secret code or cipher destined to or received from a non-American country, Chilean Government messages excepted.[51]

Bowers was pleased,[52] but some Chileans were not. To his cousin Tobias Barros, Chile's Ambassador in Berlin, the Foreign Minister explained that Transradio Chilena had informed the government that it would no longer accept ciphered messages for transmission between Axis diplomats in Chile and Axis capitals. "The U.S. Embassy was pushing for this, but we did not think it wise," said the Foreign Minister. However, as foreigners from Allied countries controlled a majority of Transradio Chilena's shares, they had been able to produce the decision. Faced with a *fait accompli* on the eve of a scheduled visit by President Ríos to Washington (scheduled for 22-29 September, although it did not actually take place because of ongoing political difficulties for President Ríos), the cabinet did not want a confrontation with the company, especially as many in Allied countries thought that the ciphered messages were costing them lives and property losses.[53]

The Italian government regarded retaliation as pointless,[54] as did Yamagata. Communications, he realized, were far more important to himself than to Chile's minister in Tokyo.[55] Von Schön and Yamagata also had a solution. From that point onward, they sent their ciphered messages to the German and Japanese Embassies in Buenos Aires, which faced no such restrictions and could forward them to Berlin or Tokyo. Effectiveness or results counted for more than dignity or strict neutrality. In a tit-for-tat reprisal, Chilean diplomats in Berlin and Rome lost the right to send ciphered messages to Santiago, but this also proved of little consequence. They simply sent their messages to Chile's Embassy in Bern, Switzerland, which then forwarded them to Santiago.[56] Only Labra in Tokyo could not communicate confidentially, and it is doubtful that he had very much to say. Cutting off the ciphered telecommunications links with Berlin, Rome, and Tokyo was a step toward the curtailment of sensitive information to the Axis, but only a diplomatic rupture could make a significant difference.

The second confrontation came in Boston, where on 8 October 1942 Under-Secretary of State Sumner Welles launched a blistering attack on the foreign policies of Argentina and Chile. Welles told his audience, people interested in foreign trade, that the U.S. was "profoundly grateful" for the assistance it had received from the other Latin American republics, eleven of which had become belligerents on the Allied side, seven of which had at least terminated diplomatic relations with Germany, Italy, and Japan. Argentina and Chile, by contrast, were acting in defiance of the Río conference and allowing their territory to be used for hostile activities against their neighbours. Because of such Argentine-Chilean non-compliance, Axis diplomats were in a position to send messages to submarine commanders. Axis submarines had then sunk without warning ships of several Latin American counties while they tried to carry goods from one such republic to another. Those same Argentine-Chilean policies had cost many Latin Americans their lives. Thereupon Welles expressed optimism that Argentina and Chile would soon mend their evil ways.[57]

Ambassador Bowers initially regarded the speech as a "heroic" pressure tactic.[58] At the same time, three past presidents rallied behind President Ríos against the ugly American who was providing their country with unwanted and unsolicited advice. *El Mercurio* editorialized that the speech,

> ...wounds our dignity [and] conflicts with the facts of the full and loyal collaboration which Chile has given to continental defence and the war effort of the United States.[59]

Individual Chilean Senators expressed disapproval.[60]

The government of Argentina also protested Welles's interpretation of events as expressed in that Boston speech, and Foreign Minister Barros issued a statement of his own. President Roosevelt had invited President Ríos to Washington, he said, as a gesture of good will, and President Ríos had accepted the invitation in the same spirit. Nevertheless, Welles had publicly accused Chile of responsibility for ship sinkings and loss of life "on remote oceans" in defiance of Chilean responsibilities as a Western Hemisphere nation. Yet there had not been a single sinking off the Pacific coast south of the Panama Canal. Chile simply could not assume responsibility for events thousands of miles away, and in any event, there was tight censorship over telecommunications. The Axis belligerents could no longer send ciphered messages to their capitals. Barros either ignored the fact that such messages were still reaching Berlin, Tokyo and Rome albeit via Buenos Aires, or he lacked the imagination to think of such a possibility—although his own diplomats in Berlin and Rome were doing something similar. The foreign minister demanded the same respect from the United States that the Allies were rendering to Switzerland, Portugal, Sweden, and Turkey.[61]

Two days later, Ríos announced a further postponement of his already postponed trip to Washington, citing the speech as the reason.[62] However, ten days later he had a major cabinet shuffle. Interior Minister Morales and

Industry Minister Schnake, both of whom favoured the rupture with the Axis, retained their positions within the cabinet. Foreign Minister Barros did not. Joaquín Fernández became Chile's new foreign minister.

As he reorganized his cabinet 21 October, President Ríos issued a public statement. Its essence was that each individual minister had made a worthy contribution to his administration. However, he needed a team, not a group of rugged individualists each headed in the direction of his own choice at any given moment. The statement concluded:

> My goal in matters of foreign policy is to align Chile on the side of the rest of the Western Hemisphere, in defence of the great principles of hemispheric integrity and the moral and philosophical values of liberty and democracy.[63]

El Llanquihue thought that the statement made good sense,[64] and El Correo de Valdivia expressed optimism that with a more harmonious cabinet than the one he had had, President Ríos could cope with the foreign and domestic challenges facing him.[65]

Some people in Santiago had no doubt as to what the cabinet shuffle meant. Bowers told President Roosevelt that Ríos had decided that his failure to break with the Axis had been a mistake and that his foreign minister had become a political liability.[66] On 21 October von Schön reported—perhaps with the aid of the same people who had told him about the "secret" Senate debates—of a verbal duel between Interior Minister Morales, who favoured the break, and Foreign Minister Barros, who did not. The political life expectancy of a Chilean cabinet minister was brief, but President Ríos' shuffle of 21 October 1942 which affected eight portfolios was without precedent in the twentieth century.[67] Ernesto Barros told cousin Tobias that his departure would be the prelude to a change in policy and the diplomatic rupture,[68] and he sent a similar message to the government of Argentina out of a sense of "duty" to respect the Argentine-Chilean accord to keep the other informed about any change in policy.[69] While El Mercurio provided extensive coverage of the cabinet shuffle in its issues of 21 and 22 October, it did not mention the question of diplomatic relations with the

Axis (or otherwise) as an issue. However, the *Times of London* saw that the departure of Ernesto Barros might well foreshadow a change in Chilean policy toward the Axis.[70]

THE LAST FEW MONTHS

Coinciding with the cabinet shuffle came a crackdown on Germans with radio transmitters. One Schaumburg-Lippe reported from Valparaíso that on 23 October the Chilean government began to arrest Germans for sending ciphered radio messages about ship movements. The detainees were free but under police surveillance, said Schaumburg-Lippe.[71] On 4 November, von Schön reported the arrest of an employee at the Valparaíso consulate-general on grounds of espionage. Von Schön ordered that given what had happened earlier at the consulate at Osorno and the influence of Interior Minister Morales, only the embassy in Santiago should receive ciphered messages.[72] Berlin agreed.[73]

It may well be that Ernesto Barros' successor, Joaquín Fernández, wanted a rupture as soon as he could find a plausible pretext. However, because Chile was a democracy and the cabinet would need Senate support for what it was doing, Fernández chose to move cautiously. Fernández knew that despite the Allied victories of 1942, he could not create a consensus if he appeared overly subservient to American pressure. He believed that the Welles speech had been a mistake. As late as 24 November, President Ríos himself said that Chile would need military and financial guarantees before it could agree to such an "extreme" step as a diplomatic rupture.[74]

Yet, for a while, it appeared that Barros' foreign policy were as strong as ever, and Bowers's first impressions of Fernández and the new cabinet were unfavourable. Regarding Fernández, he wrote to Sumner Welles:

> He impresses me as lacking in ability, character and convictions, and as being utterly without imagination or a comprehensive view of the world situation. He is clearly an opportunist, and possibly in him Ríos has just what he wants—a Minister who is willing to be a cipher, leaving everything in Ríos' hands.

Bowers thought that on the whole the entire new cabinet was "weak."[75] Within days, however, Bowers could report that at the behest of Ríos, Fernández had approached three major newspapers—*El Mercurio*, *La Hora*, and *La Nación*—to ask for editorials on behalf of the rupture. According to Bowers, *El Mercurio* responded with enthusiasm and, because of its basic conservatism, its credibility was formidable.[76] Chile was very much a part of the inter-American family, *El Mercurio* editorialized 23 October.

U.S. authorities continued to exert pressure upon the Ríos government. On 3 November, U.S. government sources leaked to United Press in Montevideo the news that on 30 June it had delivered to the Chilean government copies of seventy-one intercepted telegrams sent from Chile to Germany. Chilean newspapers published the revelations the following day. The telegrams, said United Press, indicated that German spies in Chile had been informing contacts inside Germany about schedules of ships along the west coast of South America, U.S. military assistance to South American countries, South American exports to the United States, steps taken by South American countries to defend themselves, and Chilean political news. The German spies had their base at Calle Prat #828 in Valparaíso, three blocks from the coast and within easy walking distance of Chile's principal naval base and commercial port. United Press named names: Friedrich von Schulz Hausmann, Bruno Dittmann, Jorge Hasbaldieck, Arnold Barkahm, Hans Hafbauer, Juan Aguilera, Kaste Borg, Emilio Simonsen Wice, Isabel Piderich, Ludwig von Bohlen, Sanh Blum, Erich Wichmann, Guillermo Geller, and North German Lloyd. Such details enhanced the credibility of the reports from United Press. From Valparaíso, said the newagency, spies radiated to Argentina, Peru, Colombia, Ecuador, Guatemala, Mexico, and the United States itself.[77] The following day an inside column in *El Mercurio* entitled "Chile's duty" called upon readers to forget about Sumner Welles' speech and to offer full support to the U.S. war effort. An editorial the following day called for a crackdown on the spies, and expressed confidence that the Ríos government would do so. One day later, a front page headline proclaimed, "Cordell Hull praises the Chilean government's policy of repression against spies." Like newspapers elsewhere,[78] El Mercurio also publicized the U.S. success in North Africa and expressed agreement with President Ríos's telegram of congratulations to President Roosevelt.[79]

U.S. pressure behind the scenes was intense. Because of the menace which the Axis powers represented, the United States was supplying weapons to other Latin American countries, including Peru and Bolivia. These two countries have never fully reconciled themselves to their military defeat by Chile during the 1879-1884 War of the Pacific and to their subsequent territorial cessions. The military balance of power in South America became a matter of concern to strategists in Santiago. They feared that weapons provided to Bolivia and Peru for use against the Axis might, sooner or later, point in the direction of Chile. Chile could not afford to receive fewer weapons than its neighbours to the north and northeast. Chilean officials in Washington appealed for more.

The reply from Secretary of State Cordell Hull was blunt. "The [State] Department," he said, "does not feel that it can accede to the request of the Chilean authorities that certain of the armament set forth in a list handed to the Chilean Ambassador by the Under Secretary last August be made available to Chile prior to Chile's rupture of relations with the Axis." Given Chile's limited support for the Allied cause, other Latin American governments would fail to understand why the United States was sending the weapons to Chile rather than to other republics. Finally,

> So long as Chile maintains relations with the Axis, all details regarding arms and munitions which might be sent to Chile, as well as the disposition, location and use of such arms and munitions would be immediately made known to the Axis, thus reducing materially the potential value of such arms and munitions in the defense of Chile and of the continent.[80]

From the sidelines, Ernesto Barros was critical of his successor and of President Ríos, and he had no qualms about sharing his thoughts with

Yamagata.[81] Given Yamagata's frequent contacts with the German embassy in Santiago, von Schön was undoubtedly aware of Ernesto Barros' thoughts and the new direction of Chilean foreign policy. Barros also met the Italian ambassador, Raffaele Boscarelli, to speculate upon President Ríos's probable intentions.[82]

Alerted by Ernesto Barros to the probability of a diplomatic rupture, the Axis diplomats accredited to Chile duly informed their respective governments. From Berlin, Tobias Barros warned that the German government was confused about the direction of Chilean foreign policy and that a rupture would not be without consequences.[83] Tobias Barros also visited Ernst Wörmann at Auswärtiges Amt and promised to keep fighting for German-Chilean friendship.[84] From Tokyo, Minister Labra read in the English-language *Japan Times* that Chile was in the process of abandoning its policy of neutrality.[85] Japanese government sources threatened reprisals should Chile sever diplomatic relations. "If that did happen, it would be impossible for Chile to protect her long coast line."[86] Later Tokyo warned the Chileans about "shipping losses inflicted by the German and Italian U-boats." Radio Tokyo told the people of Chile to expect "sacrifices, hardship, and loss of life."[87]

Japan's ambassador in Argentina was sufficiently concerned about the impact of a possible rupture on Japanese naval and air operations in the Pacific that within days he held discussions with Argentine Foreign Minister Enrique Ruiz.[88] The Argentine government, which had originally proposed that neither Argentina nor Chile should abandon its common front without consulting the other,[89] threatened reprisals.[90]

To bring pressure to bear upon Chile's foreign minister, Yamagata maintained contacts with other high-level Chileans. On 24 October, Yamagata held a private conversation with a former finance minister, Oscar Gajardo Villarroel, about the best way to avoid a diplomatic rupture when "President Ríos was such a weak character" and U.S. pressure was so intense.[91] Given the role of the Chilean senate in foreign policy decisions, Yamagata contacted the speaker of the senate, Florencio Durán.

Durán—who had strong fraternal feelings toward Argentina[92]—advised Yamagata to bribe senators if he wanted to maintain Chilean neutrality,[93] evidently unaware that Yamagata had been bribing politicians for some months.[94] On 2 November, ten days before the U.S. naval victory in the Solomon Islands, Yamagata warned Fernández not to change the direction of Chilean foreign policy. Yamagata was certain that Fernández's commitment to neutrality was less than that of Barros.[95]

Yamagata, Ambassador Boscarelli, and Senator Durán speculated about the contents of Fernández's first foreign policy address,[96] and in November, when some Senators were circulating a petition for a special session to debate foreign policy, the German, Italian, and Japanese diplomats did what they could to discourage them. In the absence of a debate, the Axis officials reasoned, the status quo was likely to continue, but debate might lead to rupture. For his part, Yamagata lobbied with Conservative Senators Maximiliano Errázuriz, as well as with the president of the Conservative party, Deputy Fernando Aldunate.[97] The FBI identified Senator Errázuriz as "a known pro-Axis sympathizer," past-president of the Chilean-Japanese Society, "friendly with pro-Axis interests and...associated with Japanese and Italian elements in Chile."[98]

On 9 December Yamagata again spoke to Senate Speaker Durán.[99] At first Fernández soft-pedalled the likelihood of a rupture. On 28 October, he reassured the Argentine government that he would honour the Argentine-Chilean accord to keep the other party informed of any change in foreign policy.[100] The next day he told Ambassador Barros that his appointment as foreign minister did not necessarily mean a change in foreign policy.[101] As late as 17 November, he told Chile's ambassador in Buenos Aires, Conrado Ríos, that the government had not yet decided upon a diplomatic rupture.[102] However, whatever it did decide, Fernández had told Ambassador Ríos, would "above all [be] in the interests of Chile."[103]

At the same time, Fernández and President Ríos missed a golden opportunity for humanitarian assistance which might have justified ongoing diplomatic relations with the Axis powers. Late in October, a representative of the Czechoslovakian government-in-exile, Dr. F. Pavlasek, approached Chile's minister in Ottawa, Eduardo Grove, with an urgent request. Pavlasek feared that Hitler's forces were about to invade the unoccupied part of France where Czech soldiers might face "torture or execution."[104] Those soldiers had fled their homeland when Hitler annexed it, and they had fought for France until its collapse in June 1940. They were able-bodied and capable of making a contribution to any society, said Pavlasek, but they needed immediate asylum in a neutral country. There was little hope that the Vichy regime would allow their departure for an Allied belligerent. Moreover, Czechoslovakia's government-in-exile would provide funds to guarantee that the former soldiers would not become a burden on Chilean society. Unfortunately, there was no sense of urgency in Santiago, and German forces invaded unoccupied France before Fernández or any other Chilean gave a response. Happily, some of the Czech soldiers managed to escape to Spain as German forces advanced.[105]

American victories on both battlefronts increased the probability that a diplomatic rupture would be "in the interests of Chile." The U.S. victory in the Solomon Islands on 12 November lessened the risks of reprisals from Japan. Operation Torch in Morocco and Algeria, successfully launched 8 November, had a great impact, despite the comment of Ambassador Barros that the North African campaign was but a sideshow. That the U.S. would divert its troops there was a sign of weakness, he thought, a recognition of Axis strength within Europe itself.[106] By contrast, President Ríos congratulated U.S. President Roosevelt upon the Torch victory and said that it contributed to the security of the Western Hemisphere.[107] Even before Torch, Fernández had denied cipher privileges to diplomats from Vichy France, whose government collaborated with Hitler,[108] and on 11 December, Fernández informed Ambassador Barros that Chile was closing its consulate in Vichy.[109] From Rome, Chile's chargé d'affaires, Barriga, said that the American victories made it possible that Italy might conclude a separate peace with the Allies.[110]

Bowers was happy with the apparent change in direction, although Yamagata understandably was not. Ríos remained anxious to visit the White House, he reported, and his government was arresting "nazi and Axis spies on a large scale."[111] He thought that the rupture would take place "immediately" after Ríos returned from his Washington trip.[112] Fernández explained to the U.S. ambassador that Ríos would stop in Buenos Aires on his return from Washington and try persuade Argentina also to make the break, and he reassured Bowers who feared that the Castillo government in Argentina might have the opposite effect upon Ríos.[113] Political difficulties promised to be minimal. El Mercurio's publisher, Agustín Edwards, had long promised Bowers to "work for a rupture in relations,"[114] and even El Diario Ilustrado, according to Bowers, had pledged that it would support Ríos if he were to break with the Axis.[115] In any event, Ríos did not go to Washington himself but sent two political allies who favoured the break, Raúl Morales, Minister of the Interior, and Oscar Schnake, the former presidential candidate.[116] The role of Morales proved decisive.

Immediately upon arrival at the White House 17 December, Morales told President Roosevelt "that he was the bearer of a personal message from the President of Chile that Chile had decided immediately to break diplomatic relations with the Axis governments." However, Morales—on behalf the Ríos—wanted some reassurance. Morales wondered about his country's vulnerability to submarine attacks, and President Roosevelt—and who had been Under-Secretary of the Navy during World War I and was knowledgeable about naval affairs—said that danger was minimal. At worst, some Japanese submarine could "fire a few shells on the Chilean coast, as Japan had done against the California coast some six months ago." The attack would enrage Chileans as it had Californians. Morales wondered about attacks on electrical stations, which would curtail copper production. Roosevelt instructed him to discuss the details with Sumner Welles.[117]

Later that day Morales met Hull for what appears to have been a rather unpleasant conversation. Morales wanted a pretext for the break, and Hull referred him to the Río obligations of the previous January. However, Hull also instructed U.S. military and naval personnel to assemble evidence that Axis spies in Chile were providing information which led to the sinking of Allied ships, their crews, and their passengers. Morales wanted additional protection for coal producing areas and Valparaíso, and Hull reminded him that Chileans had failed to appreciate the military assistance which the United States had already provided. Yet, President Roosevelt was ready to consider the request.[118]

On 22 December, Morales met Sumner Welles to discuss those same two points. Welles provided him with evidence which demonstrated that "American ships that had left Chile had been sunk in the Caribbean as a result of clandestine radio messages sent by German agents in Valparaíso to German military or naval agents." Some of the documentation was highly confidential, to be seen by Morales and President Ríos but by no other Chileans. On the subject of additional weaponry, Welles was less forthcoming. Chile already had received formidable supplies, said Welles, and new shipments at that point could be open to misinterpretation. Many would think that the United States had bribed the Chilean government to make the break. Additional shipments could be considered once Chile had terminated its relations with the Axis. Morales expressed satisfaction with this understanding.[119]

Morales's return to Chile 5 January 1943 received extensive publicity. At once he met senior political (including President Ríos and Foreign Minister Fernández), military, and diplomatic officials, along with the ambassadors of the United States, Brazil, and Argentina. An official statement said that President Ríos approved of everything that Morales had done, and Fernández also expressed approval.[120] On 15 January, an editorial in *La Nación* praised the government's foreign policy, which had evolved from neutrality to non-belligerence to a pending rupture with the Axis.

The government is working for the well being of the Republic, and if there is a change in foreign policy, it would be for sound reasons after mature reflexion upon the most important and long-term interests of Chile and America.

La Nación considered that any risks would lead to a safer world in the long run. Meanwhile, Chile had obligations to the its hemispheric neighbours and to humanity.

El Mercurio agreed. On 6 January 1943, *El Mercurio* columnist Cristóbal Saenz asked the rhetorical question, "Why should we break with the Axis?" Saenz then expressed admiration for liberal values, called for solidarity with Mexico and Brazil whose ships the Axis had sunk in waters close to the Western Hemisphere, and warned:

> What would be the position of Chile in the new world political and economic organization if she continues in her isolationist ways?

Military realities provided an additional incentive.

In January 1943, the German army faced disaster at Stalingrad, the British Army had won the decisive Battle of El Alamein, and American forces had captured Morocco and Algeria. Argentina's ambassador had told Fernández that as far as his country was concerned, there would be no consequences and that Chilean-Argentine relations would not be affected in any way.

Fernández told a secret session of the Chilean Senate that Chile could not afford to antagonize the United States at a time when Peru was strengthening its armed forces. Nor could Fernández ignore Bolivia. Bolivia's president refused to accept the outcome of the War of the Pacific as final, and his country's "just aspiration," for a port on the Pacific was "permanent" and "unshakeable." Bolivian authorities took advantage of Chile's lack of co-operation to lobby with other countries.[121]

Former President Carlos Ibáñez accepted the government's decision. On 15 January he said that he was breaking a self-imposed silence out of a sense of patriotism. Ibáñez said that he did not have as much information as members of the government must have. From his perspective, the rupture appeared undesirable. However, the Constitution gave the president responsibility for foreign relations, and he called upon all Chileans to rally around their president.[122]

Yet, there was considerable effort to maintain the status quo. Argentina and the Axis powers also made the most of their final weeks. On 8 January 1943, the Argentine government appealed to the Ríos administration not to cut ties with Germany, Italy, and Japan. In Yamagata's words, Argentine authorities "made a definite proposal to the Chilean Government for cooperation between the two countries with a view to preventing a break of diplomatic relations."[123] From Santiago and Buenos Aires, Tokyo learned that U.S. authorities wanted Brazilian and Mexican forces to fight for the Allies in hot weather environments (the Mediterranean and the South Pacific), where Americans might not feel comfortable.[124] Indeed, Brazilians did join the Italian campaign, and Mexicans fought in the Philippines. A Chilean journalist once stationed in Japan "acted as an informer for Yamagata."[125] In return for ongoing diplomatic relations, Japanese Foreign Minister Masayuki Tani proposed military assistance to Chile against Peru and Bolivia, its rivals of longstanding, but Yamagata thought that January 1943 was a bad time to forward the proposal. "If we were now to make such a suggestion," he wrote, "the enemy would turn it to our disadvantage." However, time ran out, although Yamagata did not blame Chileans or the Ríos government. Yamagata noted that the U.S. was in a position to promise arms and munitions to Chile and to threaten economic reprisals if that country did not conform.[126]

Former President Arturo Alessandri, who thought that rupture would lead to the shedding of Chilean blood, conducted a media offensive. One biographer has suggested that at age 75 Alesssandri's judgment was not what it had been,[127] but that is probably unfair. Alessandri made a series of arguments which were logical from the standpoint of a near pacifist. He said that he opposed totalitarianism, and his track record speaks for itself on that score. He also proclaimed himself an admirer of the United States. However, as a patriotic Chilean he continued to oppose the rupture. Neutrality, he thought, was quite compatible with Chile's hemispheric obligations until and unless there were Axis attacks upon Chilean shipping, the Panama

Canal, or the South American coastline south of the Panama Canal. To date such events had not taken place. Alessandri called for a plebiscite in which all literate Chileans of at least eighteen years of age could vote.[128]

Ernesto Barros also lobbied extensively and until the Senate voted, there was no guarantee that the break would actually occur.[129] Ambassador Tobias Barros did his best to avoid a rupture. He suggested to von Weizsäcker that he should make a trip to the front so that he could file a credible report on German victories there, thus offsetting the Allied propaganda about German setbacks. He also advised the German government to order huge quantities of saltpetre from Chile for delivery after the war, provided that Chile maintained its policy of neutrality. German authorities liked these suggestions and tried to act on them. There were repeated plans for Tobias Barros to go to the front, but the Chilean Senate made its decision before he could go there. In December 1942, the German government promised that in exchange for neutrality, Chile would be allowed to sell 300,000 tons of saltpetre in each of the five post-war years; this compared with 160,000 tons before the war. The cause, however, was hopeless. By then, no amount of lobbying or bribery could persuade President Ríos and his cabinet to reverse direction.[130]

On 19 January, the Chilean Senate voted by a margin of 30:10 with two abstentions to support the diplomatic rupture with the Axis. Those in the minority included both government and opposition senators: Miguel Cruchaga, president of the AAA; Ernesto Cruz and Pedro Opaso, from Curicó, Talca, Maule and Linares; Francisco Urrejola and Gustavo Rivera, from Ñuble, Concepción, and Arauca; Fernando Alessandri, from Tarapacá and Antofagasta; Carlos Haverbeck and Alejo Lira, from Valdivia, Llanquihue, Chiloé, Aysén, and Magallanes; Oscar Valenzuela, from O'Higgins and Colchagua; Humberto del Piño from Bío-Bío, Malleco and Cautín. Senator Maximiliano Errázuriz, president of the pro-Japan lobby and senator from Curicó, Talca, Maule and Linares abstained.[131]

A majority of the ten did not have German or Italian surnames, and they came from all parts of the country. The following day, President Ríos explained in a radio broadcast that Chile had had a longstanding moral obligation to break with the Axis and delayed only in order to establish a national consensus on the matter.

If the media represented the thinking of Chilean elites, it does not appear that the Ríos government had much to fear. The ultra-Conservative pro-Ibáñez *El Diario Ilustrado* praised President Ríos for acting in accord with the spirit of democracy. Although entitled to act on his own, he had chosen to work with the Senate. Government officials had done what was in the national interest, even if their reasons remained so sensitive that the public could not yet be told what they were.[132] *La Nación* also praised the government for its democratic, consultative approach to the problem. At the same time, it rejected Alessandri's idea of a plebiscite, bound to be divisive, at such a critical moment. Nineteen of the twenty-one republics had already acted, said *La Nación*, and it would be "inexcusable" not to offer full support to those risking their lives for "the ideals of culture, liberty, and social justice."[133]

From Chile's south, where the ethnic German influence was strong, Osorno's *La Prensa* gave thanks that the period of uncertainty had finally ended. It also said that the outcome was hardly surprising, but reminded President Ríos that Germany, Italy, and Japan were countries with which Chile had a tradition of friendship.[134] *El Correo de Valdivia* praised the President's "patriotism, inspiration and rectitude" for standing with the rest of the hemisphere in support of democracy. Nor, it added—apparently without any intention of irony—had the Ríos administration acted precipitously. It had studied the situation carefully and proceeded according to the constitution.[135] Both newspapers warned that there would be a price to pay, but like Bernardo Ibáñez, secretary-general of the Confederation of Chilean workers,136 they were willing to make sacrifices for the cause.

SUMMARY AND CONCLUSIONS

Chilean policy toward the Axis was pragmatic, not heroic. In the aftermath of Pearl Harbor, when it was not altogether clear that the United States

Navy had control of the South Pacific, caution made sense. Unless one had strong principles, it made little sense to antagonize Japan. That Rossetti would be cautious at the Río conference, when his party wanted to win the forthcoming presidential election and thought it might need the support of German-Chileans, also made sense. However, once Ríos had won the election and the United States began to win battles, it was shrewd to comply with Washington's wishes. After Midway, Guadalcanal, and the Solomon Islands, there was no doubt that the United States was the force to be reckoned with in the long run on the Pacific. The success of Operation Torch gave a similar indication on the Atlantic, although the Battle of the Atlantic itself remained to be won. The fact that Chile, unlike Argentina, faced the Pacific and not the Atlantic may help to explain the fact that Chile's rupture with the Axis preceded that of Argentina by a full year. The 1879-1884 War of the Pacific was also a major factor. Money—both the incentive of assistance from the United States and bribes paid to individuals—proved important as Chileans pondered what action to take. Certainly, in the long run, the United States could provide more money and more weapons than Argentina or, presuming that they were defeated, the Axis powers could.

In domestic terms too, Chilean policy toward the Axis was pragmatic. After the election, President Ríos did not need to concern himself with the German and Italian vote, especially as he was not eligible for immediate re-election. German attempts at subversion should have concerned any patriotic Chilean concerned about his country's sovereignty, and evidence of the connection between Chile-based spies and the sinking of Allied ships should have concerned anyone concerned about a decent, democratic future. It was unconscionable that Ernesto Barros ignored the evidence presented to him by the U.S. embassy and by Chile's Dirección General de Investigaciones, and the fact that President Ríos waited weeks to replace him after Ambassador Barros presented the facts indicates a certain timidity on his part. To limit the Axis diplomats' telegraphic privileges, even to arrest spies and house them at Zapallar, did not prevent transmission of undesirable information.

Chilean politicians were susceptible to bribes and threats from either side. While the Germans and Japanese offered cash, the White House offered a trip to Washington. Undoubtedly there were senators and cabinet ministers who did what they did from a sense of conviction, but there were many who broke ranks with their own government to communicate and plot strategy with foreign officials, both American and Axis. Parliamentarians and congressmen from many countries regard such actions as part of the democratic process, but it is more questionable for cabinet ministers and former cabinet ministers to do so. Such intrigues help explain the delay before the rupture and the rupture itself of January 1943.

Some Chileans of German or Italian ethnicity undoubtedly were involved in Nazi causes around Osorno until December 1941 and Valdivia into 1943 or later. Some did attend Nazi gatherings at Frutillar and Puerto Montt. Seminarian Tullio Franchini was an effective messenger. It is understandable that ethnic Chileans were not eager to take a stand against their family's point of origin, especially when that country continued to supply professional people.

However, even in Valdivia, Osorno, and Puerto Montt, the press had practical reasons for delaying any rupture with the Axis. Declarations of friendship for the Axis powers were rare, and those who expressed such friendship—columnist Joaquín Edwards, Senators Cruchaga and Errázuriz, Ambassador Barros—had surnames that were neither Germany, Italian, nor Japanese. Not all Axis sympathizers came from German or Italian families, and the support of those families was limited. Actions taken by the Abwehr or the German Embassy on behalf of presidential candidate Carlos Ibáñez proved futile. Even around Valdivia and Osorno, blood was thicker than politics, and Mrs. Ríos's point of origin was a higher priority than ideology. Ironically, Ibáñez and Tobias Barros would have a turn to govern in 1952, years after the defeat of Nazi Germany.

Chilean authorities could probably have made the break with the Axis more quickly than they did. Some, like Ernesto Barros, did not want to do so. Others, like Rossetti or—it would appear—President Ríos, did not realize that the political risk was minimal. Without strong U.S. pressure, President Ríos almost certainly would never have taken the plunge.

NOTES

1. Ernesto Barros did ask Tobias Barros about the Volga campaign in a late September despatch (#145), vol. 1968, ADRE.

2. Sir Basil Liddell Hart, *History of the Second World War* (London: Papermac, 1992 [1970]), pp. 363-368; Gordon Prange, *Miracle at Midway* (New York: McGraw-Hill, 1982).

3. Liddell Hart, p. 367.

4. Tobias Barros to Ernesto Barros, 28 June, #146, vol. 1969, ADRE.

5. *El Llanquihue* (Puerto Montt), 10 June 1942.

6. Yamagata to Tokyo, 24 June, #432-433, NAC.

7. Yamagata to Tokyo, 8 July, #486-487, NAC.

8. Ott, German embassy, Tokyo, to AA, RG 242, NARA, Series T-120, Reel 183, 12 July 1942, frames 88683-88684.

9. Instructions to submarine commanders, 23 Aug. 1942, frame 88732.

10. For information on the proposed visit to Washington see Bowers to FDR, 4 Sept. 1942; Memoranda of Conversation between Secretary of State Cordell Hull and Chile's ambassador in Washington, Rodolfo Michels, 10 and 14 Sept. 1942; Hull to FDR, 14 Sept. 1942, all in PSF. *El Mercurio* published President Ríos's acceptance in its issue of 15 Sept. 1942.

11. *El Llanquihue* (Puerto Montt), 15 Aug. 1942, editorial.

12. *La Prensa* (Osorno), 16 Aug. 1942.

13. Von Schön to Berlin, 9 July 1942, frame 88680.

14. Ernesto Barros to Tobias Barros, 19 Aug., #130, vol. 1968, ADRE.

15. *El Llanquihue* (Puerto Montt), 24 Aug. 1942; *La Prensa* (Osorno), 24 Aug. 1942, quoting a UP report of 23 Aug. from Santiago.

16. Bernstein, pp. 72-76.

17. Von Schön to AA, 23 Sept. 1942, frames 88760-88761.

18. Bowers to Welles, 8 Oct. 1942, Welles. The Speer letter is included with that covering letter.

19. Von Schön to AA, 1 Oct. 1942, frame 88763.

20. Ernesto Barros to Tobias Barros, 7 Oct., #155, vol. 1968, ADRE. 21. Von Schön to Berlin, 23 Sept. 1942, frames 88760-88761. See FBI, pp. 73, 79, 126-127, 152-153, 170.

22. Bowers to Welles, 15 Oct. 1942, PSF; also, FBI, p. 153.

23. Wörmann memorandum, AA, 6 Oct. 1942, frames 88764-88766.

24. Bowers to Welles, 11 Aug. 1942, PSF.

25. Orde, Santiago, to Eden, London, 16 Sept. 1941, Series A 981/1, Item CHIL 10, Canberra.

26. Message from the Foreign Office to the Prime Minister [Churchill], 29 Sept. 1942, Series A 981/1, Item CHIL 15, Canberra.

27. Yamagata to Tokyo, read 16 March 1942, HW1/418, PRO.

28. Tobias Barros, Berlin, to Santiago, 9-10 March 1942, HW1/422, PRO.

29. Yamagata to Tokyo, 31 March 1942, HW1/477, PRO.

30. Italian report from Santiago [to Rome?], 27 May 1942, HW1/615, PRO.

31. Barriga, Rome, to Foreign Minister, Santiago, 12 Nov. 1942, HW1/1090, PRO.

32. Foreign Minister Tani, Tokyo, to Yamagata, 9 Oct. 1942, HW1/971, PRO.

33. Von Schön spoke to Yamagata, who forwarded the information to his foreign office in Tokyo; Yamagata to Tokyo, 6 Aug. 1942, HW1/822, PRO.

34. Suni, Madrid, to Tokyo, 12 May 1942, HW1/500, PRO.

35. Suni to Tokyo, 6 April 1942, HW1/495.

36. Report of the Italian ambassador, Madrid, 13 May 1942, HW1/578, PRO.

37. Alba, London, to Foreign Minister, Madrid, 1 Nov. 1942, HW1/1033, PRO.

38. Viscount Templewood (Sir Samuel Hoare), *Ambassador on Special Mission* (London: Collins, 1946), pp. 15-16.

39. Patterson to Hull, 1 Aug. 1942.

40. Welles to FDR, 3 Aug. 1942, PSF.

41. Bowers to Welles, 4 Sept. 1942, Sumner Welles Papers Official Correspondence, 1920-1946, Box 46, FDR Archives, Hyde Park. Cited hereafter as Welles.

42. Bowers to Welles, 17 Sept. 1942, Welles.

43. Bowers to Welles, 18 Sept. 1942, Welles.

44. Bowers to FDR, 10 Sept. 1942, PSF.

45. Bowers to Barros, 5 Sept., vol. 2012, ADRE.

46. Bowers to Barros, 5 Sept., vol. 2012, ADRE.

47. Bowers' summary of his talks with Ríos is attached to a letter from Bowers to Barros, 2 Oct., vol. 2012, ADRE.

48. Bowers to Barros, 25 Sept., vol. 2012, ADRE.

49. Barros to Ríos, 9 Oct., #297, boveda 14, vol. 9, ADRE.

50. Peter Tennant, *Touchlines of War* (Hull, England: University of Hull Press, 1992), especially pp. 270-272. Tennant, a British propagandist based in Sweden throughout World War II, referred to Sweden's record as "somewhat inglorious" (p. 272).

51. Transradio Chilena to von Schön, 9 Oct. 1942, frame 88789.

52. Bowers to Barros, 20 Oct., ADRE.

53. Ernesto Barros to Tobias Barros, 14 Sept. (#141) and 7 Oct. (#154), vol. 1968, ADRE. See also the message sent by Ernesto Barros to Conrado Ríos, Chilean Ambassador in Buenos Aires, 6 Oct., #292, Boveda 14, vol. 9, ADRE.

54. Tokyo to Buenos Aires, 14 Oct., #963-964, NAC.

55. Yamagata to Buenos Aires, 2 Nov., #1125, NAC.

56. The file on outgoing messages from the Chilean Embassy in Berlin is vol. 1969, while that on outgoing messages from the Chilean Embassy in Rome is vol. 2044, ADRE. To see the Japanese diplomatic traffic, examine the file of Canadian intercepts, R.G. 24, vol. 20307, National Archives of Canada, Ottawa.

57. Welles's speech appears in full in *El Correo de Valdivia*, 9 Oct. 1942.

58. Bowers to FDR, 15 Oct. 1942, PSF.

59. *El Mercurio*, 10 Oct. 1942.

60. *El Llanquihue* (Puerto Montt), 10 Oct. 1942.

61. *El Correo de Valdivia*, 10 Oct. 1942.

62. A copy of Ríos's letter of 11 Oct. 1942 to President Roosevelt appeared on the front page of *El Llanquihue* (Puerto Montt), 12 Oct. 1942.

63. The statement appeared in *El Llanquihue* (Puerto Montt), 22 Oct. 1942.

64. *El Llanquihue* (Puerto Montt), 22 Oct. 1942.

65. *El Correo de Valdivia*, 23 Oct. 1942.

66. Bowers to FDR, 19 Oct. 1942, PSF.

67. Von Schön via Buenos Aires to AA, 21 Oct. 1942, frame 88818. See also Ernesto Barros to Tobias Barros, 21 Oct., #162, vol. 1968, ADRE; Sater, pp. 117-118; *Annales de la Republica*, p. 610.

68. Ernesto Barros to Tobias Barros, 21 Oct., #162, vol. 1968, ADRE.

69. Ernesto Barros to Conrado Ríos, 21 Oct., #303, Boveda 14, vol. 9, ADRE.

70. *Times of London*, 22 and 23 Oct. 1942.

71. Schaumburg-Lippe, Valparaíso, via Buenos Aires, to Berlin, 28 Oct. 1942, frame 88850.

72. Von Schön via Buenos Aires to AA, 4 November 1942 (frames 88892-88893), 7 Nov. (frames 88894-88896), and 18 Nov. (frame 88916).

73. Telegrammkontroller, 20 Nov. 1942, frame 88928. For further information about the arrests of people associated with PYL, see Hoover to Hopkins, 2 Nov. 1942, Hopkins.

74. Associated Press report from *Le Devoir* (Montreal), 24 Nov. 1942.

75. Bowers to Welles, 28 Oct. 1942, Welles.

76. Bowers to Welles, 7 Nov. 1942, Welles.

77. Published in *El Mercurio* (Santiago) and *El Llanquihue* (Puerto Montt), 4 Nov. 1942.

78. For example, *El Llanquihue* (Puerto Montt), 4 Nov. 1942.

79. *El Mercurio*, 11 Nov. 1942.

80. Hull to Bowers, 23 Nov. 1942, *FRUS, 1942*, VI.

81. Yamagata to Buenos Aires, 27 Oct. and 9 Dec., #s 1087-1088 and 1297-1300, NAC.

82. Yamagata to Tokyo, 1247, RG 24, vol. 20307, NAC.

83. Tobias Barros to Fernández, 30 Oct., #483, vol. 1969, ADRE.

84. Wörmann, AA, 23 Oct. 1942, frames 88827-88828.

85. Labra to Fernández, 21 Nov., #75, vol. 2049, ADRE.

86. Statement broadcast on Radio Tokyo, 21 Nov. 1942, 6:10 p.m., and 24 Nov. 11 a.m. recorded by the Short Wave Department of the Australian Broadcasting Commission, Melbourne; Australian Archives, Melbourne. Cited hereafter as Melbourne.

87. Radio Tokyo, 1:15 p.m., 16 Jan. 1943, Melbourne.

88. Ríos to Fernández, 31 Oct., #430, Boveda 14, vol. 10, ADRE.

89. Ernesto Barros to Conrado Ríos, 30 April, #122, Boveda 14, vol. 9, ADRE.

90. Fernández's reply to note #448 from Conrado Ríos, 13 Nov., #324, Boveda 14, vol. 9, ADRE.

91. Yamagata to Buenos Aires, 24 Oct., #1019, NAC.

92. See Durán's speech, "HAY QUE HACER EFECTIVOS LOS LAZOS HISTORICOS Y CULTURALES QUE UNEN A CHILE Y ARGENTINA" ("We ought to strengthen the historical and cultural ties which united Chile and Argentina") published on the front page of El Mercurio 13 Nov. 1942.

93. Yamagata to Buenos Aires, 24 Oct., #1002, NAC.

94. Yamagata to Tokyo, 22 June, #403-404, NAC.

95. Yamagata to Buenos Aires, 2 Nov., #1125, NAC.

96. Yamagata to Buenos Aires, 31 Oct., #1053, NAC.

97. Yamagata to Buenos Aires, 12 Nov. and 5 Dec., #1260, NAC.

98. FBI, pp. 128, 216.

99. Yamagata to Buenos Aires, 5 and 9 Dec., #1271, #1297-1300, NAC.

100. Fernández to Conrado Ríos, 28 Oct., #310, boveda 14, vol. 9, ADRE.

101. Fernández to Tobias Barros, 29 Oct. #55, vol. 1968, ADRE.

102. Fernández to Conrado Ríos, 13 Nov., #326, boveda 14, vol. 9, ADRE.

103. Fernández to Conrado Ríos, 13 Nov., #324, boveda 14, vol. 9, ADRE.

104. Dr. F. Pavlasek to Eduardo Grove, 29 and 30 Oct. and 9 Nov. 1942, vol. 1981, ADRE.

105. Pavlasek to Grove, 21 Nov. 1942, vol. 1981, ADRE.

106. Tobias Barros to Fernández, 12 Nov., #259, vol. 1969, ADRE.

107. Fernández to the Chilean Embassy in Rome, 11 Nov., s/n, vol. 2043, ADRE.

108. Fernández to Conrado Ríos, 27 Oct., #308, boveda 14, vol. 9, ADRE.

109. Fernández to Tobias Barros, 11 Dec., #196, vol. 1968.

110. Barriga to Fernández, 11 Dec., s/n, vol. 2043, ADRE.

111. Bowers to FDR, 29 Oct. 1942.

112. Bowers to FDR, 7 Nov. 1942, PSF.

113. Bowers to Welles, 14 Nov. 1942, PSF.

114. Bowers to Welles, 19 Oct. 1942, Welles.

115. Ríos to Welles, 15 Nov. 1942, PSF.

116. Ríos to FDR, 2 Dec. 1942, PSF; Bowers to FDR, 7 Dec. 1942, PSF; FDR to Ríos, 23 Dec. 1942, PSF.

117. Memorandum of Conversation by the Under Secretary of State (Welles), Washington, 17 Dec. 1942, *FRUS, 1942*, VI, pp. 41-42.

118. Hull to Bowers, 18 Dec. 1942, *FRUS, 1942*, VI, pp. 43-44.

119. Memorandum of Conversation, by the Under Secretary of State (Welles), 22 Dec. 1942, *FRUS, 1942*, VI, pp. 44-46.

120. Morales's return to Chile is described in *La Nación* (Santiago), 6 Jan. 1943; the official statement in the issue of 7 Jan.

121. Weekly Political Intelligence Summary No. 191, Foreign Office (Research Department), 2 June 1943, Series A 989/1, Item 43/145/411, Canberra.

122. *El Diario Ilustrado* (Santiago), 16 Jan. 1943.

123. Yamagata to Tokyo, 8 Jan. 1943, Diplomatic "MAGIC" Summaries, R.G. 457, vol. 1, file SRS 837, NARA, College Park. Cited hereafter as MAGIC.

124. Japanese foreign minister Tani to embassy in Buenos Aires, 11 Jan. 1943, SRS 837, MAGIC.

125. Yamagata to Tokyo, 10 Jan. 1943, SRS 837, MAGIC.

126. Yamagata to Tokyo, SRS 839, MAGIC.

127. Arenda Bravo, p. 160.

128. See, for example, *El Mercurio*, 12 Jan. 1943; *El Diario Ilustrado*, 12 Jan. 1943.

129. *FRUS, 1943*, V, pp. 795-826. See also the *New York Times*, 19-21 January 1943.

130. Regarding the trip to the front, see von Weizsäcker memoranda, 30 Oct. 1942 (frame 88862) and n.d. (frames 88863-88865); an unidentified memorandum (because of an illegible signature), n.d., (frame 88891); Wörmann memoranda, 9 Nov. (frame 88897)) and 15 Nov. (frame 88913). Regarding the sale of saltpetre, see von Weizsäcker to von Rintelen, Berlin, 2 Dec. 1942 (frame 88937); Proclamation, n.d. (frame 88938); von Rintelen to von Weizsäcker, 3 Dec. 1942 (frame 88939); von Weizsäcker to von Rintelen, 4 Dec. 1942 (frame 88940).

131. *El Diario Ilustrado* (Santiago), 20 Jan. 1943.

132. *El Diario Ilustrado* (Santiago), 20 Jan. 1943.

133. *La Nacion* (Santiago), 19 Jan. 1943.

134. *La Prensa* (Osorno), 21 Jan. 1943.

135. *El Correo de Valdivia*, 21 Jan. 1943.

136. Quoted in *La Prensa* (Osorno), 21 Jan. 1943.

CHAPTER 5

AFTERMATH AND CONCLUSIONS

CHANGES RESULTING FROM THE RUPTURE

The rupture had consequences. The Japanese government arrested Labra; the Chileans in retaliation interned Yamagata. The Association of the Friends of Germany (AAA) disbanded.[1] U.S. Vice-President Henry Wallace visited Chile and made a courtesy call upon President Ríos in March.[2] Ships manufactured in Chile transported U.S. forces to Europe,[3] and President Ríos went to the United States on an official visit.[4] The Axis and Chilean governments spent the best part of a year attempting to arrange the exchange of their respective diplomats.[5] President Ríos obliged the Colegios Alemanes (German schools) to teach a more Chilean curriculum. Ambassador Bowers reported:

> On Saturday [3 July 1943] President Ríos summoned me to the palace...As never before since I have known him, he spoke vigorously against the Germans and the Nazis. He spoke with disgust of the fact that for some years the Chileans tolerated the Germans maintaining

schools with teaching only in German. "All they were taught," he said, "was to Heil Hitler. I have prohibited that and now teaching in all the schools is in Spanish. The fact is that Germans who have been here two and three generations who are Chilean citizens are still at heart and in reality, Germans.[6]

Even the DCB, parent organization of the DJC, outlawed the use of uniforms and promised to emphasize "manual labor and homework" instead of marches.[7]

Actually, the consequences might have taken a very different twist. Japan really valued its legation with Chile. As late as 17 January 1943, Yamagata had been planning to send a husband and wife team, Señor and Señora Enrique Gallardo Nieto, on "an inspection tour" of the United States. The couple would have $5,000 to meet expenses.[8] On 19 January 1943, the day before the Chilean government actually ruptured relations with the Axis, Japanese authorities were planning a coup d'état to oust the Ríos administration and install a more friendly one. Yamagata advised the Japanese Ambassador in Buenos Aires (Tomii) that he had distributed 1,500,000 pesos ($50,000 US) in accordance with instructions from Tokyo. Nothing came of the idea after Ambassador Tomii expressed serious doubts:

> Well, if this opportunity comes after relations are severed, even if by our scheme a pro-Axis government were established, no other American nation would recognize it and it would be treated as a homeless orphan. Such a government would soon peter out. In any event, we would have almost nothing to gain.

> Accordingly, if it is impossible to carry out this machination before the break comes, I think at the moment of rupture Minister Yamagata had better tell these fellows to let the matter drop.[9]

U.S. intelligence officers who studied intercepted Japanese military traffic noted that while Yamagata threatened that a diplomatic rupture might invite Japanese naval action against Chile itself, Tomii in Buenos Aires disagreed. Anxious to maintain Buenos Aires as a listening post on the Western Hemisphere, Ambassador Tomii—whose rank was higher than that of Minister Yamagata—advised Tokyo to proceed "very prudently" in whatever it did.[10]

Nevertheless, plans for a Japanese-sponsored coup did not end at that point. Almost a month later, U.S. intelligence sources intercepted a despatch of 12 February from Tomii which outlined details of a possible coup and mentioned an unnamed "Chilean conspirator [who had] received a further substantial advance from the Japanese." The plot involved the overthrow of the Ríos cabinet but not of President Ríos himself; and while formal diplomatic relations with Japan could not be restored,

> ...the new administration will tie up with Argentina and give Japan every possible consideration, "thereby de facto restoring amicable relations with your empire."

Authors of the MAGIC intelligence series found strong circumstantial evidence that the "Chilean conspirator" was none other than defeated presidential candidate Carlos Ibáñez. First, the conspirator visited Buenos Aires late in January 1943 and discussed arrangements for the coup with Ken Usui, Third Secretary at the Japanese Embassy in Buenos Aires. On 9 February, Usui gave him 5,500,000 Chilean pesos ($177,000 US) for his supporters in case the coup failed. Ibáñez, noted MAGIC Summary Number 329, went to Buenos Aires 27 January and was still there 9 February. Secondly, when a diplomatic rupture had seemed imminent in October 1942, the Japanese Foreign Minister suggested that Yamagata "keep in touch with" Ibáñez in case any contingency plans were necessary. Thirdly, there was Ibáñez's undeniable track record as a protagonist of the Axis. He had accepted German and Japanese money to finance his presidential campaign of 1942, and "Japanese communications indicate that the General has been on intimate terms with the Germans, especially von Bohlen, the Air Attaché, who was head of the German espionage ring in Chile."[11]

Despite any advantages to the Allied cause, the rupture meant that Chilean diplomats were no longer in a position to help Poles in Italy, Jews in Croatia, or Czechs in France. Any Chilean appeals to human decency would fall upon deaf ears in Berlin, Rome, or Tokyo. However, opportunities to render assistance had not been numerous, and when they were there, Chilean authorities had not always grasped them.

ONGOING PROBLEMS

The decision to close the Axis diplomatic and consular posts won praise in the expected quarters. On 21 January, 1943, El Mercurio's editorial, "Hemispheric solidarity," lauded the decision.

> Chile has responded with honour to the call of its brothers throughout America and to the call of the democratic conscience which requires it to align itself with those who with their blood are defending the principles of liberty and justice.

The following day El Mercurio noted that the British Foreign Secretary, Anthony Eden, had expressed approval, as did King George VI himself and the presidents of most of the Latin American republics. Because, however, President Roosevelt had gone to Casablanca, Morocco, for a secret meeting with Prime Minister Churchill, he did not comment for almost a week, and Bowers found the silence from the White House "painfully embarrassing." He had sufficient trust in Ríos and Fernández that he informed the two of them, but he could not make any public explanation.[12]

The Argentine Ambassador left Chile's Foreign Ministry "with a grave face" after learning that the suspension had actually happened, although Argentine Foreign Minister Enrique Ruiz said that his country's relations with Chile would not be affected.[13] Argentine President Ramón S. Castillo made a similar assertion.[14]

Yet they were affected. When the rupture took place, Japanese officials thought that it might be possible to evacuate their no-longer-accredited diplomats from Chile to Argentina. The Argentine government refused permission "on the ground that it would be contrary to the promises which Argentina has made to the other American states."[15] By February, Argentina and Japan found themselves on a collision course over the sending of ciphered messages, and Japan was ready to make threats if it could not have its way. The Argentine government had limited the number and length of such messages, to the consternation of the Japanese Navy. Foreign Minister Shigemitsu Tani advised his embassy in Buenos Aires:

> Our Naval authorities in Argentina have a special means of gathering information on enemy countries that we cannot get in any other way, and since this is absolutely essential in the prosecution of our war, we have decided to make some sacrifices and let the Navy have a larger share of the allotted words.

This arrangement was not successful, and Tokyo wanted Buenos Aires to raise the quota of allowable ciphered words. Tani wrote to Tomii:

> If they [the Argentines] don't act as we wish, go ahead and tell them that if they do not change their policy we will have to take some retaliatory steps.[16]

Yet Argentina held firm.[17]

Ambassador Tomii predicted that "so long as Castillo is President [of Argentina] there will be no change in Argentina's neutrality in spite of the machinations of the United States,[18] and Tomii was correct. However, on 4 June 1943—after the Axis capitulation in Tunisia, Castillo fell from power in a coup d'état. The Axis diplomats appear to have been surprised by this development and, across the Atlantic, Spanish Foreign Minister Jordana explained to Japan's Minister, Suma:

> Recent reports from the diplomats of both North and South America have indicated that the [Axis] defeat in Tunisia was a very great shock to the people of Argentina and engendered in them the spirit of revolution which resulted in the above action being taken.[19]

On 12 June 1943, barely one week after Castillo's ouster, the new Argentine foreign minister sent a message to his chargé d'affaires in Berlin. In the interests of hemispheric solidarity and "the common cause of American security," he said, the Argentine government had prohibited the use of cipher "in international radio communications." This new regulation had taken effect two days earlier.[20] The German and Japanese, but not the Italian, governments protested, but in vain. The Argentine foreign minister told diplomats from the three Axis powers that economic pressure from the United States was making it increasingly difficult for Argentina to maintain neutrality.[21]

Seven months later, after the Allied victory in the Battle of the Atlantic, the expulsion of the Axis from Africa, Italy's defection to the Allied cause, and further German setbacks in the Soviet Union, Argentina followed Chile's lead and closed the Axis posts. Until that happened, the Axis belligerents could transfer some of their Chilean-based activities to Argentina and minimize the impact of their rupture with Chile.[22]

This they may have done. Certainly by April 1943, Tomii was forwarding to Tokyo the same sort of nonsense that Yamagata had been offering before the break. According to Tomii, the influence of Republican isolationists in the United States was growing. Conservative Democrats were "showing a tendency to collaborate with the Republican Party in order to check the Administration and the Army leaders....Congressional opposition to the Administration's basic policies for prosecution of the war is growing tremendously."[23] Presumably Tomii had his sources.

On 27 May 1943, Tani told his embassy in Buenos Aires:

> Argentina is our principal source of information on enemy shipping, and such information is the basis for the Imperial Navy's strategy; with the situation as it is, it is our desire that the Naval Attaché be given enough leeway in code [cipher] words to enable him to report on enemy shipping without any handicap. Priority should be given to information about ship movements, so see to it that the Naval Attaché has enough code [cipher] groups for these despatches.[24]

The loss of cipher privileges in Argentina was a serious matter.

(Argentina's new president, Edelmiro Farrell replaced Castillo as head of state. The Farrell government was so partial to the Axis that the U.S. refused to grant diplomatic recognition for several months. By then the war situation was such that Argentina was limited as to the facilities which it could offer the Axis belligerents.)

The Spanish embassy in Santiago remained a possible conduit for information to the Axis belligerents. Spain became the official protector of German and Italian interests in Chile, while Sweden assumed responsibility for those of Japan.[25] That, of course, did not mean that Spanish diplomats could not provide the Japanese with information. Within days of Pearl Harbor, the Japanese Foreign Office had asked several Japanese diplomats in neutral countries the following questions:

a. What authoritative information will the Government to which you are accredited give us?

b. What information is available from secret connections with nationals of that Government?[26]

One of the most helpful neutral governments had been that of Spain whose Foreign Minister, Ramón Serrano (Franco's brother-in-law), was an enthusiastic supporter of the Axis.[27] By 9 January 1942 Japan's legation in Madrid could advise Tokyo that "the man who is responsible for our information here" had, at Serrano's request, called on the minister "to help Japan out by planning the means of gathering intelligence reports from the United States."[28] Evidence presented in earlier chapters indicates that Spanish diplomats assisted German as well as Japanese diplomats, and not only in the United States. Spanish diplomats were able to report on ship movements, as they did in April 1942 when nationals from Axis countries sailed from Arica.[29] On 10 May 1943 Bowers said that the Spanish embassy was organizing an "Indo-American Society" to continue the work of the AAA.[30] On 1 February 1944, by which time the Allies were definitely "closing the ring" on the remaining Axis belligerents, Germany and Japan, Bowers asked Washington to use its influence to pressure Franco to "cease using Spanish diplomatic missions in Latin America in such a manner as to serve the Axis and create prejudices against the United States.[31]

Churchill too had reason for concern about Spaniards who were spying for the Axis. Intercepted Spanish and Japanese diplomatic traffic removed any doubt on the issue, and while there was no evidence of bad faith towards the host governments on the part of Juan Cárdenas and the Duke of Alba, Spanish ambassadors in Washington and London respectively, Churchill knew that what they reported to Madrid often did not stop there. On 31 March 1943, Spain's Foreign Minister—Count Francisco Gómez Jordana, the Count of Jordana—forwarded to Suma information on Anglo-American relations which Cárdenas had sent him.[32] A report of 20 April 1943 written by the Duke of Alba also found its way to Tokyo.[33]

As head of Japan's' legation in Madrid, Suma received a wide range of interesting intelligence reports from the United States. On 21 January 1943—three days before Roosevelt and Churchill revealed their presence to journalists in North Africa—Suma forwarded to Tokyo one such report from Washington. The U.S.-based correspondent said, "I learn from a very secret source that CHURCHILL has gone to North AFRICA to settle political and military questions there." Suma's source also provided information on the state of the defences along the California coast and shipments of strategic material from New York.[34] Two days later, Suma provided details on a U.S. shipping route between Trinidad, where the United States had formidable air and naval bases, and New Orleans.[35] On 27 April 1943, Suma sent Tokyo further information about convoys, again supplied by his source in Washington.[36]

Thanks to Suma, Churchill could observe that Franco's new foreign minister—Count Gómez Jordana—appeared to be no friend of the Allies. With the British seizure of Gibraltar and the Spanish-American War in mind, Jordana discounted Allied promises "to respect the sovereign rights of Spain" at the time of the Operation Torch.[37] In February 1943, Jordana offered Suma "his heartiest congratulations" after the Japanese navy had sunk "capital ships which the Americans confidently believed to be unsinkable." Jordana also told Suma that if Churchill visited the Iberian Peninsula, he personally would refuse to meet him.[38] Historian Javier Tusell has explained that Jordana's actions were more important than his rhetoric. According to Tusell, Jordana's moves from Serrano's pro-Axis policies to more neutral ones were almost "imperceptible," but they were consistent. Jordana did not want to go out of his way to antagonize the Axis,[39] and at times the Allies might have reasons not to trust him. Churchill knew that the *Abwehr* operated from Melilla in North Africa, from Madrid itself, and from Algeciras—within sight of Gibraltar.[40] Spanish archival sources indicate that Jordana wanted Spain to be truly neutral, not partial toward Axis or Allies. First, he took action to limit Spain's support of the Axis. Very soon after he replaced Serrano at the Foreign Office, Jordana wrote a memo which warned that too close an association with the Axis belligerents was not in Spain's interest. Spain, noted Jordana, had "extensive interests" in Spanish America and ought to protect them. They could be in jeopardy if Spain antagonized the United States and Latin American countries by being perceived as the "instrument of their enemies." Jordana urged "strict prudence and scrupulous caution." He also suggested a withdrawal of official support from the Spanish government for Falangist activities throughout Spanish America.[41] (Falangists, supporters of Franco, might give Franco's Spain a bad image.)

Five months later, Jordana took action which the U.S. government would have disapproved. When Chilean authorities did decide to break with the Axis, Jordana wrote to the governments of Portugal and Argentina expressing concern that the Latin bloc of neutral countries–Spain, Portugal, Argentina, Chile—which might mediate the dispute between the Anglo-Americans and the Germans, was disintegrating.[42] Furthermore, he asked Spain's ambassador to Chile, Juan Ignacio Luca de Tena, to use whatever influence he had to persuade the Ríos government not to make the break. Luca replied that Jordana must accept the rupture. It was inevitable. Bolivia and Peru had irridentist land claims against Chile dating back to the War of the Pacific, said Luca. If Chile remained out of step with the rest of the Western Hemisphere, said Luca, the Ríos government feared that other countries would ally themselves beside Peru and Bolivia, against Chile.[43]

For their part, because the Allies sought to maintain Spanish neutrality, such as it was, and to avoid active Spanish military collaboration with Germany and Italy, there were limits as to what they could do to restrain Franco and his representatives.[44] If they could not stop them within the United States and the United Kingdom, they could hardly ask other countries to sever diplomatic relations with Spain.

Fortunately such a rupture proved unnecessary. For reasons quite unrelated to Chile, Franco's government began to distance itself from the Axis early in 1943, and by mid-year, the chasm was significant. On 7 February 1943, U.S. intelligence sources in Bern, the Swiss capital, noted that Soviet victories on the eastern front were causing such minor Axis partners as Romania, Hungary, and Finland, and such neutrals as Turkey, Spain, and Sweden to reassess their foreign policies.

> Turkey, Spain and Sweden all foresee the possibility of an American-British victory, and they are all reviewing their foreign policies. Spain has apparently already changed from non-belligerency to neutrality.[45]

By April 1943, when the U.S. army in Morocco and Algeria and the British army in Egypt were forcing the German and Italian armies to retreat to Tunisia, Allied victories in North Africa appeared to be having a similar effect.[46]

U.S. intelligence was well aware of Madrid's importance as an intelligence-gathering centre for the Axis.[47] It also knew that the Axis spy agency "TO," headed by Spaniard Angel Alcazar de Velasco, forwarded considerable information from the United States and next to nothing from Chile.[48] Because of Spain's significance to the Axis war effort, Japanese authorities sought permission to elevate their legation in Madrid to an embassy and to open a consulate in Tangier, where spies could monitor Allied ships as they entered or departed from the Mediterranean.[49] Official

Washington was aware that Franco's government denied these requests.[50] (Washington also had a double agent in "TO," José María Aladrén.) Before his departure from Madrid, Aladrén had informed U.S. ambassador Carlton Hayes he was going to the United States to spy for "TO." Inside the United States, Aladrén co-operated with the FBI and other U.S. government agencies.[51] Hence, U.S. authorities had some idea of what Spanish officialdom was doing.

There is no evidence at the archives of Spain's Foreign Office, the Ministerio de Asuntos Exteriores in Madrid, that the Spanish embassy used its role as Protector of German interests in any inappropriate manner. What documents there are show that in January, 1944, Spain's embassy, under a new ambassador, the Marqués de los Arcos, became involved when the Chilean government placed restrictions on German financial institutions such as the Banco Alemán Transatlántico and the Banco Germánica de América del Sur. De los Arcos reported what was happening to his superiors in Madrid, who undoubtedly relayed the news to Berlin. Whatever evidence there may have been of Spanish espionage on behalf of Germany has disappeared.[52]

Quite independently of Allied victories, the behaviour of Japanese forces in the Philippines—until 1898 a Spanish possession—alienated Spanish sympathies. In May 1943, Jordana angrily presented Suma with a list of Spanish grievances. Japanese authorities had dropped Spanish as an official language in the Philippines while retaining English, the language of Spain's American enemy which had captured the archipelago in 1898 and which was currently fighting Japan. Bishop Miguel-Angelo Olano was being treated as a Japanese prisoner. It was next to impossible for Spaniards to send money to the Philippines, and telegraphic communications between the foreign office in Madrid and the Spanish legation in Tokyo were erratic. "The Spanish Consul in Manila isn't being treated like a consul," said Jordana. Nor, despite repeated promises of reassurance from Japanese officials could Jordana find any signs of improvement.[53]

Juan Cárdenas, Spain's ambassador to the United States, had his own reasons for anger at the Japanese. Always the professional diplomat, on 17 February 1943, Cárdenas protested misuse of the diplomatic pouch, which Japanese officials had used for sending $400 to double-agent Aladrén (whom Cárdenas did not know to be a double agent). Said Cárdenas to Jordana:

> Since the importation of banknotes is absolutely forbidden, I beg of your Excellency not to permit such shipments...because of the serious results such shipments can cause our Embassy here and the harm they can do to our interests.[54]

Politeness turned to anger when Japanese officials attempted to smuggle $15,000 worth of Japanese pearls into the United States in the Spanish diplomatic pouch. Such activities, warned Cárdenas, would jeopardize Spanish interests.[55] As the Axis cause deteriorated, there were definite limits to Jordana's willingness to render assistance. When the short-lived Argentine government of General Pedro P. Ramírez banned the sending of ciphered radio messages 10 June 1943, Suma asked Jordana whether Spanish diplomats would forward such messages on behalf of Japan. Jordana refused to co-operate.[56]

For reasons of self-interest, Spanish support for the Axis waned, and this soon became evident to Axis officials—as well as to Americans in the intelligence community who intercepted Spanish and Axis diplomatic messages. Late in April 1943, Spain withdrew from its role as Protector of German interests in Chile and transferred its responsibilities to Switzerland.[57] The following month, Suma explained to his government why Spain was "turning away from the Axis." By then the Allies had ousted the Axis from Tunisia and controlled all North Africa. Spaniards no longer feared a German invasion of Spain, but Allied forces were close at hand.[58] Japan's foreign minister and Mussolini's ambassador to Japan had already drawn similar conclusions.[59] Not long thereafter, German officials in Berlin were thinking along the same lines.[60] The fall of Mussolini's government in the summer of 1943 reinforced the developing chasm between the pragmatic government of Generalíssimo Franco and his erstwhile Axis partners.[61] In October 1943, Spain reverted from its self-proclaimed status of non-belligerency to neutrality.[62]

The rupture was certainly not a panacea. According to U.S. intelligence sources, on 20 January 1943—hours before the rupture took effect—Yamagata advised: "We have a simple means for communication between Chile and Argentina, which can be safely used following the break in relations." Nor was Yamagata bluffing. On 7 March Yamagata—still in Chile—sent ciphered messages to Tomii for forwarding to Tokyo.[63]

At the same time, Nazi organizers continued to meet throughout southern Chile, and in December 1943 Bowers lamented "that Nazi organizations in Chile continue to operate clandestinely, that the Germans connected with these organizations have little or no fear of action against them on the part of the Chilean Government; ...and that the Nazis in Chile plan to carry on the campaign of National Socialism even though Germany is defeated."[64] Espionage by Axis agents continued to be a cause for concern throughout 1944.[65]

Despite the rupture, an estimated 400 people connected with the German embassy remained active within Chile. Bowers wanted them "out of the country" and regarded their departure as "our primary object in asking [for] a rupture of relations. That the British Embassy would oppose their repatriation struck him as "absurd," for "there is every indication that they may remain and continue their work." A Spanish ship scheduled to sail from Buenos Aires in May would not be making the trip until July, lamented Bowers, and he suspected that Franco was deliberately assisting the Axis belligerents. The longer the 400 remained in Chile, the greater their usefulness to the Axis cause would be. Fernández favoured the departure of the 400, said Bowers, and the U.S. embassy in Madrid might ask the Spanish government to move more quickly.[66] President Roosevelt replied that he would discuss the matter with Lord Halifax, the British ambassador in Washington, but warned that the 400 might be less dangerous in Chile than in Germany, where

...they would immediately be put to work to relieve the increasingly acute manpower shortage in that country. The German government is, as you know, most anxious to have these people come home.[67]

Bowers remained convinced that German diplomats were still in a position to do harm in Chile. On 10 May he told President Roosevelt that Allied victories in North Africa had

...convinced the most stubborn pro-Nazis here that Hitler is completely lost. The pro-German element has been scotched and unable to do much, its organization proscribed.[68]

However, on 8 June, he reiterated his complaints about the ongoing presence of the 400 and the obstructionist activities of the British embassy in keeping them there. Fernández wanted them out, said Bowers, but the British kept finding "flaws in the arrangement." The latest British pretext was that the Germans might carry undesirable documents or strategic materials in their luggage. Bowers strongly disagreed: "Better far a hundred tons of copper in the baggage and these men out, than the copper in Chile and these men in."[69] Even after the diplomats had sailed back to Europe in September 1943, eleven months after closure of the notorious German consulate in Valdivia, Bowers referred to that south Chilean city as "the German and pro-Nazi section" of Chile.[70] President Ríos agreed that Valdivia remained "a problem," where there were too many Nazis whose first loyalty was to Hitler rather than to Chile.[71]

Nor did the diplomatic rupture resolve the problem of German-sponsored clandestine radio stations. Radio station PYL remained on the air until its discovery at Quilpué 27 October 1943.[72] It was action by Chile's police, not the closure of the German embassy, which terminated PYL. Moreover, PYL was not the only outlet of its kind in Chile. PQZ continued to function for an additional sixteen months.

Bolivian foreign policy, which had influenced Ríos and Fernández in their decision to break with the Axis, continued to concern Fernández throughout 1943. At the end of March, Bolivia decided to declare war upon the Axis, and its government suggested that the other four nations liberated by Bolívar—Venezuela, Colombia, Ecuador, and Peru—should do likewise. Fernández thought that such declarations of war would not strengthen the Allied cause militarily, and he charged:

> Bolivia wishes to declare war in order to obtain U.S. support for her claims to a seaport and to justify building up military strength in preparation for a possible conflict with Chile.[73]

In September, Fernández visited Río de Janeiro to discuss Chilean-Bolivian relations with Brazilian authorities and to win support.[74] The Axis belligerents were not the only foreigners who alarmed the government of Chile in 1943.

In 1944 the FBI's J. Edgar Hoover outlined the facts about PQZ to Harry Hopkins, Special Assistant to President Roosevelt. Hoover's report included pictures and names of "the many espionage agents and the equipment used by them in the operation of extensive German espionage activities in Santiago, Chile." Chilean authorities made the discoveries and made the documentation available to Ambassadors Bowers, who in turn gave it to the FBI. On 15 February 1944, the Chilean government began to arrest more than ninety people, "including persons of German nationality, Chileans of German descent and Chilean nationals."

According to Hoover, the ninety sought "security information" about the United States and other countries of the Western Hemisphere and also planned a campaign of sabotage. Documents linked the ninety to German embassy officials who had been in Santiago, and the operation continued to function long after the embassy staff's repatriation. Chilean authorities found $174,150 in U.S. currency, plus an additional $27,000 in Argentine and Chilean currency and bonds.[75]

Months after the break, Ambassador Bowers thought that "many" officers in the Chilean army continued "to be...pro-Nazi."[76] In 1944, Hoover told Hopkins that high ranking Chilean military officers, including the Army Chief of Staff, appeared to be involved with PQZ and its activities. So problematic was the Army situation, said Hoover, "that President Ríos has become alarmed and may stop further investigation of this case." Almost certainly one officer submitted reports to Ludwig von Bohlen, a.k.a. Bach, until von Bohlen left Chile in September 1943.[77] Events of the 1950s and 1970s confirm Bowers's impression of ongoing Nazi values among some army officers.

Bowers regarded Allied military victories as more important than the rupture itself in winning Chilean good will and minimizing Axis influence. The liberation of North Africa in the first half of 1943 was a first step.[78] On 9 June 1944, he told President Roosevelt that the United States had won considerable good will in Chile by "taking Rome...without destroying any of the religious or historic buildings."[79] Two and one-half months later, he reported pro-American demonstrations following the liberation of Paris. The demonstrators ignored the British, said Bowers.[80]

EPILOGUE

Chile did not actually enter the war until February 1945, by which time the State Department was threatening that failure to enter the war would mean Chile's exclusion from the United Nations. Fernández found the pressure from Washington "meaningless and possibly embarrassing." Members of the Ríos administration regretted that it came at a time when there was no obvious reason for a declaration of war and feared that Senators and others would think that the Ríos administration lacked the will or ability to protect Chilean interests.[81] Chile's principal contribution to the Allied effort had been the sale of copper at prices well below the market value.[82]

Even then German espionage continued, headed by the veteran spy Albert Julius von Appen, a.k.a., "Apfel" until his arrest in March 1945. Von Appen was a businessman with the Hamburg-American Line for South America, not a diplomat, and his network extended into Peru, Argentina, Brazil, Colombia, and Venezuela. Chilean authorities first arrested him in October 1942 when they smashed PYL, then released him. After Chile's declaration of war and subsequent "ship disasters," they arrested him again. With the war in Europe almost over, Von Appen confessed that,

> ...he had been instructed in sabotage at a school at Charlottenburg, Germany, in 1939. He came to South America equipped with explosives and codes and organized a ring with associates in the countries mentioned above. Von Appen has stated that since October, 1942...he has divorced himself from the sabotage activities and that no sabotage has ever been committed by his organization.

Concluded J. Edgar Hoover, "Von Appen's confession reveals the scope of German plans for sabotage in South America, and also reflects that these plans have not been effective."[83]

For various reasons, Ríos did not manage to visit the United States until the autumn of 1945, by which time President Roosevelt had died and President Harry Truman was the one to receive him. The first Chilean president to make a state visit to Washington, Ríos also visited Canada and thirteen Latin American countries on the same trip. He was not well when he travelled, and he died the following year.[84]

Nazi influence in the army—and elsewhere—remained a problem for the rest of the twentieth century. Carlos Ibáñez did win Chile's presidential election of 1952—taking less than half the vote in a field of four candidates. In January 1954, Ibáñez appointed as his Foreign Minister none other than Tobias Barros, former Chilean Ambassador to Hitler's Germany and winner of the Order of the German Eagle. In June of that same year, Barros became Minister of Defence. Under his leadership, one could not anticipate a purge of Nazi sympathizers in the armed forces. Because relations with Argentina had been tense, within days of taking office President Ibáñez sent Conrado Ríos back to Argentina as Chile's ambassador. Argentine President Juan Perón (1946-1955) had welcomed Nazis and Nazi sympathizers to Argentina as possible modernizers. When Perón fell in 1955 and went into exile, some of these people thought that they should migrate again, and some went to Chile. Given his World War II track record, it would have been out of character for Conrado Ríos to be concerned about such matters.

Of Nazis who may have moved from Argentina to Chile when Perón fell, the most notorious has to be Walter Rauff. Rauff had been an SS captain who found more efficient ways to exterminate Jews with gas. Transferred to Italy to take charge of intelligence operations, he was there when the war ended. Assisted by Bishop Alois Hudal, an Austrian who headed a Roman Catholic college in Rome, he helped fugitive Nazis to escape. In 1949, his mission accomplished, he too went to South America, first to Buenos Aires, then to Punta Arenas in Chile. There he operated a fish-packing plant. The Pinochet régime appointed him a director of DINA, its secret police, and when the Israelis requested Rauff's extradition, Pinochet's foreign minister replied that it was "inappropriate to expel a [Chilean] citizen who has lived 20 years in the country."[85]

The values of the AAA survived within the Chilean armed forces long after World War II. In 1986—less than eleven years after Franco's death—the present author visited the Alcazar, a fortress in Toledo, and read the notices there. From 21 to 28 July 1936, forces loyal to Spain's democratically elected republican government besieged the Alcazar. Forces loyal to Generalíssimo Franco, then engaged in an attempt to destroy the republican government, withstood the siege and, almost three years later, won the Civil War. In January 1973, nine months before Pinochet's coup, the Chilean army congratulated Franco and his Falangists for withstanding the siege. The Chilean air force followed suit in 1975, as did the Carabineros (Chilean police) in 1976. Others who congratulated the Falangists for defeating the "Communists" included branches of the Argentine military and Spanish veterans of the Blue Division, who had fought beside German forces on the Soviet front between 1941 and 1944.

Naziism has other manifestations in modern Chile. Chilean Nazis still commemorate their failed Putsch of 5 September 1938. Men dressed in brown shirts and black boots march each year to the place in the Santiago General Cemetery where Swastikas surround a small-scale replica of the

Washington Monument. Engraved on the monument are the names of the fifty-five Nazis who died in 1938.[86] Canadian author Lake Sagaris identifies Sergio Onofre Jarpa, appointed Pinochet's Minister of the Interior 10 August 1983, as a former member of Chile's Nazi party.[87]

In July 1989, four months before the Berlin Wall opened, General Pinochet told a couple of Chilean journalists, Raquel Correa and Elizabeth Subercaseaux, that Communists worried him considerably more than did Nazis. "Hitlerism has disappeared," he said. "Stalinism has not."[88] That Hitler's heritage survived through Rauff, Onofre Jarpa, and those who celebrated the events of 5 September 1938 appeared of little concern.

Despite the legacy of death, torture, and questionable associates, General Pinochet remains popular in parts of Chile. In February 1997, he vacationed in the resort community of Puerto Varas, 1000 kilometres south of Santiago. He and his entourage (family and bodyguards without uniforms) rented rooms at the Hotel del Lago, but the hotel continued business as usual. It remained possible simply to wander in from the street, order drinks at the bar, and guess who might be a guard. "Everything we have we owe to him," said one resident. "Only Communists dislike him. Before he assumed power, food was in such short supply that people lined up at 5 a.m. to buy what they could. Now our stores and supermarkets have everything."

From Puerto Varas, General Pinochet and his bodyguards made a surprise trip to Puerto Montt, twenty kilometres to the south. They travelled in a cavalcade with windows blackened, so that nobody from the street could tell which car was Pinochet's, and guards talked on cellular phones. However, they made unexpected visits to Puerto Montt's ultramodern Paseo del Mar shopping mall and the Central Café. Women surged past his bodyguards to hug and kiss the army commander. "Pleased to see you, General!" was the common greeting. There was widespread applause throughout the cafe, and the customers' only regret was they did not have their cameras to record the occasion.[89]

Carlos Cerda is a Chilean novelist who spent the Pinochet years in East Germany. In 1990, when East Germany collapsed and General Pinochet vacated Chile's presidency, Cerda returned home. In 1993, he released what has become a best-seller, *To Die in Berlin*, now in its fourth edition. In one scene, a Chilean refugee named Mario visited the East German community of Weimar. Weimar, his East German guide noted, was home to such distinguished and civilized Germans as Göthe and Schiller. It was close to Buchenwald, one of Hitler's death camps. Many residents of Weimar were totally unaware of what was happening at Buchenwald. So it must also be in Chile, suggested the East German guide. Many Chileans saw what they wanted to see, equally unaware of the horrors of the Pinochet régime, where thousands were tortured or executed, and many more were driven into exile. How right the fictitious guide was!

It would not be fair to hold Germans or Chileans of German extraction responsible for any surviving Nazi legacy in Chile. Few were insiders of the Pinochet régime. Walter Rauff and like-minded people would have had no influence without extensive support from people whose ethnicity was not German. Reports indicate that most of those who parade into the Santiago General Cemetery each 5 September "do not have blond hair." That is appropriate. Most of the fifty-five who died on that date in 1938 did not have German names.

CHILE AND THE GERMAN CONNECTION TODAY

The bloodshed which some of Bernardo Philippi's contacts had feared overcame Germany between 1914 and 1945. One can argue that the horrors continued in part of Germany until 1989. Happily, as many German-Chileans thought at the time of the Third Reich, Germany was greater than Hitler, and the Federal Republic of Germany has been a postive force, in Chile as in the world as a whole.

As the twentieth century ends, Germany's profile in southern Chile remains highly visible. There is an imposing German Church in Osorno, half a block from the Plaza de Armas. The Federal Republic of Germany has a consulate on Juan Mackenna, one of Osorno's main streets. In the midst of an obviously German section of Puerto Montt stands a modern Iglesia Alemana, built when Karl Steybe was pastor. In Frutillar, the Federal Republic of Germany helped to finance a German colonial museum the size of a city block. Its many buildings and expansive gardens replicate the lifestyle of the nineteenth century pioneers. German Chileans have earned a reputation as effective firefighters. There is even a Confederation of Compañías Chileno-Alemanas de Bomberos (German-Chilean Companies of Firefighters).

Throughout the length of Chile's Tenth Region, as the area from Valdivia to Chiloé has become, the German government subsidizes German schools—each described as a *Deutsche Schule* or *Colegio Alemán*. The flag of the Federal Republic of Germany flies alongside the Chilean flag outside the Deutsche Schule of Valdivia, the nation's most successful school in terms of academic performance in the 1996 Academic Aptitude Tests.[90] The schools encourage Spanish-German bilingualism. Teachers from Germany teach in those schools, and the German-born and -educated rector of the German Institute in Osorno, Dr. Ulrich Rammer, has expressed pleasure that the German language has some relevance to Chile. Dr. Rammer promotes educational goals with which few would argue—an ability to think for oneself and make informed decisions. While most students at the German schools have German ancestors, other Chileans can and do attend.

German architecture is ubiquitous throughout the Tenth Region, and most communities have a German Club (*Deutscher Verein/Club Alemán*) and a German medical clinic (*Clínica Alemán*). Since the Pinochet régime privatized the local hospital, the Clínica Alemán is the only semi-public facility available in Puerto Varas where patients can stay. *Deutsche Welle* is available on cable television. Although there are no German-language newspapers published in the Tenth Region, the Santiago weekly, *Der Condor*, is available. A columnist named Schlager who writes for *El Diario*

Austral in Osorno and *El Llanquihue* in Puerto Montt encourages Chileans to celebrate their ties with Germany.

There is much to celebrate. The German presence is now something to be welcomed, not feared. The German government which spends money and displays interest in Chile is the benign Federal Republic of Germany. Like most Germans anywhere, German-Chileans regard the Third Reich as a bad memory, if they think of it at all. A publication of late 1996 from Osorno which celebrates the 150th anniversary of the arrival of Chile's first German settlers totally ignores events of 1933-1945. Neither the German ambassador to Chile, Dr. Werner Reichenbaum, nor Dr. Rammer, both of whom wrote in German, nor the German-Chileans, all of whom wrote in Spanish, made any reference to that unfortunate period.

Nor do they mention Chile's connection with Communist East Germany, officially known from 1949 to 1990 as the German Democratic Republic. During the Pinochet years, many refugees fled to East Germany, and one of them, Leonardo Yáñez, married a daughter of East German leader Erich Honecker. As a result of that liaison, the Honecker parents moved into daughter Sonia's home in the Santiago suburb of La Reina once East Germany collapsed, only months after the return of democracy to Chile. The Honeckers apparently felt that they had little in common with the German-Chileans of the Tenth Region, and residents of the Tenth Region heartily reciprocated that sentiment.

Karl Anwandter disliked authoritarian government. Georg Aubel, one of the earliest settlers, wrote in 1847, "We have come to a land of freedom." That is the prevailing attitude across the Tenth Region today. Yet, during the Third Reich Germans and Germany represented a threat, not a positive asset, for Chile and the Western Hemisphere.

COMMENTARY

One must be impressed by the evidence marshalled by Ambassador Bowers and FBI director J. Edgar Hoover (who relied on Bowers for much of his information). They knew about Spanish activities, Nazi sympathizers in the

Chilean Army, and ongoing Nazi activities. Events justified the lobbying which Bowers had done to close the embassies. Spanish diplomats could do some of the undercover work for German, Italian, and Japanese officials, and clandestine German radio stations could continue to operate. However, German schools became less subversive, the AAA became less reputable, and the radio stations had to cope with what they had rather than rely on fresh infusions of funds, training, and direction. Spain's government, for reasons unrelated to Chile, began to distance itself from the Axis.

Obviously Bowers had a different perspective from that of the White House, which had to think in global rather than local terms. Given the harm that the Axis diplomats could do, whether they remained in Chile as embassy officials or guests of the state, it is obvious that he would want them out of the country. British authorities and President Roosevelt, however, had to consider their possible contribution to the war effort elsewhere. Given the behaviour of Spanish diplomats, it is understandable that he would seek greater pressure upon Franco. However, London and Washington had to remember the importance of Spanish non-belligerence at a time when Hitler alone presented a formidable challenge.

Given ongoing tensions, including territorial disputes, it certainly was in Chile's interest to cement the relationship with Brazil. From that standpoint alone, the rupture made sense. Still, it is understandable that Chilean diplomats, like Bernstein, would be affected by their immediate environment as well as by any ideological baggage which they might have been carrying. Those stationed in Brazil, site of the Río conference and a World War II belligerent, might be expected to support policies favoured by the Brazilian government. This was especially to be expected of a diplomat named Bernstein who regarded the Axis as "barbarous to an unprecedented degree."[91] At the same time, given his association with former President Ibáñez and his lifelong interest in cordial Chilean-Argentine relations, it was hardly surprising that Ambassador Conrado Ríos in Buenos Aires offered conflicting advice.

There were also no simple solutions to complicated situations. The Axis belligerents did receive information from Chilean sources which threatened the Allied cause. It would have been irresponsible for the Allies to ignore what German, Italian, and Japanese officials were doing and were capable of doing. The rupture left many unresolved problems, but it limited the chances of new damages and dangers and made possible the elimination of certain existing ones. In the end, Allied military victories and Chilean good will counted for more than the closure of Axis diplomatic and consular posts in Chile.

CONCLUSIONS

Closure of the Axis diplomatic and consular posts was a wise policy for President Roosevelt's administration to pursue. It seriously curtailed, although it did not end, Axis capacity for espionage. It strengthened the hand of the Chilean government with regard to schools and lessened the possibility of a German state-within-a-state in southern Chile. It weakened (although it did not destroy) the respectability of Nazi Germany throughout Chile.

Until January 1943, the Axis belligerents benefited from their diplomatic ties, even if commerce with Chile had come to an end. As long as possible, they sought to maintain what links they could. However, they could not take reprisals. There was little choice but to accept the restrictions on ciphered messages, and they could not punish Chile militarily without jeopardy to their interests in Argentina. After the rupture, intelligence gathering necessarily became more difficult.

The United States enjoyed several advantages in its rivalry with the Axis powers in Chile. Restrained as Cordell Hull was during the presidential campaign of 1942, the U.S. had more money—public and private—to spend in Chile than did the Germans, Italians, or Japanese. Other great powers had already broken with one or more of the Axis belligerents, as had most of the Latin American republics. The values of the Allies were considerably more attractive to most Chileans than were the values of the Axis powers.

Fears of U.S. support for Bolivia helped persuade the Chilean government to sever diplomatic relations with the Axis. The rupture then had maximum impact because Allied victories in Europe, North Africa, and the Pacific, as well as Japanese actions in the Philippines, helped to neutralize Argentina and Franco's Spain.

Moreover, to achieve their objective—an end to Axis espionage and subversion in Chile—the U.S. embassy relied upon more than the closure of the Axis diplomatic posts and consulates. Ambassador Bowers struggled to create good will for the United States, by providing weaponry, by influencing the media, by saving an historic church, and by inviting President Ríos and others to Washington. Chilean good will was vital to the isolation of the Axis powers. Successive Allied military victories convinced an increasing number of Chileans that the U.S. would be on the winning side, and that it would not be wise to have antagonized the winner.

NOTES

1. Bowers to Hull, 30 Jan. 1943, *FRUS, 1943*, V, p. 806; see also the *New York Times*, 1 Feb. 1943.

2. *New York Times*, 27-31 March and 1-4 April, 1943.

3. Bowers, p. 121.

4. Bowers, pp. 325-327.

5. Vol. 2093, ADRE; Tobias Barros, II, pp. 428-440.

6. Bowers to Welles, 5 July 1943, PSF.

7. Converse, p. 122.

8. MAGIC Summary No. 306, 26 Jan. 1943, Box 3.

9. MAGIC Summary No. 305, 25 Jan. 1943, Box 3.

10. MAGIC Summary No. 309, 29 Jan. 1943, Box 3.

11. MAGIC, Summary No. 329, 18 Feb. 1943, Box 3.

12. Bowers to FDR, 1 Feb. 1943, PSF. The text of President Roosevelt's congratulatory letter to President Ríos, dated 26 Jan. 1943, is available in the Official File Box 429, PSF.

13. *New York Times*, 21 Jan. 1943.

14. *El Mercurio*, 22 Jan. 1943.

15. MAGIC Summary No. 313, 2 Feb. 1943, Box 3.

16. Magic Summary No. 332, 21 Feb. 1943, Box 3.

17. MAGIC Summary No. 427, 27 May 1943, Box 5.

18. MAGIC Summary No. 337, 26 Feb. 1943, Box 3.

19. MAGIC Summary No. 438, 7 June 1943, Box 5.

20. MAGIC Summary No. 447, 16 June 1943, Box 5.

21. MAGIC Summary No. 452, 21 June 1943, Box 5.

22. For an interpretation of the impact of Chile's diplomatic rupture on Argentina, see Gary Frank, *Struggle for Hegemony in South America: Argentina, Brazil, and the United States during the Second World War* (Miami: Center for Advanced International Studies, University of Miami Press, 1979), pp. 35, 41, 46, 67, 68.

23. MAGIC Summary No. 400, 30 April 1943, Box 4, citing a despatch of 16 April from Tomii.

24. MAGIC Summary No. 427, 27 May 1943, Box 5.

25. Bowers to FDR, 1 Feb. 1943, PSF.

26. MAGIC Summary No. 304, 24 Jan. 1943, vol. I, file SRS 847, MAGIC.

27. Herbert Feis, *The Spanish Story; Franco and the Nations at War* (New York: Knopf, 1948); Max Gallo, *Spain under Franco: A History*, trans. Jean Stewart (New York: Dutton, 1974). See also Antonio Marquina, "L'Espagne et la Deuxième Guerre Mondiale: L'Etape de Ramón Serrabi Suñer et Ministère des Affaires Etrangères,: *Guerres Mondiales et Conflits Contemporains*, CLVIII (1990), pp. 5-22; Javier Tusell, "L'Espagne et la Deuxième Guerre Mondiale: L'Etape Jordana," *ibid.*, pp. 23-39.

28. MAGIC summary No. 304, 24 Jan. 1943, vol. I, file SRS 847, MAGIC.

29. Madrid to Tokyo, 24 April, #s 168 and 169, NAC.

30. Bowers to FDR, 10 May 1943, PSF.

31. Bowers to the State Department, 1 Feb. 1944, PSF.

32. Suma to Tokyo, 31 March 1943, HW1/1557, PRO.

33. Suma to Tokyo, 20 April 1943, HW1/1632, PRO.

34. Suma to Foreign Minister, Tokyo, 21 Jan. 1943, HW1/1332, PRO.

35. Suma to Foreign Minister, Tokyo, 23 Jan. 1943, HW1/1332, PRO.

36. Suma to Foreign Minister, Tokyo, 27 April 1943, HW1/1655, PRO.

37. Suma to Foreign Minister, Tokyo, 17 Nov. 1942, HW1/1137, PRO.

38. Suma to Foreign Minister, Tokyo, 8 Feb. 1943, HW1/1359, PRO.

39. Javier Tusell, "L'Europe et la Deuxième Guerre Mondiale: L'Etape Jordana," *Guerres Mondiales et Conflits Contemporains*, CLVIII (April 1990), pp. 23-39, especially pp. 27 and 34. The word "imperceptible" appears on p. 34.

40. *Abwehr* report from Melilla to Madrid, 9-10 Nov. 1942, HW1/1075; *Abwehr* report from Madrid, 28 Oct. 1942, HW1/1044; *Abwehr* report from Algeciras to Madrid, 11 March 1943, HW1/1476, PRO.

41. Memo "Política Exterior–Problems de Actuación de Falange en el Extranjero," written by Jordana, Madrid, 8 Sept. 1942, Leg. R, Caja 1370, Exp. 9, Ministerio de Asuntos Exteriores, Madrid.

42. Jordana, Madrid, to Spanish Ambassador, Lisbon, 15 Jan. 1943; Jordana, Madrid, to Spanish Ambassador, Buenos Aires, 15 Jan. 1943; Leg. R, Caja 1372, Exp. 1, Ministerio de Asuntos Exteriores, Madrid.

43. Luca de Tena, Santiago, to Jordana, Madrid, 16 Jan. 1943, Leg. R, Caja 1372, Exp. 1, Ministerio de Asuntos Exteriores, Madrid.

44. Carlton J.H. Hayes, *Wartime Mission in Spain, 1942-1945* (New York: Macmillan, 1945); Herbert Feis, *The Spanish Story: Franco and the Nations at War* (New York: Alfred A. Knopf, 1948); Templewood, pp. 15-16.

45. MAGIC Summary No. 318, 7 Feb. 1943, Box 3.

46. Interception of a message from the Argentine ambassador to Spain, intercepted by U.S. intelligence and reported in MAGIC Summary No. 398, 28 April 1943, Box 4.

47. MAGIC Summary No. 323, 12 Feb. 1943, Box 3.

48. MAGIC Summary No. 318, 7 Feb. 1943, Box 3; No. 334, 23 Feb. 1943, Box 3; No. 393, 23 April 1943, Box 4.

49. MAGIC Summary No. 323, 12 Feb. 1943, Box 3.

50. MAGIC Summary No. 416, 16 May 1943, Box 5; No. 426, 26 May 1943, Box 5.

51. MAGIC Summary No. 335, 24 Feb. 1943, Box 3.

52. Arcos, Santiago, to the Foreign Minister, Madrid, 24 Jan. 1944, 17 Feb. 1944, 24 April 1944; Leg. R, Caja 5749, Exp. 25, Ministerio de Asuntos Exteriores, Madrid.

53. MAGIC Summary No. 426, 26 May 1943, Box 5. These were not new problems. See MAGIC Summary No. 329, 18 Feb. 1943, Box 3.

54. MAGIC Summary No. 335, 24 Feb. 1943, Box 3. See also MAGIC Summary No. 31;7, 6 Feb. 1943, Box 3.

55. MAGIC Summary No. 437, 6 June 1043, Box 5.

56. MAGIC Summary No. 477, 16 July 1943, Box 6.

57. MAGIC Summary No. 401, 1 May 1943, Box 5.

58. MAGIC Summary No. 416, 16 May 1943, Box 5.

59. MAGIC Summary No. 409, 9 May 1943, Box 5.

60. MAGIC Summary No. 454, 23 June 1943, Box 5.

61. MAGIC Summary No. 489, 28 July 1943, Box 6; No. 504, 12 Aug. 1943, Box 6; No. 507, 15 Aug. 1943, Box 6.

62. Stuart E. Eizenstat (co-ordinator), *U.S. and Allied Wartime and Postwar Relations and Negotiations with Argentina, Portugal, Spain, Sweden, and Turkey on Looted Gold and German External Assets and U.S. Concerns about the Fate of the Wartime Ustasha Treasury* (Washington: Department of State, 1998), pp. 59-61.

63. MAGIC Summary No. 358, 19 March 1943, Box 4.

64. Bowers to Hull, 20 Dec. 1943, *FRUS, 1943*, V, p. 825.

65. *FRUS, 1944*, VII, pp. 788-802.

66. Bowers to FDR, 1 May 1943, PSF.

67. FDR to Bowers, 19 May 1943, PSF.

68. Bowers to FDR, 17 May 1943, PSF.

69. Bowers to Welles, 8 June 1943, PSF.

70. Bowers to Cordell Hull, 28 Dec. 1943, PSF.

71. Bowers to Welles, 5 July 1943, PSF.

72. Bowers to Fernández, 18 Jan. 1944, *FRUS, 1944*, VII, p. 789.

73. MAGIC Summary No. 386, 16 April 1943, Box 4.

74. MAGIC Summary No. 553, 30 Sept. 1943, Box 6.

75. Hoover to Hopkins, 14 June 1944, R.G. 24, Papers of Harry L. Hopkins, Box 144, FDR.

76. Bowers to Hull, 3 June 1943, *FRUS, 1943*, V, p. 820.

77. Hoover to Hopkins, n.d. but probably Feb. 1944, R.G. 24, Papers of Harry L. Hopkins, FBI Reports, Chile, Box 141, FDR.

78. Welles to FDR, 10 May 1943, PSF.

79. Bowers to FDR, 9 June 1944, PSF.

80. Bowers to FDR, 24 Aug. 1944, PSF.

81. Bowers to Hull, 5 Dec. 1944 and Bowers to President Roosevelt, 12 Dec. 1944, *FRUS,1944*, VII, pp. 691, 697. See also *FRUS, 1945*, pp. 755-770.

82. Drake in Bethell, p. 116.

83. Hoover to Hopkins, 31 March 1945, Papers of Harry L. Hopkins, Box 141, FDR.

84. Germán Gamonal, p. 18.

85. Jorge Camarasa, Odessa al Sur: La Argentina Como Refugio de Nazis y Criminales de Guerra (Buenos Aires: Planeta, 1955), p. 34.

86. The present author has visited the Nazi monument in the Santiago General Cemetery, although not on September 5.

87. Sagaris, p. 205.

88. Raquel Correa and Elizabeth Subercaseaux, *Ego Sum* (Santiago: Planeta, 1996), p. 57.

89. The author observed for himself General Pinochet's visit to Puerto Varas. The report of his visit to Puerto Montt comes from *El Llanquihue* (Puerto Montt), 22 Feb. 1997.

90. *El Llanquihue* (Puerto Montt), 14 and 15 Jan. 1997.

91. Bernstein, p. 76.

INDEX

FREEDOM FIGHTERS

Anarchist Intellectuals, Workers, and Soldiers in Portugal's History

João Freire

translated by
Maria Fernanda Noronha da Costa e Sousa

Some eighty years ago, Portugese libertarians were organized under the banner of syndicalism. This movement deeply marked the history of Portugal. *Freedom Fighters* examines anarchist ideas and how these arrived in Portugal, and how the anarchist program gained popularity with both the working class and intellectuals, people who believed in the slogan 'with neither God nor master.'

This fascinating history is traced from the beginning of the 20th century through the Spanish Civil War and the Second World War. The role of the anarchists during Salazer's dictatorship is examined with much previously unknown documentation. Of particular interest is the history of the anarchists during the 1974 'Carnation Revolution' and during Portugal's emergence as a contemporary liberal democracy.

> *Freedom Fighters* is now, and will remain for a long time, a necessary book to any who look to do new research on the subject.
> —*Miguel Serras Pereira*, Público, *Lisbon*

> A coherent and solid work on Portuguese anarchism.
> —*Alfredo Margarido*, Anais, *Lisbon*

Freedom Fighters fills a large gap in the history and sociology of Portugal. Much of the analysis and documentation presented in this important work will help the contemporary reader to understand Portugal today.

JOÃO FREIRE is a professor of Sociology at the University of Lisbon.

216 pages, photographs
Paperback ISBN:1-55164-138-0 $24.99
Hardcover ISBN:1-55164-139-9 $53.99

HOW THE FIRST WORLD WAR BEGAN
The Triple Entente And The Coming Of The Great War Of 1914-1918

Edward E. McCullough

The current dogma concerning the origins of the First World War supports the militarist myth that wars are caused by stupid, evil, aggressive nations on the other side of the world who refuse to get along with the good, peaceful people on this side.

This book attempts to understand the real causes of war and to dissociate propaganda from historical fact. By reviewing the events of the pre-1914 period, the responsibility of Germany for the outbreak of the war is reconsidered.

It begins with a short account of the situation after the Franco-Prussian War, when France was isolated and Germany secure in the friendship of all the other Great Powers, and proceeds to describe how France created an anti-German coalition. The account of the estrangement of England from Germany attempts to correct the usual pro-British prejudice and to explain the real causes of this development. This book is unique in its approach to the German Empire of 1871-1918.

> Historian Edward McCullough pulls no punches in this controversial book. He offers new insights into the Great War. A must read for anyone interested in world history. —*St. Catherine Standard*

For 32 years, EDWARD E. McCULLOUGH has taught as a university teacher in Montrèal and he is currently Professor Emeritus at Concordia University. He has spent the past fifteen years working on this book; his research work on European history which constitutes one of his main fields of interests has already been published in two reviews.

368 pages, bibliography, index
Paperback ISBN: 1-55164-140-2 $28.99
Hardcover ISBN: 1-55164-141-0 $57.99

BOOKS OF RELATED INTEREST

Anarchist Collectives, *by Sam Dolgoff*
Anarchist Papers, revised *by Dimitri Roussopoulos*
Certainties and Doubts, *by Anatol Rapoport*
Every Life Is a Story, *by Fred H. Knelman*
Fateful Triangle, *by Noam Chomsky*
Fugitive Writings, *by Peter Kropotkin*
Great French Revolution, *by Peter Kropotkin*
How to Take an Exam, *by Bertell Ollman*
Humorous Sceptic, *by N.Anthony Bonaparte*
Imperialism and Ideology, *by John Laffey*
Islamic Peril, *by Karim H. Karim*
Legacy of the New Left, *by Dimitrios Roussopoulos*
Living With Landmines, *by Bill Purves*
Modern State, *by J. Frank Harrison*
Nationalism and Culture, *by Rudolf Rocker*
Perspectives on Power, *by Noam Chomsky*
Rethinking Camelot, *by Noam Chomsky*
Writers and Politics, *by George Woodcock*
Year 501, *by Noam Chomsky*
Zapata, *by Peter E. Newell*

send for a free catalogue of all our titles
BLACK ROSE BOOKS
C.P. 1258, Succ. Place du Parc
Montréal, Québec
H3W 2R3 Canada
or visit our web site at: http://www.web.net/blackrosebooks

To order books:
In Canada: (tel) 1-800-565-9523 (fax) 1-800-221-9985
email: utpbooks@utpress.utoronto.ca

In United States: (tel) 1-800-283-3572 (fax) 1-651-917-6406

In UK & Europe: (tel) London 44 (0)20 8986-4854 (fax) 44 (0)20 8533-5821
email: order@centralbooks.com

Printed by the workers of
MARC VEILLEUX IMPRIMEUR INC.
Boucherville, Québec
for Black Rose Books Ltd.